# Leading Across Differences:
# Cases and Perspectives

Edited by

Kelly M. Hannum
Belinda B. McFeeters
Lize Booysen

**Pfeiffer**
A Wiley Imprint
www.pfeiffer.com

Casebook ISBN: 9780470467169

Facilitator's Guide Set ISBN: 9780470563359

| | |
|---|---|
| Acquiring Editors: | Lisa Shannon |
| Assistant Editor: | Marisa Kelley |
| Marketing Manager: | Tolu Babalola |
| Director of Development: | Kathleen Dolan Davies |
| Developmental Editor: | Susan Rachmeler |
| Production Editor: | Michael Kay |
| Editor: | Rebecca Taff |
| Manufacturing Supervisor: | Becky Morgan |

Printed in the United States of America

Printing   10  9  8  7  6  5  4  3  2  1

# About Pfeiffer

Pfeiffer serves the professional development and hands-on resource needs of training and human resource practitioners and gives them products to do their jobs better. We deliver proven ideas and solutions from experts in HR development and HR management, and we offer effective and customizable tools to improve workplace performance. From novice to seasoned professional, Pfeiffer is the source you can trust to make yourself and your organization more successful.

**Essential Knowledge** Pfeiffer produces insightful, practical, and comprehensive materials on topics that matter the most to training and HR professionals. Our Essential Knowledge resources translate the expertise of seasoned professionals into practical, how-to guidance on critical workplace issues and problems. These resources are supported by case studies, worksheets, and job aids and are frequently supplemented with CD-ROMs, websites, and other means of making the content easier to read, understand, and use.

**Essential Tools** Pfeiffer's Essential Tools resources save time and expense by offering proven, ready-to-use materials—including exercises, activities, games, instruments, and assessments—for use during a training or team-learning event. These resources are frequently offered in looseleaf or CD-ROM format to facilitate copying and customization of the material.

Pfeiffer also recognizes the remarkable power of new technologies in expanding the reach and effectiveness of training. While e-hype has often created whizbang solutions in search of a problem, we are dedicated to bringing convenience and enhancements to proven training solutions. All our e-tools comply with rigorous functionality standards. The most appropriate technology wrapped around essential content yields the perfect solution for today's on-the-go trainers and human resource professionals.

**Pfeiffer**
www.pfeiffer.com
*Essential resources for training and HR professionals*

## ABOUT THE CENTER FOR CREATIVE LEADERSHIP

The Center for Creative Leadership (CCL) is a top-ranked, global provider of executive education that develops better leaders through its exclusive focus on leadership education and research. Founded in 1970 as a nonprofit, educational institution, CCL helps clients worldwide cultivate creative leadership—the capacity to achieve more than imagined by thinking and acting beyond boundaries—through an array of programs, products, and other services.

Ranked in the top ten in the *Financial Times* annual executive education survey, CCL is headquartered in Greensboro, North Carolina, with campuses in Colorado Springs, Colorado; San Diego, California; Brussels, Belgium; and Singapore. Supported by more than five hundred faculty members and staff, it works annually with more than twenty thousand leaders and three thousand organizations. In addition, sixteen Network Associates around the world offer selected CCL programs and assessments.

CCL draws strength from its nonprofit status and educational mission, which provide unusual flexibility in a world where quarterly profits often drive thinking and direction. It has the freedom to be objective, wary of short-term trends, and motivated foremost by its mission—hence our substantial and sustained investment in leadership research. Although CCL's work is always grounded in a strong foundation of research, it focuses on achieving a beneficial impact in the real world. Its efforts are geared to be practical and action oriented, helping leaders and their organizations more effectively achieve their goals and vision. The desire to transform learning and ideas into action provides the impetus for CCL's programs, assessments, publications, and services.

## CAPABILITIES

CCL's activities encompass leadership education, knowledge generation and dissemination, and building a community centered on leadership. CCL is broadly recognized for excellence in executive education, leadership development, and innovation by sources such as *BusinessWeek, Financial Times, The New York Times,* and *The Wall Street Journal.*

## OPEN-ENROLLMENT PROGRAMS

Fourteen open-enrollment courses are designed for leaders at all levels, as well as people responsible for leadership development and training at their organizations. This portfolio offers distinct choices for participants seeking a particular learning environment or type of experience. Some programs are structured specifically around small group activities, discussion, and personal reflection, while others offer hands-on opportunities through business simulations, artistic exploration, team-building exercises, and new-skills practice. Many of these programs offer private one-on-one sessions with a feedback coach.

For a complete listing of programs, visit http://www.ccl.org/programs.

## CUSTOMIZED PROGRAMS

CCL develops tailored educational solutions for more than one hundred client organizations around the world each year. Through this applied practice, CCL structures and delivers programs focused on specific leadership development needs within the context of defined organizational challenges, including innovation, the merging of cultures, and the development of a broader pool of leaders. The objective is to help organizations develop, within their own cultures, the leadership capacity they need to address challenges as they emerge.

Program details are available online at http://www.ccl.org/custom.

## COACHING

CCL's suite of coaching services is designed to help leaders maintain a sustained focus and generate increased momentum toward achieving their goals. These coaching alternatives vary in depth and duration and serve a variety of needs, from helping an executive sort through career and life issues to working with an organization to integrate coaching into its internal development process. Our coaching offerings, which can supplement program attendance or be customized for specific individual or team needs, are based on our ACS model of assessment, challenge, and support.

Learn more about CCL's coaching services at http://www.ccl.org/coaching.

## ASSESSMENT AND DEVELOPMENT RESOURCES

CCL pioneered 360-degree feedback and believes that assessment provides a solid foundation for learning, growth, and transformation and that development truly happens when an individual recognizes the need to change. CCL offers a broad selection of assessment tools, online resources, and simulations that can help individuals, teams, and organizations increase their self-awareness, facilitate their own learning, enable their development, and enhance their effectiveness.

CCL's assessments are profiled at http://www.ccl.org/assessments.

## PUBLICATIONS

The theoretical foundation for many of our programs, as well as the results of CCL's extensive and often groundbreaking research, can be found in the scores of publications issued by CCL Press and through the center's alliance with Jossey-Bass, a Wiley imprint. Among these are landmark works, such as *Breaking the Glass Ceiling* and *The Lessons of Experience,* as well as quick-read guidebooks focused on core aspects of leadership. CCL publications provide insights and practical advice to help individuals become more effective leaders, develop leadership training within organizations, address issues of change and diversity, and build the systems and strategies that advance leadership collectively at the institutional level.

A complete listing of CCL publications is available at http://www.ccl.org/publications.

## LEADERSHIP COMMUNITY

To ensure that the Center's work remains focused, relevant, and important to the individuals and organizations it serves, CCL maintains a host of networks, councils, and learning and virtual communities that bring together alumni, donors, faculty, practicing leaders, and thought leaders from around the globe. CCL also forges relationships and alliances with individuals, organizations, and associations that share its values and mission. The energy, insights, and support from these relationships help shape and sustain CCL's educational and research practices and provide its clients with an added measure of motivation and inspiration as they continue their lifelong commitment to leadership and learning.

To learn more, visit http://www.ccl.org/community.

## RESEARCH

CCL's portfolio of programs, products, and services is built on a solid foundation of behavioral science research. The role of research at CCL is to advance the understanding of leadership and to transform learning into practical tools for participants and clients. CCL's research is the hub of a cycle that transforms knowledge into applications and applications into knowledge, thereby illuminating the way organizations think about and enact leadership and leader development.

Find out more about current research initiatives at http://www.ccl.org/research.

For additional information about CCL, please visit http://www.ccl.org or call Client Services at (336) 545-2810.

# CONTENTS

# FOREWORD

*Maxine Dalton*
*Marian Ruderman*

How do you teach people who often differ from one another on a variety of dimensions such as nationality, religion, race, and gender to work effectively together? Kelly Hannum, Belinda McFeeters, and Lize Booysen invite people to learn to collaborate across differences through the use of real-life vignettes and theoretical perspectives. *Leading Across Differences: Cases and Perspectives* offers thirteen cases based on real incidents in organizations in conjunction with analytical tools for addressing the dynamics of difference in organizations. This book challenges the reader to apply social science concepts to the very real implications of different social identity groups working together in organizations.

*Leading Across Differences* is a product of the Leadership Across Differences (LAD) Project, a study of the leadership necessary to guide an organization in the face of social identity-based conflicts. Social identity conflicts involve clashes stemming from differences between groups based on ethnicity, religion, immigration, and gender. Such conflicts cut to the core of who we are and what we value. They have the ability to fester and slowly eat away at the fabric of an organization. Rarely addressed and difficult to resolve, social identity conflicts are often reflective of tensions and conflicts between different groups embedded in the larger society. Social identity conflicts are a serious problem that threaten organizational morale and reputation as well as individual dignity.

The LAD research team, including a large group from the Center for Creative Leadership as well as colleagues from France, Jordan, the United States, Brazil, Germany, South Africa, India, Israel, Spain, and Singapore, approached the study of social identity conflicts in a variety of ways, the centerpiece of which was a qualitative study of social-identity conflicts in twenty organizations in ten different countries, each of which had historically experienced serious identity-based conflicts. In each organization, we collected data with a critical incident approach. Participants were asked to describe organizational events they had witnessed that they believe involved identity group conflict. There were asked to describe the conflict, who took leadership roles, what they did, and how they did it. The interviews assessed what formal and not-so-formal leaders did behaviorally as they attempted to resolve the conflict. Although the stories were collected from a research perspective, we realized early that they had great instructional value as well. The stories provide a realistic look at the ease with which social identity conflicts can occur, escalate, and threaten an organization. *Leading Across Differences* fictionalizes the stories, changing the names and identifying features of both the individuals and organizations involved but retaining the essence of the conflict and its causes.

These cases illustrate both the kinds of situations that result in social identity conflict and the many different approaches for addressing them. The cases clarify the difficulty that non-dominant groups have in trusting the motives of even the most well meaning leader who comes from a different group. They demonstrate the critical role of simple acts of respect and the importance of organizational policies, practices, and norms in preventing the emergence of social identity group conflict. These cases also illustrate the cynicism that can fester when attention to social identity conflicts takes the form of window-dressing. The questions following each case are intended to help readers identify the root of the problem, interpret the situation, and consider alternative resolution strategies. Through their teaching experiences, Hannum, McFeeters, and Booysen realized the power these cases have in creating honest discussions about differences.

Although the cases form the heart of the book, Hannum, McFeeters, and Booysen have supplemented them with carefully selected theoretical chapters, each providing a set of ideas from which to discuss the cases. Written by noted scholars, these chapters offer a series of perspectives for understanding the conflicts between groups in organizations. The editors pull these views together so the reader can appreciate the many different paths for understanding and addressing social identity conflict.

The editors believe that the cases, exercises, and concepts in this volume can teach practices for managing the discord and conflict among different social identity groups in the workplace. These cases are compelling, and the lessons they illustrate can be applied in real-life situations. They provide a safe way of addressing dangerous issues. In combination with the conceptual chapters, they make the complex discussable and therefore actionable. The book provides a solid basis for understanding how to diagnose, address, and resolve social identity conflicts in the workplace.

# PREFACE

The cases and ideas expressed in this book are drawn from the Leadership Across Difference research project. Our research began in 2001 and continued through 2008. The international research team included Center for Creative Leadership faculty and research partners at various institutions around the world. We conducted our research using a multi-method research design. We gathered survey, interview, and archival data from for-profit and nonprofit organizations. We wanted to better understand what contributed to social identity tensions and conflicts in organizations and explore what leadership responses were desired and which were used. To learn more about this research, you can visit our website at http://www.ccl.org/leadership/research/lad/.

We decided to create a casebook based on our research as a practical way to share the interesting things we were learning and to prompt informed dialogue. Our goal was to help facilitate learning in a way that would enrich lives and lead to more effective organizations and, ideally, a more effective global society.

This book results from the efforts of many people. Information about the individuals who contributed directly is included in the contributors section at the back of this book. However, many other individuals have shaped the information in this book. We would like to thank the organizations and individuals who contributed their stories, which form the foundation of this casebook, but remain unnamed to honor our agreements with them. We also want to thank our research collaborators who played an active role in the Leadership Across Differences project, including Chris Ernst, Kathryn Cartner, Rachael Foy, Bill Gentry, Sarah Glover, Michael Hoppe, Vijayan Munusamy, Patty Ohlott, Marian Ruderman, Joan Tavares, Maxine Dalton, Ancella Livers, Robbie Soloman, Jeff Yip, Donna Chrobot-Mason, David Dinwoodie, Claude Levy-Leboyer, Jonna Louvrier, Muhsen Makhamreh, Stella Nkomo, Lilach Sagiv, Sigmar Malvezzi, Shalom Schwartz, Peter Smith, and Tammy Rubel.

The organizations listed below provided support, making it possible to gather the information reflected in this book, and we are very grateful for their support.

- Blue Cross–Blue Shield
- Bristol-Myers Squibb Company
- CARE
- Chubb
- ConocoPhillips
- GlaxoSmithKline
- Greensboro Fire Department
- Lutheran Family Services
- Mercy Corps
- Merrill Lynch
- Singapore Economic Development Board
- Swiss Re
- Syngenta
- Verizon
- Virginia State University
- Warner Foundation
- Z. Smith Reynolds Foundation

Finally, our ability to create this book was greatly enhanced by the support, encouragement, and understanding of our family and friends. Kelly would like to thank her parents—Elizabeth Hannum and Wallace Hannum; her stepmother, Nancy Kiplinger; and her siblings—Rebecca Rogers, Bryan Rogers, and Wallace

Hannum–for their love and support. She also thanks her chosen family—Keith and Dylan Erikson—for making it fun to come home and for not setting anything on fire. Belinda would like to thank her husband, Forrest McFeeters; parents, Franklin and Bettie Bennett; and siblings Felecia Bennett-Giles and Jabbar Bennett, for their continuous love and support. Lize would like to thank her partner, Karin Hougaard, and her daughter, Claris Pienaar, for rescuing her from being doomed to the obscurity of everlasting bookishness.

October 2009

Kelly Hannum
Belinda McFeeters
Lize Booysen

# Introduction

We live in an increasingly interdependent world, a world in which people with different histories, perspectives, values, and cultures are brought together in a variety of ways and in a variety of places. Educational institutions, for-profit organizations, governmental agencies, and many other types of workplaces are serving and employing people representing an ever-widening array of backgrounds. In some instances, groups of people who know very little about each other are working together. Differences in perspectives and behaviors can be hard to understand, confusing, or just seem wrong. An example of this can be found in Case 6, where workers from India are brought to the United States. The Indians try to adapt to U.S. customs, but find it difficult, while the U.S. workers feel threatened and resent the situation. In other instances, groups who have shared a sometimes troubling history are brought together to learn or work together. There are often ingrained ideas and stereotypes that may be connected to strong negative feelings and beliefs. An example of this is in Case 1, where long-standing racial tensions lead to an argument between two students. In either context, it is not surprising that misunderstandings, tensions, and conflicts arise and have an impact on workplace morale and productivity. But leading across differences is more than avoiding or responding to the sometimes negative consequences of differences; it is also about capturing a diversity of perspectives and ideas to foster creativity and to identify and improve products and services. Most organizations and institutions now realize that customers, partners, and employees want to see themselves reflected in the organization; therefore it is imperative to foster inclusion in order to effectively accomplish the following objectives:

- Attract, hire, retain, and promote talented employees with a variety of skills, abilities, and perspectives
- Enhance the ability to create new business opportunities (products and services)
- Earn the respect and loyalty of customers, suppliers, partners, and employees
- Maintain marketplace leadership

Despite the growing challenges and opportunities created by our interconnected world, many people do not know how to lead through situations in which there are misunderstandings or conflicts rooted in differences. These types of tensions and conflicts are usually emotionally charged and very confusing. It is not clear who should take action or what, if any, action should be taken. Very little time is spent preparing leaders for this aspect of their role. We believe that this is, in part, because there are few practical resources that offer solutions that are grounded in research.

## PURPOSE

The need for practical, relevant, and usable information about how to lead across differences is growing. In this book we provide examples of and perspectives on concepts and situations important to leading across differences. The differences addressed are steeped in social identities, such as those related to gender, religion, race, ethnicity, and country of origin. We have included the differences most commonly referenced in our research. However, there are far more differences, and combinations of differences, than could be addressed in a single volume. While the types of differences may, or may not, match your own context, the dynamics of difference are likely to be similar.

People learn from experience. By our providing the experiences of others and information to help translate those experiences in this book, readers will be better prepared for similar situations they may face or may better understand experiences they have already had. We do not provide readers with the "right" answers; rather, we provide strategies to help readers better understand themselves and their context so they might develop effective and appropriate responses to different situations.

## AUDIENCE

The primary audience for this casebook is individuals with teaching or training responsibilities for new or budding managers, supervisors, or leaders who will be (or are) leading and working in groups with varied social identity groups represented. The casebook may be used in both academic and organizational settings. The casebook is written in a way that managers and leaders can read and reflect on the material as part of a self-study; but to reap full benefit, it is helpful to engage with others in discussions of the ideas and events shared in this book. The use of the cases and information in the casebook can be supported by using the processes shared in the Facilitator's Guide and Instructor's Guide.

## THE ORGANIZATION OF THIS BOOK

This book is divided into four parts: (1) the Leadership Across Differences Framework, (2) cases, (3) perspective chapters, and (4) exercises. A glossary, a list of resources, and references are also included at the back of the volume.

Accompanying materials include a Facilitator's Guide and an Instructor's Guide. The Facilitator's Guide provides information about how to select and utilize the cases as well as facilitation ideas for group debriefings of the individual exercises in the casebook and group exercises. The Instructor's Guide provides additional information, such as sample course syllabi, specific to using the casebook in an academic setting and five sets of PowerPoint presentations. Instructors (college professors) are invited to download these free materials from the following site:

www.wiley.com/college/hannum

If you are a trainer (and not a college professor), please send an email to the following address to receive your free copy of these materials:

pfeiffertraining@wiley.com

### Leadership Across Differences Framework

We adapted a framework created by The Leadership Across Differences research team for describing the connections between the factors and processes that are important to understand when leading in a context of social identity difference in organizations (see Figure I.1). This framework is described in detail in Part 1.

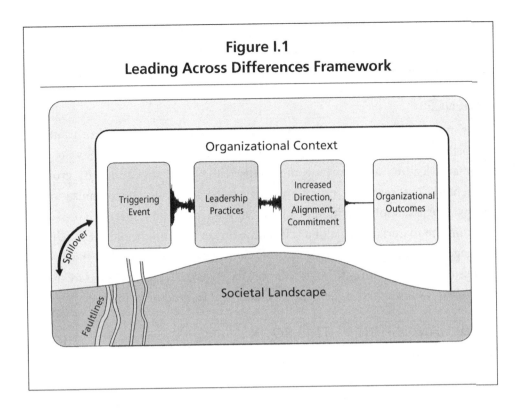

**Figure I.1**
**Leading Across Differences Framework**

Organizational Context

Triggering Event

Leadership Practices

Increased Direction, Alignment, Commitment

Organizational Outcomes

Spillover

Societal Landscape

Faultlines

## Cases

The cases in this book are based on interviews of more than one hundred people in twenty organizations on five continents conducted as part of the Leadership Across Differences research. The individual names, organizational names, and other identifying information have been removed in order to protect the confidentiality of research participants. All names used in the cases are pseudonyms. Some of the cases in this book are based on events gathered from different sources and do not reflect a single event or situation but rather a composite of multiple events and situations. There are two reasons we have taken this approach: (1) interviews may not have provided the detail needed to create a compelling case, and (2) the information from the interview may be too specific to ensure confidentially or to provide a case that would be applicable in multiple settings.

The cases in this book are short enough to be read and discussed in a session of an hour or more. You may choose to focus on only one aspect of a case if time is limited. Likewise, you may choose to use the cases as a starting point for a much larger discussion of broad concepts and issues that takes place over multiple sessions.

We have created the cases and supporting instructional materials to be flexible enough to meet multiple learning needs and formats. More supporting information can be found in the Facilitator's Guide and Instructor's Guide. All of the cases in this book follow the same format. Each case includes the following elements:

- A title,
- The type of trigger,
- The type of organization,
- Recommended chapters,
- A detailed description of the context and the event, and
- Discussion questions.

The discussion questions provided with each case are there for reference and to prompt deeper thinking about the case—*there are no right answers to these questions*. You may choose to create your own discussion questions based on your learning objectives. It is not essential to discuss all of the questions, and not all of the questions may be relevant to the key concepts and points you want to address. You may also want to use discussion questions as prompts for private or shared reflections. For instance, participants could write private journal entries or post their comments on shared blogs. The expert commentary provided in the Perspectives section is intended to provide more information about the key concepts underlying the cases. The information in the Perspectives chapters can be made more tangible by examining it in the context of the cases and the cases can be more general when thought of in the broad terms outlined in the Perspectives chapters. In that way the two sections support one another.

The case matrix (see Table 1) provides the following information about each case: country in which the case takes place, type of organization (FP = for profit or NP = nonprofit), type of trigger (for a brief description, see Part 1; for more detail, see the chapter on triggers in Part 3), and the social identities (gender, race, religion, nationality, class, sexuality, language, immigrant status, education, and age) that are most closely related to the case. Social identities most relevant to the case are noted with dark gray shading, while those with secondary relevance to the case are noted with light gray shading. In some instances, more than one social identity was found to have the same or similar relevance to the case study. In these cases, multiple identities are noted with the appropriate shading. Social identities that are not relevant to the cases are not shaded. The matrix is intended to help users of the book identify cases that may be most relevant for their context.

# Table 1
## Case Description Matrix

| Case Number | Country | Org. type | Trigger | Gender | Race | Religion | Nationality | Class | Sexuality | Language | Immigrant Status | Education | Age |
|---|---|---|---|---|---|---|---|---|---|---|---|---|---|
| 1 | South Africa | NP | Differential Treatment | □ | ■ | | | | | | | | □ |
| 2 | Singapore | FP | Insult/ Humiliating Act | | | | ■ | | | | ■ | | |
| 3 | United States | NP | Differential Treatment | | | ■ | | | □ | | | | |
| 4 | Hong Kong | FP | Assimilation | | ■ | ■ | | | | | | | |
| 5 | Hong Kong | FP | Different Values | | | | ■ | | | | | | |
| 6 | United States | FP | Assimilation | | □ | | ■ | | | □ | | | |
| 7 | South Africa | FP | Assimilation | | | | | | | □ | | | |
| 8 | South Africa | FP | Differential Treatment | ■ | | | | | | | | | |
| 9 | Jordan | FP | Differential Treatment | | | | ■ | | | | ■ | | |
| 10 | Brazil | FP | Assimilation | ■ | | | | | | | | | |
| 11 | Jordan | NP | Simple Contact | | | ■ | | | | | | | |
| 12 | United States | NP | Differential Treatment | | | | | | ■ | | | | |
| 13 | France | FP | Differential Treatment | | | | | ■ | | | | ■ | |

## Perspectives

The perspective chapters have been written by experts from different countries with different areas of expertise. These perspectives offer readers insights into new ways of thinking about situations. Learning to effectively work across differences represents not only a challenge, but also an opportunity for innovation and for more holistic approaches to problem solving, particularly complex problems that require multiple perspectives to find an effective solution. The ability to think and act in different ways increases one's leadership repertoire.

The first few chapters in Part 3 provide a foundational understanding of the core concepts running throughout the cases. We recommend that you read the first four chapters before reading and discussing the cases. In Chapter 1, Dr. Nkomo provides an overview of social identity and the dynamics of in-group versus out-group thinking. In Chapter 2, Drs. Ruderman and Chrobot-Mason describe the categories of triggering events from which the cases shared were drawn. In Chapter 3, Drs. Homan and Jehn provide an overview of organizational faultlines. Chapter 4 describes different categories of leadership practices one could use to lead within contexts of difference. Subsequent chapters go more deeply into the concepts illustrated in the cases. In Chapter 5, Dr. Schwartz describes his theory of the underlying cultural values that help frame our attitudes and behaviors. In Chapter 6, Dr. Pittinsky discusses his theory about two very different approaches to difference: xenophobia and allophilia. In Chapter 7, Drs. Van Dyne, Ang, and Livermore, describe the concept of cultural intelligence. In Chapter 8, Dr. Essed shares her thinking about how the issues raised in these cases connect with social justice and dignity. In Chapter 9, Dr. Livers and Mr. Solomon introduce the concept of "miasma" and describe the additional pressures often experienced by individuals in a non-dominant category. In Chapter 10, Drs. Bhawuk and Munusamy link the notion of one's self-concept and approach to leadership to culture. In Chapter 11, Dr. Weber builds on the previous chapters and introduces the notion of leader authenticity. And finally in Chapter 12, Mr. Yip describes the notion of leading in a context of paradox.

## Exercises

This section of the book contains individual exercises designed for self-study or for use in a training or classroom setting. The learning objectives, materials needed, and instructions are provided for each exercise. In general, the exercises prompt deeper reflection about oneself, others, and the context in which the relationship is embedded. This section helps one apply the information in the cases and chapters to one's own context.

## HOW TO USE THIS BOOK

The sections of this book are intended to work together. The Introduction and Leading Across Differences Framework provide a minimum understanding in order to frame the cases and summarize how the various core elements fit together. The Cases provide an external stimulus to prompt discussions about the challenges of and opportunities and approaches for leading across differences. The chapters provide an overview of key concepts that underlie or are reflected in the cases and framework. The chapters can be read before or after the cases, although we recommend that you read the first four chapters before reading and discussing the cases. The exercises are designed to be completed by an individual (group exercises and group debriefing ideas for individual exercises are included in the Facilitator's Guide). Completing the exercises can help make the concepts clearer and help one apply the information in the casebook to one's context. While the cases can be read and discussed without reading the chapters or completing the exercises, to get the full benefit of the book one should read all of the chapters and complete at least some of the exercises.

# PART ONE

# Leadership Across Differences Framework

The Leadership Across Differences Framework (see Figure P.1) is based on a metaphor of geological faultlines. Geological faultlines are cracks in the earth. Stress or pressure on the plates creates a fault, which may be active or dormant. Lau and Murnighan (1998, 2005) suggest that organizational faultlines in groups are analogous to geological faults in the Earth's crust: they are always present; they create various levels of friction as boundaries rub together, pull apart, grind, and collide; and yet they may go unnoticed without the presence of an external force. Lau and Murnighan define faultlines as "hypothetical dividing lines that may split a group into subgroups based on one or more attributes" (1998, p. 328). When the pressure between groups becomes too great, often because of a triggering event or series of events, the faultline becomes active and the groups separate into "us" and "them."

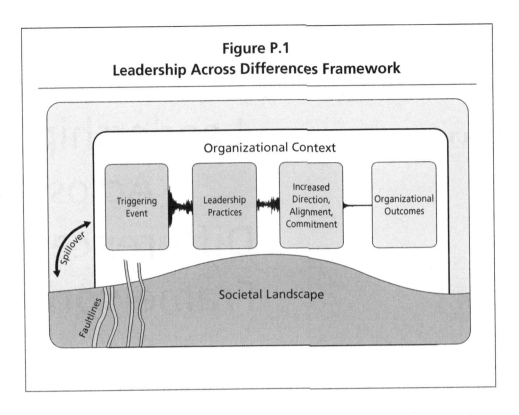

**Figure P.1**
**Leadership Across Differences Framework**

Organizational Context

Triggering Event

Leadership Practices

Increased Direction, Alignment, Commitment

Organizational Outcomes

Spillover

Faultlines

Societal Landscape

The focus of the Leadership Across Differences framework is organizations, although the concepts included in the framework allude to the broader context of communities and societies, represented by the "societal landscape." The "leadership practices" represent how leadership prepares for and responds to faultlines and triggering events. Increased direction, alignment, and commitment indicate the three primary outcomes of leadership and are believed to contribute to organizational outcomes. The degree to which a diverse group has a shared direction, is engaging in work aligned with that direction, and is committed to achieving a shared goal is an indicator of effective intergroup leadership (Drath, McCauley, Palus, Van Velsor, O'Connor, & McGuire, 2008). The arrow for spillover represents the notion that what happens in society can spillover into organizations and what happens in organizations can spill over into society. For example, the long-lasting tension between Malaysia and Singapore influenced the relationships in the work team discussed in Case 2, and the local bombings described in Case 11 led to heightened tensions within the organization. Similarly, a major organizational scandal can have an impact on society. There can also be positive spillover. For example, if groups can learn to work well together and learn together in organizations and educational institutions, they may be better able to live well together in society. In this way, organizations and educational institutions represent a naturally occurring place for interventions that lead to improved effectiveness not only within their "walls" but also within society more broadly. Allport's (1954) *The Nature of Prejudice* suggested that bringing together individuals from opposing groups, under certain conditions, could reduce intergroup prejudice. His perspective is better known as *contact theory*—that positive contact with someone different can reduce one's prejudice about that person's group in general. In Case 13 the effect of the contact hypotheses can be seen in the dilemma of the manager. While the dynamics of spillover are not the focus of this book, we mention them here partly because they represent an opportunity for increasing the positive impact of leadership within organizations and educational institutions.

Our framework provides a broad context for understanding how social identity is part of the fabric of organizations as well as the factors that lead to (and help learn from and reduce) social identity tensions in organizations. There are multiple, complex factors associated with leading across differences, far too many to adequately address in a single publication. As editors, we have distilled concepts from multiple fields in order to illuminate the critical aspects of the cases described in this book and have provided readers with a list of "Recommended Reading" to assist those who want to know more. In the paragraphs below, we provide an overview of the elements of the framework. Many of the concepts introduced here are addressed more thoroughly in the perspective-giving topical chapters. We refer you to those chapters as appropriate.

## SOCIETAL LANDSCAPE

Social factors influence social identity development and awareness as well as provide the context for more deeply understanding the relationship between different social identity groups—including tensions between groups. For instance, the changes in the post-apartheid societal landscape in South Africa are clearly evident in Cases 1, 7, and 8. It is important to note that, as organizations operate globally, there are likely to be multiple values, histories, and environments represented in a single organization. In that way the societal landscape of an organization may have multiple layers.

One of the driving aspects of the societal landscape is cultural values. Cultural values are socially shared, abstract ideas about what is good, right, and desirable in a society or other bounded group. There may be very different cultural values represented in the Indian office than in the U.S. office of the same organization. For another example, see how cultural values influence the perception of employees in Case 6. Shalom Schwartz's chapter offers a deeper insight into cultural values. Todd Weber's chapter on values and authenticity shows how leadership can be influenced by values.

Another key component of the landscape is identity group history, which is the history of the relationship between social identity groups in society at large including tenure, recency, and the intensity and nature of past conflict. These tensions underpin *intergroup anxiety* (Stephan & Stephan, 1985). The formal and informal political environment is also a factor in the societal landscape. This includes the degree to which different identity groups have access to power and voting rights and the extent to which there is "free press," active labor organizations, and community organizing. The laws as well as informal justice systems of the country or countries in which an organization is located, including labor relations, determine workplace policies and behaviors. These laws influence the relationships between groups within an organization, for instance, the effect of the implementation of equal opportunity legislation in South African organizations, as described in Case 7. Also of interest is the ability of various social identity groups to access the justice system and the application of the laws to various social identity groups. The chapter on social identity by Stella Nkomo and the chapter on Social Justice and Dignity by Philomena Essedare are useful in understanding these dynamics.

Employment trends also have an impact on organizations. For example, the percent of the population that is unemployed and the type of work available to different groups influences the degree to which workers can easily change jobs, and thus the degree to which they are willing to put up with unpleasant situations at work. The differential treatment between the Palestinians and Jordanians, as discussed in Case 9, illustrates these inequities rather well. The extent to which the employable population is diverse has an impact on the opportunity for diversity within the organization. And finally, the degree of religious tolerance and the extent to which different religious groups are represented in the country or countries in which an organization is located is likely to influence the degree of religious tolerance or tension within the organization, as can be seen in Cases 3 and 4.

## ORGANIZATIONAL CONTEXT

Organizational factors provide the next layer of context and may or may not reflect broader societal elements. These factors shape behavioral norms and values within the organization itself. An organization's mission and values indicate what an organization seeks to accomplish and the values by which is operates. In our study, a working assumption was that the superordinate goal of nonprofit organizations is some type of "greater good," while profitability is the primary superordinate goal for for-profit organizations. Mission and values influence the nature of social identity group relations. A nonprofit mission (for example, feeding hungry children) may make the day-to-day tensions between different social identity groups seem "less important" in the greater context of what they are trying to achieve. As another example, economic factors in society (for example, the need for a job) may make profitability an important enough goal to put aside or tolerate differences.

The extent to which the primary work of an organization requires interdependent and cooperative work will influence how essential intergroup leadership is to achieving organizational outcomes. Organizations vary from having work that is highly technical, task-oriented, and independent to highly adaptive and interdependent. Interdependent work may require different social groups to work together (leading to increased contact), while independent work may allow for greater separation of different social identity groups (which may lead to infrequent triggers because of the lack of interaction). The nature of the work may also vary by unit in the organization. For example, the manufacturing aspect of work may be technical, task-oriented, and independent, while the marketing function is adaptive and interdependent.

## SPILLOVER

The process by which social identity differences in the society at large influence organizational dynamics is called spillover. The extent or means by which spillover impacts organizational dynamics is influenced by a number of different organizational elements, for example, an organization's mission and values. An example of spillover could be a news report about a riot involving different nationalities. Individuals within an organization may come to work feeling angry about the situation and may blame one nationality or the other and be particularly sensitive to comments about national identity. Similarly, changes or events in the organization have the capacity to change society. A simple example is that issues faced by organizations may lead to the creation of new laws. Spillover captures the dynamic relationship between an organization and the broader society or community in which it exists.

## FAULTLINES

Faultlines are the dynamics of multiple demographic attributes that can potentially subdivide a group. Faultlines may or may not be active in an organization, but they are always present. To use another metaphor, faultlines may act like simmering pots that are not yet boiling over, but if the heat (or tension) is increased, they would begin to boil. A trigger (described in the next section) serves to activate or exacerbate a faultline. When a faultline is active, it becomes more difficult for organizations to achieve shared direction, alignment, and commitment. To learn more about faultlines, read the chapter in Part 3 by Homan and Jehn. Organizational learning paradigms can help an organization to continuously learn and appropriately transform itself given its changing realities. There are a number of different approaches organizations can take toward learning. Organizational learning includes the concepts of single loop versus double loop learning, as well as espoused theories versus theories in action from Chris Argyris' work.

## TRIGGERING EVENT

Triggers can be an action or series of actions that make an inequity or inequality, related to social identity, noticeable. A trigger is an event that involves at least two social identity groups, men and women, for example, and that causes social identity to become activated in varying degrees. For an event to be a trigger, at least two members from the same identity group attribute the event or action to their social identity group or the social identity group of the other party. Triggers are described in more detail in the chapter by Ruderman and Chrobot-Mason. Table 1 (previously presented) links the cases with the specific trigger event(s) in each case.

Table 2 provides a description and example of each of the five triggers that we found in our research.

## Table 2
## A Typology of Triggers

| Trigger | Description | Example |
|---|---|---|
| *Differential Treatment* | Occurs when one group perceives that another group has an advantage when it comes to the allocation of resources, rewards, opportunities, or punishments | Men are given preference over women for key assignments |
| *Assimilation* | Occurs when the majority group expects that others will act just like them; there is an expectation that non-dominant groups will blend into the dominant culture | Use of a language associated with a particular group and exclusionary of other groups |
| *Insults or Humiliating Acts* | Occurs when a comment or behavior devalues or offends one group relative to another | An offensive comment about someone from another identity group is made in the form of "you people" |
| *Different Values* | Occurs when groups have decidedly different values; a clash of fundamental beliefs regarding what is wrong and what is right | A group of employees is unable to accept a job-related assignment because of religious beliefs |
| *Simple Contact* | Occurs when anxiety and tension between groups is high in the broader society; simple contact between these groups triggers a faultline | A terrorist attack occurs, resulting in high anxiety and distrust between national groups who must work together |

## LEADERSHIP PRACTICES

Leadership practices are actions addressing (or intended to prevent) social identity conflicts in organizations. Leadership practices can be taken by an individual, group, or organization. They can be taken by any person in the organization regardless of formal authority, although they are likely to use different strategies. Leadership practices are organized into three distinctly different underlying beliefs about the organization's role in managing cross-group relationships: (1) that the organization should have no role at all in such relationships (Hands Off); (2) that it is the responsibility of the organization to direct and control such relationships (Direct and Control); and (3) that the organization's role is to create the right conditions for relationships to develop in a healthy manner (Cultivate and Encourage). These practices are more fully described in the Leadership Practices chapter as well as in a forthcoming book by Ernst and Chrobot-Mason. Although organizational actions may be influenced by all three beliefs, our data suggest that many organizations adopt one predominant belief that guides the prevention of and initial response to social identity conflicts.

## INCREASED DIRECTION, ALIGNMENT, AND COMMITMENT

Leadership practices are often aimed at reducing tension and increasing effective collaboration between different social identity groups. These practices should increase the shared direction, alignment, and commitment among different social identity groups as an outcome and indicator of effective intergroup leadership and thus a proximal outcome of leadership practices. Increased direction, alignment, and commitment among different social identity groups is the bridge between leadership practices and organizational outcomes. If leadership practices are not resulting in increased direction, alignment, and commitment among different social identity groups, the likelihood of positive organizational outcomes is reduced.

## ORGANIZATIONAL OUTCOMES

Although not examined in our research, organizational outcomes represent an important aspect of the framework. The goal of organizations is not to have effective leadership—but to produce positive results, for which effective leadership is necessary. We believe creating direction, alignment, and commitment among different social identity groups is a step toward enhancing organizational or institutional outcomes. In turn, clarity about the desired organizational outcomes may help produce direction, alignment, and commitment by focusing social identity groups toward a shared outcome or creating a boundary within which groups are willing to operate collectively.

# Cases

The following cases are based on interviews conducted as part of the Leadership Across Differences research project. The individual names, organizational names, and other identifying information have been removed in order to protect the confidentiality of research participants. Some of the cases do not reflect a single event or situation but rather a composite of multiple events and situations.

The cases are short enough to be read and discussed in a session of an hour or more. You may choose to focus on only one aspect of a case if time is limited. Likewise, you may choose to use the cases as a starting point for a much larger discussion of broad concepts and issues that takes place over multiple sessions. All of the cases in this book follow the same format. Each case includes the following elements:

- A title,
- The type of trigger,
- The type of organization,
- Recommended chapters,
- A detailed description of the context and the event, and
- Discussion questions.

The discussion questions are there for reference and to prompt your thinking—*there are no right answers to these questions*. It is not essential to discuss all of the questions—not all of the questions may be relevant to the key concepts and points you want to address. You may also want to use discussion questions as prompts for private or shared reflections. For instance, participants could write private journal entries or post their comments on shared blogs. The chapters in the Perspectives section provide more information about the broader context of the case. You may choose to read these chapters before or after the cases, although we recommend that you read the first four chapters before reading and discussing the cases.

Part 2 contains the following cases:

Case 1: Race and Respect

Case 2: Water Crises

Case 3: Floating Holidays

Case 4: Not My Weekend

Case 5: It's Their Fault

Case 6: The Scent of Difference

Case 7: Not Catching On

Case 8: Glass Ceiling at Big Boy Toys

Case 9: Super Drugs

Case 10: The Right to Be Pregnant

Case 11: Local Bombing

Case 12: Benefits Battle

Case 13: Francois' Dilemma

# Race and Respect

**Trigger: Differential Treatment**

**Organization: A university (nonprofit) in South Africa**

**Recommended Chapters:**

- Chapter 1: Social Identity: Understanding the In-Group/Out-Group Group Phenomenon by Stella M. Nkomo

- Chapter 2: Triggers of Social Identity Conflict by Marian N. Ruderman and Donna Chrobot-Mason

- Chapter 3: Organizational Faultlines by Astrid C. Homan and Karen A. Jehn

- Chapter 4: Leadership Practices Across Social Identity Groups by Marian N. Ruderman, Sarah Glover, Donna Chrobot-Mason, and Chris Ernst

- Chapter 5: Cultural Values by Shalom Schwartz

- Chapter 8: Social Justice and Dignity by Philomena Essed

- Chapter 9: Miasma: The Dynamics of Difference by Ancella B. Livers and Robert F. Solomon, Jr.

## THE CASE

This case takes place at a mid-sized university in South Africa. The majority of students and employees are White South Africans, and the rest are Black South Africans. The university prides itself on equal opportunity and fair and non-biased behavior. It attempts to instill these beliefs in all employees and staff. The university seeks greater diversity and inclusiveness of its staff and students. However, there have been concerns about unequal hiring and enrollment practices at the university for quite some time. A great deal of tension is present between white and black faculty and staff members at the university.

The situation described takes place during a lecture in a first year course. The majority of students in the class are white. The average student age is eighteen years old. The situation primarily takes place between an older, black, female student in the class (Maria), who is also a member of the university staff, and a popular white male student (Mark).

Maria overheard Mark negatively gossiping about her with classmates. She could not hear exactly what he was saying, but had heard him say offensive things in the past like, "I'm sick of taking classes with people who should be cleaning my kitchen." Maria was frustrated, because she had heard similar comments many times before. She decided to verbally confront Mark during class. In an angry tone, she yelled, "Wake up! This is the new South Africa. I can take you to court for this." The professor noticed the confrontation and asked the two to step outside of the class with him to resolve the issue. He asked his assistant to continue the lecture. The students began to talk among themselves, wondering whether Mark was in trouble. The professor's assistant, who was a co-worker and friend of Maria, attempted to continue with the lesson. The students asked the assistant whether Mark was going to be in trouble. The assistant responded by saying that if he did something wrong, administrators would deal with it appropriately. He advised the students to bring their attention back to the lecture, but the students' minds were preoccupied with what had just occurred. One could hear rumblings from many of the students suggesting that Maria was wrong to confront their classmate and that she was too outspoken. The three black students in the class thought Mark's sense of humor was derogatory but did not say anything about the situation. They didn't agree with how Maria handled the situation, but could understand why she was angry with Mark. When the professor returned, the assistant asked him how everything went. The professor advised that things had been sorted out.

Mark's father was an administrator at the university and was upset when he heard about the incident with his son. He complained to the dean, a white male, and the dean filed a complaint against Maria. A few days later, Maria's director called her into her office and advised that she had to stand before a disciplinary hearing because of her confrontation with Mark in class.

After the hearing, the dean fired Maria. Some believed the dean's decision seemed extreme and unfair. Others believed the dean made a just and fair decision. There was a lot of speculation and conversation about what was really going on.

A year later, the professor's assistant (who is Maria's friend), ran into the dean at a conference. The two spent a few minutes catching up, and just as they were about to end their conversation, the dean said to the professor's assistant, "By the way, I made a mistake regarding Maria's dismissal. Could you communicate my apologies to her and let her know that I am sorry?"

## DISCUSSION QUESTIONS

### Core Questions

- What are the social identity tensions expressed in the case?
- Discuss how you think the different social identities might perceive the tensions expressed in the case. How does this incident represent what is going on in the greater society?
- What about the situation was handled well?
- What could have been handled better or differently?
- How do the different social identities of the players contribute to their power and influence?
- What if Mark and Maria's social identities were switched?
- What role did leadership play in this situation? What role could it have played?
- Describe how different leadership practices might lead to different outcomes.
- Discuss the leadership or absence of leadership in the case.

### Reflective Questions

- Pick the character who is most different from you and reflect on how you would feel if you were in his or her position.
- Pick the character who is most similar with you and reflect on how you would feel if you were in his or her position.
- Who in the case would you feel the least comfort in leading and why?

### Case-Specific Questions

- Do you think the outcome would have been the same if the dean were a black woman? In what way?
- How might individuals or the university work toward resolving any additional distrust and/or division this case may have contributed to?

- What do you think contributed to the silence of the black students in the class?

- What impact do you think the dean's apology would have?

- How do the events that took place in the case relate to xenophobia (a dislike or fear of people who are different from oneself)?

- What steps can be taken to support a perspective of allophilia (a positive orientation toward the members of a particular group seen as different or "other")?

# Water Crises

**Trigger: Insult/Humiliating Action**
**Organization: Large, multinational organization in Singapore**
**Recommended Chapters:**

- Chapter 1: Social Identity: Understanding the In-Group/Out-Group Group Phenomenon by Stella M. Nkomo

- Chapter 2: Triggers of Social Identity Conflict by Marian N. Ruderman and Donna Chrobot-Mason

- Chapter 3: Organizational Faultlines by Astrid C. Homan and Karen A. Jehn

- Chapter 4: Leadership Practices Across Social Identity Groups by Marian N. Ruderman, Sarah Glover, Donna Chrobot-Mason, and Chris Ernst

- Chapter 5: Cultural Values by Shalom Schwartz

- Chapter 7: Cultural Intelligence: A Pathway for Leading in a Rapidly Globalizing World by Linn Van Dyne, Soon Ang, and David Livermore

- Chapter 9: Miasma: The Dynamics of Difference by Ancella B. Livers and Robert F. Solomon, Jr.

## THE CASE

This case takes place in a large multinational organization in Singapore. Singapore was ejected from the Malaya Federation in 1965 after a series of race riots. There have been tensions between Malaysia and Singapore ever since. A group of colleagues were waiting for a business meeting to begin and were talking about recent news coverage of a heated dispute over water prices that Singapore was having with Malaysia. Malaysia supplies Singapore with half its daily water needs. Malaysia wanted to renegotiate the previously fixed price of water. Singapore is charging industries a higher rate and making a profit, and Malaysia feels it should also be earning more. Singapore is willing to renegotiate the water price. However, they want the negotiation to be part of a larger deal addressing multiple issues lingering since the 1965 expulsion. Malaysia only wants to discuss the water price.

Someone made a remark indicating that, "You know Malaysia is being childish about the whole situation. The Foreign Minister of Malaysia is being unreasonable. Why can't we settle things once and for all? They are just jealous because we're better off now that we're not part of their country any more—it's their own fault." Most of the group members agreed and continued to gripe about the situation. One of the team members, Stacey, spoke up and advised that she was Malaysian. She defended the foreign minister and his position, as well as Malaysia. After she finished speaking, the room went silent. Some apologized and indicated they forgot that she was Malaysian. Others said nothing.

After the meeting, tensions were high. Team members felt uncomfortable interacting with Stacey. During team meetings, she had little to say and collaborated at a minimum with team members. The team manager noticed the change in behavior and asked individual team members about the tension she observed and why Stacey was not interacting with the team as she had before. Different team members were concerned and explained the situation to the manager, providing different perspectives.

## DISCUSSION QUESTIONS

### Core Questions

- What are the social identity tensions expressed in the case?
- Discuss how you think the different social identities might perceive the tensions expressed in the case. How does this incident represent what is going on in the greater society?
- What about the situation was handled well?
- What could have been handled better or differently?
- How do the different social identities of the players contribute to their power and influence?
- What role did leadership play in this situation? What role could it have played?

- Describe how different leadership practices would have led to a different outcome.
- Discuss the leadership/absence of leadership in the case.

**Reflective Questions**
- Pick the character who is most different from you and reflect on how you would feel if you were in his or her position.
- Pick the character who is most similar to you and reflect on how you would feel if you were in his or her position.
- If you were the leader, how would you have handled the situation?
- How would you feel if the people you worked with assumed you had opinions and values like theirs because your differences were not visible?

**Case-Specific Questions**
- Should someone in the meeting have done more to resolve the situation? What could he or she have done?
- What would be a culturally intelligent way for the team manager to handle the situation?
- How does the group's assumption (that Stacey was Singaporean, rather than Malaysian) reflect the impact of assumptions that groups tend to make about group members?
- How can one demonstrate sensitivity (fairness) in situations in which there may be invisible differences?
- What role did cultural values play in this case?

# Floating Holidays

**Trigger: Differential Treatment**
**Organization: Nonprofit organization in the United States**
**Recommended Chapters:**

- Chapter 1: Social Identity: Understanding the In-Group/Out-Group Group Phenomenon by Stella M. Nkomo
- Chapter 2: Triggers of Social Identity Conflict by Marian N. Ruderman and Donna Chrobot-Mason
- Chapter 3: Organizational Faultlines by Astrid C. Homan and Karen A. Jehn
- Chapter 4: Leadership Practices Across Social Identity Groups by Marian N. Ruderman, Sarah Glover, Donna Chrobot-Mason, and Chris Ernst
- Chapter 6: Approaches to Difference: Allophilia and Xenophobia by Todd L. Pittinsky
- Chapter 8: Social Justice and Dignity by Philomena Essed
- Chapter 9: Miasma: The Dynamics of Difference by Ancella B. Livers and Robert F. Solomon, Jr.
- Chapter 11: Leader Values and Authenticity by Todd J. Weber

## THE CASE

Rachel moved from the northeastern part of the United States to the south to begin a new job. Shortly after beginning her new position, she was surprised when she found out that the company was closed for Good Friday since Good Friday was not a national holiday. Rachel took issue with Good Friday being a company holiday. It was the first time Rachael had worked for a company in which it was assumed that everyone was a Christian. There was no policy that provided employees with an option to choose a different religious day as a paid holiday in the case that one was of a different faith. An employee could discuss taking a different day off with his or her supervisor and seek the supervisor's approval. Since Rachel is Jewish, she preferred taking Yom Kippur off instead of Good Friday, the Christian holiday. She believed that she should not have to ask for a supervisor's permission to do so since individuals are not required to ask for permission to take Good Friday or Christmas off.

Rachel suggested that the company change the Good Friday day off from a paid holiday to a floating holiday, in which individuals could choose to take the day off or not. Her rationale includes the fact that the company currently gives employees ten days off a year for holidays, three of which are Christian celebrations.

In response, Rachel's manager told her that because so many employees would be in an uproar if Good Friday were taken away as a paid holiday, she should forget about the idea and accept what had been the company norm for so many years. He added, "Ideally, we wouldn't close for just the Christian holidays, but that's not the case. The majority of employees are Christian, so the majority rules. Besides, you don't lose by having Good Friday off." Rachel became angry and continued to argue her point that Good Friday should be a floating holiday, an optional day off for employees. In haste, she yelled, "This company needs to make up its mind about what it will stand for. For a company that has such a strong Christian belief system, why does it promote same-sex partner benefits?"

## DISCUSSION QUESTIONS

### Core Questions

- What are the social identity tensions expressed in the case?

- Discuss how you think the different social identities might perceive the tensions expressed in the case. How does this incident represent what is going on in the greater society?

- What about the situation was handled well?

- What could have been handled better or differently?

- How do the different social identities of the players contribute to their power and influence?

- What role did leadership play in this situation? What role could it have played?

- Describe how different leadership practices would have led to a different outcome.
- Discuss the leadership/absence of leadership in the case.

## Reflective Questions
- Pick the character who is most different from you and reflect on how you would feel if you were in his or her position.
- Pick the character who is most similar to you and reflect on how you would feel if you were in his or her position.
- If you were the leader, how would you have handled the situation?
- How would you feel if the people you worked with assumed you had values like theirs because your differences were not visible?
- How would you feel if your invisible social identity was insulted (by people who did not know)?

## Case-Specific Questions
- Discuss the implications of basing company policy and procedures on the practices and beliefs of majority groups.
- What is suggested by Rachel's last comment? Why do you think she made the comment?
- What was threatening about the situation? Why do you think so?
- If someone from the dominant group is threatened, how does it affect the dynamics?
- How can groups be inclusive about celebrations when different groups have different customs?
- How is respect demonstrated or not demonstrated in this case?

# Not My Weekend

**Trigger: Assimilation**

**Organization: Large corporation in Hong Kong**

**Recommended Chapters:**

- Chapter 1: Social Identity: Understanding the In-Group/Out-Group Group Phenomenon by Stella M. Nkomo

- Chapter 2: Triggers of Social Identity Conflict by Marian N. Ruderman and Donna Chrobot-Mason

- Chapter 3: Organizational Faultlines by Astrid C. Homan and Karen A. Jehn

- Chapter 4: Leadership Practices Across Social Identity Groups by Marian N. Ruderman, Sarah Glover, Donna Chrobot-Mason, and Chris Ernst

- Chapter 5: Cultural Values by Shalom Schwartz

- Chapter 7: Cultural Intelligence: A Pathway for Leading in a Rapidly Globalizing World by Linn Van Dyne, Soon Ang, and David Livermore

## THE CASE

This case takes place in the Hong Kong office of a large multinational financial company called OneStop. The company has just acquired another, smaller financial company called HelpU. The company is under a lot of pressure to meet its planning deadlines. It is critical that all employees effectively work together. The managers at the company have planned a retreat for employees in order to articulate shared values and do some team-building exercises. The retreat will take place off-site over a weekend. Managers have stressed the importance of each employee attending the retreat. It is common practice for the managers of OneStop to meet on weekends, but it is not common for employees to have to work on weekends.

Some employees were upset about the event taking place over the weekend because it will interfere with other plans. Some individuals spoke to their managers and told them that they would not be able to attend the retreat because they would be at church. Others indicated they had family commitments, such as a child's birthday, visiting a family member at the hospital, and attending a funeral. Mr. Wong, originally from HelpU, granted permission for employees to not attend the retreat in order to attend church but did not accept other excuses. Employees were confused and frustrated that some excuses were accepted, while others were not.

## DISCUSSION QUESTIONS

### Core Questions
- What are the social identity tensions expressed in the case?
- Discuss how you think the different social identities might perceive the tensions expressed in the case. How does this incident represent what is going on in the greater society?
- What about the situation was handled well?
- What could have been handled better or differently?
- How do the different social identities of the players contribute to their power and influence?
- What role did leadership play in this situation? What role could it have played?
- Describe how different leadership practices would have led to a different outcome.
- Discuss the leadership/absence of leadership in the case.

### Reflective Questions
- If you were the leader, how would you have handled the situation?
- How would you feel if the people you worked with assumed you had values like them, because your differences were not visible?
- How would you feel if your invisible social identity was insulted (by people who did not know)?

**Case-Specific Questions**

- What does the common practice of working over weekends say about an organization's culture and expectations of employees?

- If you were a manager, would you have accepted the excuse of attending church? Why or why not?

- If you were a manager, would you have accepted the excuses related to family roles (child care, elder care, family celebrations)? Why or why not?

- To what extent should an organization mandate consistency in terms of what is an accepted excuse versus allowing managers be able to make their own determinations? What are the consequences of the different approaches?

- How does an organization maintain consistency regarding decisions about work hours when employees have different preferences?

# It's Their Fault

**Trigger: Different Values**
**Organization: For-profit marketing firm in Hong Kong, with representatives from multiple company sites in various countries**
**Recommended Chapters:**

- Chapter 1: Social Identity: Understanding the In-Group/Out-Group Group Phenomenon by Stella M. Nkomo
- Chapter 2: Triggers of Social Identity Conflict by Marian N. Ruderman and Donna Chrobot-Mason
- Chapter 3: Organizational Faultlines by Astrid C. Homan and Karen A. Jehn
- Chapter 4: Leadership Practices Across Social Identity Groups by Marian N. Ruderman, Sarah Glover, Donna Chrobot-Mason, and Chris Ernst
- Chapter 5: Cultural Values by Shalom Schwartz
- Chapter 6: Approaches to Difference: Allophilia and Xenophobia by Todd L. Pittinsky
- Chapter 7: Cultural Intelligence: A Pathway for Leading in a Rapidly Globalizing World by Linn Van Dyne, Soon Ang, and David Livermore
- Chapter 11: Leader Values and Authenticity by Todd J. Weber
- Chapter 12: Leading Through Paradox by Jeffrey Yip

## THE CASE

This case takes place at a large for-profit organization. Over the course of one year, employees of an international marketing firm with offices in six different countries met in Hong Kong to discuss a new logo and slogan for the marketing firm. Their goal was to enhance the current logo and slogan to better appeal to the company's diverse clientele. Twenty-five representatives from five countries attended the sessions designed to bring together diverse perspectives. Lin Yi, a manager based at the host location in Hong Kong, was the liaison and team leader for the group.

During the meeting, individuals met in small groups to brainstorm ideas for the new design of the logo and slogan and, on the surface, meetings seemed to be going reasonably well. After each gathering, however, one could overhear conversations of groups of participants making fun of and insulting other groups' suggestions, so much so that certain cultural groups dreaded attending the meetings because they anticipated having a negative experience.

For example, one of the Canadian participants began a discussion about how the company might design the new logo to appeal to a diverse group of clientele. She added her perspective on how she thought Canadian clientele would respond. This seemed to generate good discussion during the meeting as others talked about how clientele from their countries might respond. After the meeting, however, the Canadian participant overheard the Korean participants discussing the comments she had made, indicating that her idea was "ridiculous and would not work!" After hearing these comments, the Canadian participant was upset and annoyed with the Korean participants. She had nothing further to say to them and was unreceptive to their ideas throughout the remaining time on the project.

Groups formed based on which country individuals were from. Conflict arose among the different groups. The groups could not agree on ways in which work should get done and how people were expected to interact with each other. For example, some cultural groups were more blunt and straightforward than others, which occasionally offended individuals from other cultures, as they were not accustomed to or did not understand the direct tone used. Misunderstandings between the groups resulted in heightened tension and conflict. There were also differences about when work should happen. For example, the meetings were scheduled daily from 8 a.m. to 5 p.m. However, some participants tried to encourage others to stay beyond 5 p.m. to finish projects and discussions or to get a head start for the next day. Their suggestions for extending the day were not well-received by all. Other members of the team took extended breaks and did not arrive at the scheduled time.

Lin Yi, in his role as liaison and team leader, tried to rotate throughout the groups to have lunch with them and continue the discussions. Many times lunch conversations became griping sessions and opportunities for participants to complain about each other, either directly to Lin Yi or to one another. It was always the "other group's fault." Lin Yi was regularly placed in a position in which he was trying to smooth things over among groups.

## DISCUSSION QUESTIONS

### Core Questions

- What are the social identity tensions expressed in the case?
- Discuss how you think the different social identities might perceive the tensions expressed in the case.
- What about the situation was handled well?
- What could have been handled better or differently?
- How do the different social identities of the players contribute to their power and influence?
- What role did leadership play in this situation? What role could it have played?
- Describe how different leadership practices would have led to a different outcome.
- Discuss the leadership/absence of leadership in the case.

### Reflective Questions

- Pick the character who is most different from you and reflect on how you would feel if you were in his or her position.
- Pick the character who is most similar to you and reflect on how you would feel if you were in his or her position.
- If you were the leader, how would you have handled the situation?
- How would you feel if the people you worked with assumed you had values like them, because your differences were not visible?
- How would you feel if your invisible social identity was insulted (by people who did not know)?

**Case-Specific Questions**

- How was ethnocentrism (the tendency to believe that one's culture is superior to other cultures) reflected in this case?

- Discuss the expectations of how individuals and groups interact at work. What are the "hot buttons" for you in terms of what is or is not acceptable?

- What different strategies can leaders employ to manage competing values and practices among group members?

# The Scent of Difference

**Trigger: Assimilation**
**Organization: Large for-profit corporation in the United States**
**Recommended Chapters:**

- Chapter 1: Social Identity: Understanding the In-Group/Out-Group Group Phenomenon by Stella M. Nkomo
- Chapter 2: Triggers of Social Identity Conflict by Marian N. Ruderman and Donna Chrobot-Mason
- Chapter 3: Organizational Faultlines by Astrid C. Homan and Karen A. Jehn
- Chapter 4: Leadership Practices Across Social Identity Groups by Marian N. Ruderman, Sarah Glover, Donna Chrobot-Mason, and Chris Ernst
- Chapter 5: Cultural Values by Shalom Schwartz
- Chapter 6: Approaches to Difference: Allophilia and Xenophobia by Todd L. Pittinsky
- Chapter 7: Cultural Intelligence: A Pathway for Leading in a Rapidly Globalizing World by Linn Van Dyne, Soon Ang, and David Livermore
- Chapter 8: Social Justice and Dignity by Philomena Essed
- Chapter 9: Miasma: The Dynamics of Difference by Ancella B. Livers and Robert F. Solomon, Jr.

## THE CASE

A decrease in profits and an increase in expenses have forced Source One, a distribution company, to reorganize. As part of the reorganization, many older white, male employees were replaced by younger workers from India who would work for cheaper wages at the same location. Tension developed between employees who continue to work at the location and the new Indian employees, who now have their former colleagues' positions. The U.S. employees resent the Indian workers and are worried they will lose their jobs to them.

U.S. employees feel they must struggle to hold on to their traditions and ways of doing things because the immigrants hired by SourceOne have brought different ways of doing things. Race is a salient issue from the Indian perspective. One staff member from India noted that, "If you are white/caucasian, that is good, and if you are not, then you have to work harder." Neither side thinks things are going well. Indians are trying to adapt to U.S. customs, but finding it difficult. The U.S. workers feel threatened and resent the situation.

Employees work in small- to medium-sized cubicles next to one another. There is a break room with a microwave next to their work area, where employees can take breaks and heat their food. Some Indian delicacies include curry and other fragrant spices. Some U.S. employees believe the smell of Indian food is too strong, making it difficult for them to enjoy their own food. These employees have complained to HR about the smell of food, but no specific action has been taken. More conflict occurs when groups of Indians speak in their native tongue to one another in the hallways. Most U.S. employees do not understand what is being said and are offended because they assume that the Indians are speaking negatively about them.

## DISCUSSION QUESTIONS

### Core Questions

- What are the social identity tensions expressed in the case?
- Discuss how you think the different social identities might perceive the tensions expressed in the case.
- What about the situation was handled well?
- What could have been handled better or differently?
- How do the different social identities of the players contribute to their power and influence?
- What role did leadership play in this situation? What role could it have played?
- Describe how different leadership practices would have led to a different outcome.
- Discuss the leadership/absence of leadership in the case.

**Reflective Questions**

- Pick the perspective that is most different from your own and reflect on how you would feel if you were in that position.

- Pick the perspective that is most similar to yours and reflect on how you would feel if you were in that position.

- If you were the leader, how would you have handled the situation?

**Case-Specific Questions**

- Who feels threatened in this situation? Why do you think this is?

- If someone from a dominant group is threatened, how does it affect the dynamics? What about individuals from a non-dominant group(s)?

- What can be done, if anything, to address the sense of being threatened?

- Is there anything that might be construed as insulting? If so, what and why?

- What is difficult about integrating two cultures?

- What can be done to help the integration go well?

- What does this case illustrate in terms of the dynamics of two cultures coming together? What are the different dynamics and experiences depending on whether a group is dominant or non-dominant?

# Not Catching On

**Trigger: Assimilation**
**Organization: Large software company in South Africa**
**Recommended Chapters:**

- Chapter 1: Social Identity: Understanding the In-Group/Out-Group Group Phenomenon by Stella M. Nkomo

- Chapter 2: Triggers of Social Identity Conflict by Marian N. Ruderman and Donna Chrobot-Mason

- Chapter 3: Organizational Faultlines by Astrid C. Homan and Karen A. Jehn

- Chapter 4: Leadership Practices Across Social Identity Groups by Marian N. Ruderman, Sarah Glover, Donna Chrobot-Mason, and Chris Ernst

- Chapter 8: Social Justice and Dignity by Philomena Essed

- Chapter 9: Miasma: The Dynamics of Difference by Ancella B. Livers and Robert F. Solomon, Jr.

## THE CASE

South Africa has established affirmative action employment laws that give preference to black South Africans over white South Africans to redress historical disadvantages due to apartheid. White South Africans now believe they receive fewer advancement opportunities because of their skin color. In a software company located in South Africa, there is a belief that people are moved into jobs without the necessary prerequisite training, causing performance problems that become confounded with racial issues. Historically, company management has been all white, with white men filling the top managerial positions. In addition, middle and low-level positions are filled by black Africans, who typically do not have degrees. The current employment practices have contributed to the tension throughout the company. For example, employees generally separate by race when they socialize. For example, black employees and white employees do not eat lunch together. Members of each group sit together and speak in their own language.

Betty, a white female South African manager, has worked for the company for twenty-five years. She does not endorse past segregation practices and feels that everyone should be treated equally. Betty manages three major projects, which keep her extremely busy. Martha is a white female South African district manager and is Betty's boss. She has been with the company for about ten years and is responsible for the progress and support of Betty's area as well as five other areas.

Betty indicates that one of the most difficult parts of her job is training the black South African employees. For the most part, she feels that training is difficult because of language barriers. South Africa has eleven official languages. English is the official language for business. However, English is often the second or third language spoken by South Africans. The time constraints make her job even more challenging. The manager who was initially responsible for training new employees took a position with another company. It is now Betty's responsibility to complete the training, in addition to her other work.

Ketshiwe, a twenty-five-year-old black South African woman, had completed one week of a six-week training course before the previous trainer's departure. Betty is responsible for training the remaining five weeks. Betty is strict with Ketshiwe and has little patience while instructing her. Individuals hired for Ketshiwe's position typically have at least five years of experience in software development; Ketshiwe has two years of experience. Betty complains to others about Ketshiwe and insinuates that she was hired for the job solely because of her race. Although Betty never communicates her concerns to Ketshiwe directly, she discusses her frustration with the district manager and others within the company.

As soon as Ketshiwe finishes the training and begins to serve clients, complaints from the processing team, who are primarily white females, come to Betty. They indicate that the majority of Ketshiwe's service requests are wrong. They indicate they are not surprised that Ketshiwe makes so many mistakes; it is typical of the work of black South Africans. The team suggests that no matter how much training they've had, black South Africans have difficulty with "catching on." The discussion turns into a complaint session. A white South African employee says that, because more blacks are hired than whites, her son will have to leave the country to get a good job.

# DISCUSSION QUESTIONS

### Core Questions

- What are the social identity tensions expressed in the case?
- Discuss how you think the different social identities might perceive the tensions expressed in the case. How does this incident represent what is going on in the greater society?
- What about the situation was handled well?
- What could have been handled better or differently?
- How do the different social identities of the players contribute to their power and influence?
- What role did leadership play in this situation? What role could it have played?
- Describe how different leadership practices would have led to a different outcome.
- Discuss the leadership/absence of leadership in the case.

### Reflective Questions

- Pick the character who is most different from you and reflect on how you would feel if you were in her position.
- Pick the character who is most similar to you and reflect on how you would feel if you were in her position.
- If you were the leader, how would you have handled the situation?

### Case-Specific Questions

- What is the impact of affirmative action laws on organizations? What would be the impact of not having affirmative action laws?
- How might affirmative action measures differ depending on whether a minority group is being integrated into a majority group or a majority group is being integrated into minority group?
- How does a history of strained relations among groups affect workplace relationships between those groups?
- How do group stereotypes affect workplace relationships?

# Glass Ceiling at Big Boy Toys

**Trigger: Differential Treatment**
**Organization: A for-profit manufacturing organization in the United States**
**Recommended Chapters:**

- Chapter 1: Social Identity: Understanding the In-Group/Out-Group Group Phenomenon by Stella M. Nkomo

- Chapter 2: Triggers of Social Identity Conflict by Marian N. Ruderman and Donna Chrobot-Mason

- Chapter 3: Organizational Faultlines by Astrid C. Homan and Karen A. Jehn

- Chapter 4: Leadership Practices Across Social Identity Groups by Marian N. Ruderman, Sarah Glover, Donna Chrobot-Mason, and Chris Ernst

- Chapter 8: Social Justice and Dignity by Philomena Essed

- Chapter 9: Miasma: The Dynamics of Difference by Ancella B. Livers and Robert F. Solomon, Jr.

- Chapter 11: Leader Values and Authenticity by Todd J. Weber

- Chapter 12: Leading Through Paradox by Jeffrey Yip

## THE CASE

This case takes place in a U.S. company that employs over one thousand individuals of varying ethnicities and manufactures a variety of toys. Due to its competitive pricing, the company is now experiencing a significant backlog and needs its customer service and production staff to work as much overtime as possible to catch up with the demand. Carol, a white customer service representative, has been working overtime for more than three months. She has been with the company for three years and is considered to be a valued employee and top performer. She often mentors new staff.

During a team meeting, Carol's manager, a white male, announced that a new supervisor position would be available in their department. After the meeting, Carol asked her manager whether he thought she had a good chance at getting the position, given her skills and experience. He told her that he thought she had an excellent chance. Carol's manager also gave her tips to enhance her chances of getting the position.

Carol was excited! She knew she was giving it her all by continuing to work the overtime and following her boss's advice. The time came for the decision to be made about the supervisor position. Her interview had gone well and she felt good about the position. However, to Carol's surprise, the offer was extended to a white man from a different department who had limited customer service experience. He also happened to play on a sports team with her boss. Carol was crushed. She had worked hard and followed her manager's advice to prepare for the position. When she inquired about the decision, she was told that this person was "more suitable" for the supervisor position. To gain another perspective, Carol spoke with a colleague who was aware of the situation. She asked the colleague what he thought, and he said it was very strange and seemed to be unfair. Although Carol strongly believes that she is more qualified for the supervisor position, she remains as a customer service representative working for the new supervisor and trying to accept him as her boss.

## DISCUSSION QUESTIONS

### Core Questions
- What are the social identity tensions expressed in the case?
- Discuss how you think the different social identities might perceive the tensions expressed in the case. How does this incident represent what is going on in the greater society?
- What about the situation was handled well?
- What could have been handled better or differently?
- How do the different social identities of the players contribute to their power and influence?
- What role did leadership play in this situation? What role could it have played?

- Describe how different leadership practices would have led to a different outcome.
- Discuss the leadership/absence of leadership in the case.

**Reflective Questions**
- Pick the character who is most different from you and reflect on how you would feel if you were in his or her position.
- Pick the character who is most similar to you and reflect on how you would feel if you were in his or her position.
- If you were the leader, how would you have handled the situation?

**Case-Specific Questions**
- At the end of the case, Carol accepts the situation. What impact might this situation have on how she views her role within the organization? What are other ways she might have handled the situation?
- Why do you think the other candidate got the job?
- Explain how psychological, structural, and power issues might influence hiring and promotion decisions.
- What should organizations do to address these dynamics?

# Super Drugs

**Trigger: Differential Treatment**
**Organization: For-profit pharmaceutical company in Jordan**
**Recommended Chapters:**

- Chapter 1: Social Identity: Understanding the In-Group/Out-Group Group Phenomenon by Stella M. Nkomo

- Chapter 2: Triggers of Social Identity Conflict by Marian N. Ruderman and Donna Chrobot-Mason

- Chapter 3: Organizational Faultlines by Astrid C. Homan and Karen A. Jehn

- Chapter 4: Leadership Practices Across Social Identity Groups by Marian N. Ruderman, Sarah Glover, Donna Chrobot-Mason, and Chris Ernst

- Chapter 5: Cultural Values by Shalom Schwartz

- Chapter 8: Social Justice and Dignity by Philomena Essed

- Chapter 9: Miasma: The Dynamics of Difference by Ancella B. Livers and Robert F. Solomon, Jr.

## THE CASE

Super Drugs is a small pharmaceutical company located in Jordan. It employs just over three hundred individuals, primarily Jordanians and Palestinians. The company is made up of mostly men with very few women. Jordanian staff are primarily in the upper-level positions, while Palestinian employees hold the middle and lower-level positions.

Jordanian and Palestinian employees spend some social time together, but relations are tense because of a perception of favoritism. Over the last three months, Sami and three of his Palestinian colleagues applied for two new positions within the company. They have each been with the company for at least seven years, have positive performance records, and a good work ethic. None of them received the positions they applied for and were given no explanation other than that the decision had been made and was final. A Jordanian was hired for each of the positions instead. The Jordanians had less experience and less tenure with the company than Sami and his colleagues, who now feel discriminated against. They are unsure of their future with the company.

In addition, Sami was told that he would receive extra pay for working overtime, which he has not received. He approached his manager, Khalil, about this issue. Khalil is Jordanian and makes all of the hiring and salary decisions or has input on them. He has been working for the company for twenty years and is good friends with all of the managers in upper-level positions. The culture is such that hiring and promoting individuals from one's own group is seen as an expression of loyalty and is expected.

Khalil told Sami that he could not give him extra pay because of the financial status of the company. Sami assumed that this was true for all employees, but one day he overheard some of his Jordanian co-workers discussing the overtime work they had done, and how the extra pay has really made a difference. Hearing this, Sami decided to ask his fellow Palestinian co-workers if they were receiving extra pay for overtime work. They told him that they were not. They also discussed the positions they had each applied for and been denied for seemingly invalid reasons. The group grew increasingly frustrated.

## DISCUSSION QUESTIONS

### Core Questions

- What are the social identity tensions expressed in the case?
- Discuss how you think the different social identities might perceive the tensions expressed in the case. How does this incident represent what is going on in the greater society?
- What about the situation was handled well?
- What could have been handled better or differently?
- How do the different social identities of the players contribute to their power and influence?
- What role did leadership play in this situation? What role could it have played?

- Describe how different leadership practices would have led to a different outcome.
- Discuss the leadership/absence of leadership in the case.

**Reflective Questions**
- Pick the character who is most different from you and reflect on how you would feel if you were in his position.
- Pick the character who is most similar to you and reflect on how you would feel if you were in his position.
- If you were the leader, how would you have handled the situation?

**Case-Specific Questions**
- Discuss the importance of equal treatment in hiring and salary decisions.
- What should the Palestinian workers do now?
- Discuss the differences and similarities between loyalty and favoritism. What are the advantages and disadvantages of each?
- How are these concepts seen differently in collectivistic or individualistic societies?
- How might differential treatment contribute to more extreme forms of discrimination?

# The Right to Be Pregnant

**Trigger: Assimilation**

**Organization: For-profit financial institution in Brazil**

**Recommended Chapters:**

- Chapter 1: Social Identity: Understanding the In-Group/Out-Group Group Phenomenon by Stella M. Nkomo

- Chapter 2: Triggers of Social Identity Conflict by Marian N. Ruderman and Donna Chrobot-Mason

- Chapter 3: Organizational Faultlines by Astrid C. Homan and Karen A. Jehn

- Chapter 4: Leadership Practices Across Social Identity Groups by Marian N. Ruderman, Sarah Glover, Donna Chrobot-Mason, and Chris Ernst

- Chapter 5: Cultural Values by Shalom Schwartz

- Chapter 8: Social Justice and Dignity by Philomena Essed

- Chapter 9: Miasma: The Dynamics of Difference by Ancella B. Livers and Robert F. Solomon, Jr.

## THE CASE

Angela works for a large financial institution in Brazil. She is a consumer banking representative in the Customer Service division. She is five months pregnant and has been having a difficult pregnancy. She has missed several days from work because of this. There is no official company policy specifically regarding pregnancy-related illnesses. In Angela's division, pregnancy-related illness is not perceived the same as being sick generally. Other female employees who have had difficult pregnancies have been told they needed to come to work anyway. Women feel they don't have the "right" to be pregnant if it causes them to miss work.

Angela's manager Jose expresses his concern about her being absent from work. Angela explains that her absences are because of what she is experiencing with the pregnancy. Nevertheless, Jose complains to other managers about the situation. The situation has become gossip across the company. Some agree with Jose's point of view, and others support Angela. The gossip continues and Angela is now feeling disregarded. She is wondering why no one in management is doing anything to resolve this issue.

After giving birth, she returns to work for about a month and is later dismissed from the company; the reasons for her dismissal are not clear and more rumors spread.

## DISCUSSION QUESTIONS

### Core Questions
- What are the social identity tensions expressed in the case?
- Discuss how you think the different social identities might perceive the tensions expressed in the case. How does this incident represent what is going on in the greater society?
- What about the situation was handled well?
- What could have been handled better or differently?
- How do the different social identities of the players contribute to their power and influence?
- What if the social identities were switched?
- What role did leadership play in this situation? What role could it have played?
- Discuss the leadership/absence of leadership in the case.

### Reflective Questions
- Pick the perspective that is most different from yours and reflect on how you would feel if you were in that position.
- Pick the perspective that is most similar to yours and reflect on how you would feel if you were in that position.
- If you were the leader, how would you have handled the situation?

**Case-Specific Questions**

- What was threatening to Angela about the situation?

- What are the implications of the organization not having specific policies?

- Should pregnancy-related illnesses be treated the same as other kinds of illness? What are the implications of either approach?

- What if Jose's job is contingent on his division's productivity, and Angela missing work due to her pregnancy has reduced productivity? How can Jose balance the paradox of being seen as a productive manager with being seen as a supportive manager in this situation?

# Local Bombing

**Trigger: Simple Contact**
**Organization: Nonprofit school in Jordan**
**Recommended Chapters:**

- Chapter 1: Social Identity: Understanding the In-Group/Out-Group Group Phenomenon by Stella M. Nkomo
- Chapter 2: Triggers of Social Identity Conflict by Marian N. Ruderman and Donna Chrobot-Mason
- Chapter 3: Organizational Faultlines by Astrid C. Homan and Karen A. Jehn
- Chapter 4: Leadership Practices Across Social Identity Groups by Marian N. Ruderman, Sarah Glover, Donna Chrobot-Mason, and Chris Ernst
- Chapter 5: Cultural Values by Shalom Schwartz
- Chapter 6: Approaches to Difference: Allophilia and Xenophobia by Todd L. Pittinsky
- Chapter 8: Social Justice and Dignity by Philomena Essed
- Chapter 9: Miasma: The Dynamics of Difference by Ancella B. Livers and Robert F. Solomon, Jr.

## THE CASE

Over 90 percent of the Jordanian population is Muslim, with a very small percentage of Christians. This case takes place at one of the few Christian schools in Jordan. The school's mission is centered on working across religions in service of the poor. Unlike most schools in Jordan, which are predominately Muslim, both Muslim and Christian faiths are represented among the employees and the students. The school administrators, who are all Christian, believe there are no problems related to religious differences. Although Christian and Muslim holidays are honored, there are no formal policies or procedures related to religious differences.

After weeks of conflict between Christians and Muslims throughout Jordan, several local Christian churches are bombed. These bombings cause a major stir and, in response, frequent demonstrations are held.

A couple of weeks after the bombing incidents, Muslim and Christian teachers were discussing the bombings and speculating about why the churches were attacked and who was responsible for the attacks. The conversation became heated when some said that government agencies were responsible for the attacks, while others blamed extremists groups.

Teachers who had been friends and colleagues for years began to change their attitudes toward one other. They began to feel the differences between them and harbor ill feelings toward one other. As a result of these tensions, and ongoing gossip, some teachers began to feel alienated. A few teachers resigned from their positions.

## DISCUSSION QUESTIONS

### Core Questions

- What are the social identity tensions expressed in the case?
- Discuss how you think the different social identities might perceive the tensions expressed in the case. How does this incident represent what is going on in the greater society?
- What about the situation was handled well?
- What could have been handled better or differently?
- How do the different social identities of the players contribute to their power and influence?
- What role did leadership play in this situation? What role could it have played?
- Discuss the leadership/absence of leadership in the case.

### Reflective Questions

- Pick the perspective that is most different from yours and reflect on how you would feel if you were in that position.

- Pick the perspective that is most similar to yours and reflect on how you would feel if you were in that position.
- If you were the leader, how would you have handled the situation?

**Case-Specific Questions**
- What was threatening about the situation? Why do you think so?
- In this case, the dominant group in the school is different from the dominant group in the society at large. How does this affect the social identity dynamics in the school?
- What role could or should an organization play when larger events cause conflicts and tensions within the organization?
- If there were specific organizational policies on religious differences, would it have made a difference in this case? Why or why not?
- The school's values and mission are specifically based on religious inclusion. Explain how and why social identity conflict managed to polarize these seemingly integrated groups in this organization?
- What are the advantages and disadvantages of acknowledging group differences in organizations?
- What are the advantages and disadvantages of not acknowledging group differences in organizations?

# Benefits Battle

**Trigger: Differential Treatment**
**Organization: Nonprofit organization in the northeast part of the United States**
**Recommended Chapters:**

- Chapter 1: Social Identity: Understanding the In-Group/Out-Group Group Phenomenon by Stella M. Nkomo

- Chapter 2: Triggers of Social Identity Conflict by Marian N. Ruderman and Donna Chrobot-Mason

- Chapter 3: Organizational Faultlines by Astrid C. Homan and Karen A. Jehn

- Chapter 4: Leadership Practices Across Social Identity Groups by Marian N. Ruderman, Sarah Glover, Donna Chrobot-Mason, and Chris Ernst

- Chapter 5: Cultural Values by Shalom Schwartz

- Chapter 6: Approaches to Difference: Allophilia and Xenophobia by Todd L. Pittinsky

- Chapter 7: Cultural Intelligence: A Pathway for Leading in a Rapidly Globalizing World by Linn Van Dyne, Soon Ang, and David Livermore

- Chapter 8: Social Justice and Dignity by Philomena Essed

- Chapter 9: Miasma: The Dynamics of Difference by Ancella B. Livers and Robert F. Solomon, Jr.

- Chapter 11: Leader Values and Authenticity by Todd J. Weber

- Chapter 12: Leading Through Paradox by Jeffrey Yip

## THE CASE

This organization is a nonprofit community-based support organization located in the northeastern part of the United States. It is made up of a diverse group of individuals and has a founder and CEO who is well known for being a civil rights advocate and a leader in consumer rights. The mission of the organization is to help individuals get out of financial difficulty.

The incident takes place during a human resource committee meeting designed to set policies and new rules for employees. Policy decisions on health insurance, life insurance, and various internal guidelines are addressed by this committee. Meetings are open for all employees to attend. Initial recommendations are made by the committee and are then forwarded to the CEO for final approval.

During the meeting, there is a discussion about the company's health insurance policy. An employee, who is believed to be a heterosexual, asked about health insurance coverage for same-sex domestic partners. After the question was raised, people in the meeting immediately began to take sides based on religious beliefs and how this change would affect them.

One employee says, "It is a shame that we have to sacrifice the level of coverage for our spouses, just so a few people can have access to benefits." After hearing this, other employees begin to express their unwillingness to sacrifice the level of benefits their spouses could have.

Word traveled across the organization and other employees began to form their own opinions. Some people were willing to sacrifice coverage for the sake of equal benefits among all employees. Others were against offering same-sex domestic partner benefits for various reasons, including the possibility that the benefits would not be used, personal mindsets toward sexual preference, and various religious beliefs. Some were even caught in the middle due to their religious beliefs and their support for fairness and equality.

The work of the organization was disrupted. Employees were visiting each other's offices, asking for one another's opinions, and gossiping about what different people had said in the human resource meetings. After the third meeting about the insurance benefit, the CEO made a statement indicating that he would not tolerate discriminatory acts against anyone.

Shortly thereafter, the human resource committee negotiated with the insurance carrier for several weeks to choose the best health insurance options for the company. They specifically sought to avoid having employees sacrifice coverage due to any changes in the policy, while striving for equal benefits for all.

## DISCUSSION QUESTIONS

### Core Questions

- What are the social identity tensions expressed in the case?
- Discuss how you think the different social identities might perceive the tensions expressed in the case. How does this incident represent what is going on in the greater society?
- What about the situation was handled well?
- What could have been handled better or differently?
- How do the different social identities of the players contribute to their power and influence?
- What role did leadership play in this situation? What role could it have played?
- Discuss the leadership/absence of leadership in the case.

### Reflective Questions

- Pick the perspective that is most different from yours and reflect on how you would feel if you were in that position.
- Pick the perspective that is most similar to yours and reflect on how you would feel if you were in that position.
- If you were the leader, how would you have handled the situation?
- How would you feel if the people you worked with assumed you had values like them, because your differences were not visible?
- How would you feel if your invisible social identity was insulted (by people who did not know)?

### Case-Specific Questions

- How can a value of equality/fairness be reconciled with a conviction that certain beliefs or actions are wrong?
- How can you treat someone fairly even if you do not agree with what he or she believes or is doing?

- If you had to make a choice between fairness and equality or living according to your moral values, which would you choose and why? What would you consider when making that choice?

- What is the minimum level of respect that should be shown to all, and how would you show it?

- Treating each other with respect is often articulated as an organizational value. How can this be reflected in organizational policies and practices?

# Francois' Dilemma

**Trigger: Differential Treatment**
**Organization: For-profit insurance company in France**
**Recommended Chapters:**

- Chapter 1: Social Identity: Understanding the In-Group/Out-Group Group Phenomenon by Stella M. Nkomo
- Chapter 2: Triggers of Social Identity Conflict by Marian N. Ruderman and Donna Chrobot-Mason
- Chapter 3: Organizational Faultlines by Astrid C. Homan and Karen A. Jehn
- Chapter 4: Leadership Practices Across Social Identity Groups by Marian N. Ruderman, Sarah Glover, Donna Chrobot-Mason, and Chris Ernst
- Chapter 5: Cultural Values by Shalom Schwartz
- Chapter 6: Approaches to Difference: Allophilia and Xenophobia by Todd L. Pittinsky
- Chapter 8: Social Justice and Dignity by Philomena Essed
- Chapter 9: Miasma: The Dynamics of Difference by Ancella B. Livers and Robert F. Solomon, Jr.
- Chapter 11: Leader Values and Authenticity by Todd J. Weber

## THE CASE

This case takes place in a large, multinational insurance company in France. Francois manages a diverse department of about forty people. He is responsible for IT Services. He feels he and his department are treated as second-class citizens inside the company. Employees in the Product Development, Research, and

Marketing departments tend to have higher levels of education and are clearly move valued within the organization.

The company has a history of valuing educational level more than competence and experience. Managers are seen as superior. People with less education and those in lower levels of the company are not valued and feel disempowered. As a manager and because of his education, Francois feels he is at least sometimes listened to within the company and can speak out. However, his department is not invited to important meetings or asked for input into critical decisions. In fact, when they are invited to meetings, it is often to listen to other departments talk about their goals and accomplishments.

During management team meetings, his recommendations are ignored, while similar recommendations from the research manager are considered brilliant. At a recent meeting, all departments except for his were asked to present their progress and planning reports. It's as if the work of his group does not matter. Francois observed that in other departments, the lower-level workers are not listened to, even when they have good ideas, because they do not have university degrees. Francois doesn't agree with this approach to management. He feels the people doing the job are likely to know the job best and are a source for important information. The employees in his department are complaining to him about this "second-class" treatment from other departments. Recently, the company provided bonuses to Product Development, Research, and Marketing workers, while his department received nothing. Several employees have already left the company, even when they did not have other job prospects. One employee said he liked working for Francois, but he was sick of being treated like a donkey by the organization. Francois sees the situation as one ingrained in the company culture and doesn't know what to do about it.

## DISCUSSION QUESTIONS

### Core Questions

- What are the social identity tensions expressed in the case?
- Discuss how you think the different social identities might perceive the tensions expressed in the case. How does this incident represent what is going on in the greater society?
- What about the situation was handled well?
- What could have been handled better or differently?

- How do the different social identities of the players contribute to their power and influence?
- What role did leadership play in this situation? What role could it have played?
- Describe how different leadership practices would have led to a different outcome.
- Discuss the leadership/absence of leadership in the case.

**Reflective Questions**
- Pick a group that is most different from you and reflect on how you would feel if you were in that position.
- Pick the character who is most similar to you and reflect on how you would feel if you were in his or her position.
- If you were the leader, how would you have handled the situation?

**Case-Specific Questions**
- What are the faultlines in this company?
- What can the company do to reduce the tension between groups?
- What is the organizational impact of workers feeling disempowered?
- Why does Francois seem to be the only manager concerned about the treatment of lower-level workers?
- Is it important for organizations to include all levels of employees in decision making? Why or why not?

# PART THREE

# Perspectives

The chapters in this section have been written by experts from different countries with different areas of expertise. These perspectives offer readers insights into new ways of thinking about situations. Learning to effectively work across differences represents not only a challenge, but also an opportunity for innovations and for more holistic approaches to problem solving, particularly complex problems that require multiple perspectives to find an effective solution.

The first few chapters provide a foundational understanding of the core concepts running throughout the cases. We recommend that you read the first four chapters before reading and discussing the cases. In Chapter 1, Dr. Nkomo provides an overview of social identity and the dynamics of in-group versus out-group thinking. In Chapter 2, Drs. Ruderman and Chrobot-Mason describe the categories of triggering events from which the cases shared were drawn. In Chapter 3, Drs. Homan and Jehn provide an overview of organizational faultlines. Chapter 4 describes different categories of leadership practices one could use to lead within contexts of difference. Subsequent chapters go more deeply into the concepts illustrated in the cases. In Chapter 5, Dr. Schwartz describes his theory of the underlying cultural values that help frame our attitudes and behaviors. In Chapter 6, Dr. Pittinsky discusses his theory about two very different approaches to difference: xenophobia and allophilia. In Chapter 7, Drs. Van Dyne, Ang and Livermore describe the concept of cultural intelligence. In Chapter 8, Dr. Essed shares her thinking about how the issues raised in these cases connect with social justice and dignity. In Chapter 9, Dr. Livers and Mr. Solomon introduce the concept of "miasma" and describe the additional pressures often experienced by individuals in a non-dominant category. In Chapter 10, Drs. Bhawuk and Munusamy link the notion of one's self-concept and approach to leadership to culture. In Chapter 11, Dr. Weber builds on the previous chapters and introduces the notion of leader authenticity. And finally, in Chapter 12, Mr. Yip describes the notion of leading in a context of paradox.

# Social Identity: Understanding the In-Group/Out-Group Group Phenomenon

*Stella M. Nkomo*

---

**Keywords**: social identity, social identity theory, in-groups, out-groups, self-categorization, multiple identities, simultaneity of identities, social identity conflict, faultlines

**Key Points**

- Social identity theory (SIT) is a cognitive theory that holds that individuals tend to classify themselves and others into social categories and that these classifications have a significant effect on human interactions. Social identity theory is concerned with both the psychological and sociological aspects of group behavior and explains the psychological basis of group behavior, group association, and intergroup discrimination. It is composed of three elements:
  - Categorization (self-categorization): Individuals often put others (and themselves) into categories. Labeling someone as white, homosexual, rich, or Hindu are ways of saying other things about these people.
  - Identification: Individuals also associate with certain groups (in-groups), which serve to bolster their self-esteem.

- Comparison: Individuals compare their groups with other groups, seeing a favorable bias toward the in-group to which they belong (positive discrimination), and competing with out-groups to which they do not belong.
- The elements of identification and comparison can lead to in-group favoritism and out-group derogation, stereotyping, and social identity conflict.
- Individuals have multiple identities (black, female, academic, mother), which they belong to simultaneously.
- The relative importance of group identities may vary over time and context.
- Social identity theory provides compelling theoretical and empirical evidence of the role of social identity in how people think about themselves and others as members of a group.

## Related Exercises

- Exercise 1: Mapping Your Social Identities
- Exercise 3: Identifying Faultlines
- Exercise 4: Cultural Values
- Exercise 5: Approaches to Difference
- Exercise 7: Your Leadership Practices

## Related Cases

- Case 1: Race and Respect
- Case 2: Water Crises
- Case 3: Floating Holidays
- Case 4: Not My Weekend
- Case 5: It's Their Fault
- Case 6: The Scent of Difference
- Case 7: Not Catching On
- Case 8: Glass Ceiling at Big Boy Toys
- Case 9: Super Drugs
- Case 10: The Right to Be Pregnant
- Case 11: Local Bombing
- Case 12: Benefits Battle
- Case 13: Francois' Dilemma

During the post-World War II period up until the early 1970s, social psychology suffered a "crisis of confidence" (Hornsey, 2008). Theoretical explanations for some of the worst expressions of intergroup relations—such as the Holocaust and other atrocities—tended to blame internal psychological processes and were viewed as overly simplistic and individualistic, ignoring the role played by social context (Hornsey, 2008). Out of this crisis, psychologists developed a number of theories explaining how individuals perceive themselves and others as members of different social groups. Social identity theory (SIT) is one of the most prominent and well researched of the intergroup theories that emerged. It was developed by European social psychologist Henry Tajfel (1972) as a vehicle for explaining how people think about themselves as members of social groups as well as how they behave in intergroup contexts. Tajfel defined social identity as "the individual's knowledge that he belongs to certain social groups together with some emotional and value significance to him of this group membership" (1972, p. 272). Social identity theory helps leaders understand the potential effects of diversity on groups and individuals in organizations as well as the strategies to improve intergroup relations across difference. In this chapter, I provide an overview of social identity theory, focusing particularly on the in-group/out-group phenomenon.

With his colleague, John Turner, Tajfel conducted numerous experiments to test, validate, and extend social identity theory. They explored how people categorize themselves as members of a social group, the emotional and behavioral effects of social group membership on individual identity, and the intergroup dynamics resulting from social group comparisons (Hornsey, 2008; Tajfel & Turner, 1979). In the last two decades, literature about social identity processes in organizations and its application to understanding diversity in organizations has grown substantially (Abrams & Hogg, 2004; Ashforth & Mael, 1989; Brickson, 2000; Christian, Porter, & Moffitt, 2006; Ensari, Christian, & Miller, 2006; Hogg & Terry, 2000; Nkomo & Stewart, 2006; Tsui, Egan, & O'Reilly, 1992).

Social identity theory provides a means of understanding how diverse groups in organizations might behave and interact. Groups, organizations, and societies are never entirely homogeneous. Instead, they consist of diverse groups whose identities are based in part on social categories such as gender, race, ethnicity, age, religion, nationality, socioeconomic status, and other dimensions. Some of these identities are visible (for example, gender, race, and age), while others are less visible (for example, sexual orientation and socioeconomic status). According to social identity theory, group memberships influence the way individuals think about themselves (self-concept) and others. Individuals engage in a process of self-categorization by identifying the social groups to which they belong. For example, I think of myself as being an academic, an African-American, and a woman; like everyone else, I belong to several different social groups that make up my social identity.

The relative importance of these group identities may vary over time and context. The immediate social context influences the relative importance of different group memberships. For example, being African-American may not be as salient when I am working with a majority of African-Americans. On the other hand, if I am the only African-American in a work group, being African-American becomes more significant to me and perhaps to others. The salience of my African-American identity can also be triggered by events in the larger social context. A racial attack on a church in a predominantly African-American neighborhood may evoke my African-American identity in the workplace. In addition to the context, the particular salience of any group identity is also influenced by one's personality (Stryker, 2007).

The norms and values of the salient groups that individuals belong to influence their perceptions, behaviors, and values based on the degree of identification with a group. For example, in the Water Crises Case, Stacey, the only Malaysian on her team, defended the foreign minister and his position as well as her country in the dispute. This suggests that Stacey's group membership (being Malaysian) is important and salient to her and influences how she views the dispute.

It is important to emphasize that an individual's self-concept is not based on a single group membership and may not match how he or she is categorized by others (Nkomo & Stewart, 2006). When we meet individuals for the first time, we often quickly place them within social categories. Even though my identity as an African-American may not be particularly salient to me, others may assign significance to it and respond to me as a member of that group. Social categorization helps us to simplify and make sense of the complex social world in which we all live and work. By grouping people into social categories, we can anticipate what to expect and how we should behave toward them (Hogg & Terry, 2000).

Social identity is clarified through a comparative process. Most individuals strive for a positive self-concept and therefore want to belong to valued groups in society. One way to achieve this is to think of the groups to which we belong as special and positive and to think of the groups to which we do not belong as negative or not as good as our group (Hogg & Terry, 2000). If we accept Tajfel's (1972) idea that people are motivated to have a positive self-concept, it follows that people should be motivated to think of the groups they belong to as better. This dynamic is captured in the theory of in-groups and out-groups.

Tajfel (1972) demonstrated the power of in-group and out-group membership in a series of experiments during which he divided individuals based on trivial differences; in this case he created "overestimators" and "underestimators" on the basis of their estimates of the numbers of dots on a page. The overestimators were designated as the "in-group." He found the mere process of making active "us and them" distinctions could evoke certain predictable behaviors by in-group members toward out-group members (Hornsey, 2008). In-group members depersonalized members of the out-group; out-group members were no longer viewed as individuals but as representatives of the out-group—they became "one of them." Members of the in-group maintained social distance from the out-group. In-group bias can be expressed in a number of behaviors toward out-group members, some of which are aggressive and negative, while others are more benign (Hogg & Terry, 2000). Some of the aggressive behaviors include prejudice, discrimination, ethnocentrisms, and negative stereotyping. Extreme xenophobia can lead to actions like genocide and ethnic cleansing. Examples of this extreme include the Holocaust, wherein Jewish people, among others, were murdered because of their social identity, and the genocide in Rwanda, where Tutsi people were slaughtered by the dominant Hutus. More benign examples of in-group/out-group interactions are displaying solidarity with one's in-group, wearing a t-shirt with the group's name, or harmless intergroup competition like rooting for the home team at a sports tournament (Hogg & Terry, 2000). The positive outcomes of in-group/out-group behaviors are bonding within a group and enhanced self-esteem; however, as evidenced in the examples above, the outcomes are not always positive.

It is critically important for leaders to understand that many factors external and internal to an organization can intensify in-group/out-group dynamics for better or for worse. The "Triggers of Social Identity Conflict" chapter in this book describes events that have been found to heighten social identity tension in organizations. Intergroup dynamics in any setting including organizations are influenced by societal and organizational factors. In-group/out-group dynamics are likely to be exacerbated when the in-group/out-group membership in society is similar to that in organizations; when the dominant and valued groups in society are the same as the dominant and valued groups inside organizations (see the "Organizational Faultlines" chapter in this book for more information).

For instance, in the United States, white males dominate management and leadership positions, consistent with their status in the larger society. In South Africa under apartheid, black South Africans who were lowest on the racial hierarchy established by apartheid were relegated to menial and unskilled positions and employed as cheap labor, while white men held the highest paying professional and managerial jobs (Booysen, 2007). In societies that have experienced conflict between social identity groups, people often more strongly identify with and are emotionally invested in their membership in those social identity groups (Hornsby, 2008). For example, the ongoing conflict between Israelis and Palestinians in the Middle East and the Tamils and Sinhalese in Sri Lanka make those social identity groups (Israeli, Palestinian, Tamil, or Sinhalese) more salient.

Social categories are not equally important in terms of the kinds of experiences individuals have in organizations. Social categories like race, gender, ethnicity, religion, sexual orientation, and age are often referred to as primary dimensions of diversity because of their immutable character as well as the stigmas attached to being a member of non-dominant groups. Being gay, lesbian, bisexual, or transsexual in an organization in which heterosexuals dominate and hold powerful positions will often create more oppressive in-group and out-group dynamics than those that may occur between in-group/out-groups based on functional categories (for example, marketing versus accounting). Because individuals have multiple group identities, as illustrated earlier, they can be part of either the in-group or out-group depending on context. The likelihood of experiencing discrimination, stereotyping, and exclusion in an organization also increases when out-group status correlates with employment status. If there are few Hispanics in an organization and they all work as janitors, negative stereotyping and discrimination will likely increase toward them. Or if all of the women in an organization hold clerical positions, perception of their suitability for non-clerical positions will be reinforced by stereotypes of women.

Social identity theory and research offer a number of strategies and behaviors leaders can use to mitigate the effects of in-group/out-group dynamics; many of these strategies and behaviors are described in the Leadership Practices chapter in this book. Leaders need to recognize how their individual behavior can be significant in intergroup contexts. Where leaders are perceived to be members of the in-group, there is particularly high potential to influence perceptions, attitudes, and behaviors of in-group members toward out-groups (Hogg & Terry, 2000).

At a basic level, social identity theory suggests the importance of demographic diversity in organizations. High demographic homogeneity in an organization with a low presence of diverse people may strengthen in-group identity and power to the detriment of underrepresented groups (out-groups) (Cox, 1993). If underrepresented groups feel marginalized or stigmatized, they may be less motivated and committed to the organization or, at worst, exit the organization. In the Water Crises case referred to earlier, Stacey withdraws from participating in the work team. Research has shown that well-managed diverse groups contribute positively to organization performance and also increase the opportunities for organizations to reach diverse markets and customers (Ely & Thomas, 2001; van Knippenberg & Haslam, 2003). Attracting, retaining, and effectively leveraging a diverse workforce is critical to success in a globalized marketplace (Cox, 2001).

In summary, social identity theory provides compelling theoretical and empirical evidence of the role of social identity in how people think about themselves and others as members of a group. Empirical experiments by Tajfel (1972) and others illustrated how even meaningless social categories can evoke "us and them" behavior among in-group members toward the out-group. These types of interactions are even more volatile when group differentiation is based on socio-demographic categories embedded within long-standing historical and cultural clashes. However, at the same time, social identity theory also provides insight into the strategies leaders can use in leading across difference.

# Triggers of Social Identity Conflict

*Marian N. Ruderman*
*Donna Chrobot-Mason*

**Keywords:** Triggers, faultlines, assimilation, simple contact, different values, insult or humiliating act, differential treatment

**Key Points**

- Social identity conflicts are triggered by events that activate latent tensions in society. Such tensions may result from disparities of wealth and power or a long history of intergroup conflict and distrust.

- There are five types of events that trigger social identity conflicts in organizations: differential treatment, different values, assimilation, insults or humiliating actions, and simple contact.

- Social identity conflicts are emotional in nature—they get at the heart of who we are and what we believe.

- A general strategy for considering these questions is to try to gain a deeper understanding of social identity issues in the organization. This may allow for the recognition of potential triggers.

## Related Exercises

- Exercise 1: Mapping Your Social Identities
- Exercise 2: Your Experience with Triggers
- Exercise 3: Identifying Faultlines
- Exercise 4: Cultural Values
- Exercise 5: Approaches to Difference
- Exercise 6: Cultural Intelligence
- Exercise 7: Your Leadership Practices
- Exercise 8: Examining Your Leadership Networks
- Exercise 9: Taking a New Perspective

## Related Cases

- Case 1: Race and Respect
- Case 2: Water Crises
- Case 3: Floating Holidays
- Case 4: Not My Weekend
- Case 5: It's Their Fault
- Case 6: The Scent of Difference
- Case 7: Not Catching On
- Case 8: Glass Ceiling at Big Boy Toys
- Case 9: Super Drugs
- Case 10: The Right to Be Pregnant
- Case 11: Local Bombing
- Case 12: Benefits Battle
- Case 13: Francois' Dilemma

---

Conflicts stemming from social identity occur when disagreements between two people are rooted in the social identities of one or both parties (Chrobot-Mason, Ruderman, Weber, Ohlott, & Dalton, 2007). These conflicts, which typically start with a small group of people, can spread to include many more people in the organization.

Social identity conflicts are triggered by events that activate latent tensions in society. Such tensions may result from disparities of wealth and power or a long history of intergroup conflict and distrust. These underlying tensions in organizations are called *faultlines*—lines that divide people into distinct groups (Lau & Murnighan, 1998; see also the "Organizational Faultlines" chapter in this book). Typically, people in an organization categorize others into groups of people "like me," who are on my side of the faultline, and people who are "unlike me" on the other side of the faultline. Tajfel and Turner (1986) explain that this tendency to categorize people this way is part of human nature. This is the basic notion of in-group/out-group psychology (see the "Social Identity" chapter for more information). Similar to an earthquake caused when faultlines in the Earth's crust are activated, there can be a "quake" splitting members of an organization into groups resulting in polarization when faultlines are activated in the workplace.

Active faultlines, such as hostility between men and women, make it difficult for work groups and organizations to pursue common goals and to align resources. They also contribute to the deterioration of trust and commitment in the organization. What appears to be a simple feud between two employees can morph into a large clash between groups of workers, slowing down the productivity and effectiveness of an organization. This is because even a simple feud can evoke intense feelings of threat between two groups, leading those involved to view the situation and the relationship between groups as a fierce competition for status, clout, and esteem in the organization.

## FIVE TYPES OF TRIGGERS

Chrobot-Mason, Ruderman, Weber, and Ernst (2009) identify five types of events that trigger social identity conflicts in organizations: differential treatment, different values, assimilation, insults or humiliating actions, and simple contact. Understanding these events is a first step in trying to address them. These events highlight differences in social identity (for example, gender, race, culture, sexual orientation) as they activate faultlines. *Triggers* act as a sign that tension originating in society at large may be psychologically threatening to particular social identity groups in the organization. Triggers "wake up" dormant faultlines. The cases in this book are examples of situations that triggered faultlines. In this chapter we describe the five types of events that trigger social identity conflict and provide ideas about what leaders can do about them.

*Differential treatment* occurs when dominant and non-dominant groups perceive that they are treated differently. Groups can become polarized when resources or punishments are perceived as being differentially distributed. For example, there may be a pay gap between men and women in an organization or a feeling that a group of Muslim immigrants is unduly punished for taking breaks that coincide with their religious practice of prayer at sunset. Members of the organization feel threatened because they feel poorly treated relative to others. Some examples we have seen include certain racial groups feeling undervalued because they receive less desirable offices, promotions being more commonly given to people who "looked" like the boss, and reprimands going to people with darker skin than those in power. A common complaint on college campuses is that police may be more likely to suspect youths of certain social identity groups of crimes than members of other groups; suspicion is not equally distributed. Differential treatment activates a faultline when people become concerned that there is favoritism or bias. Distribution decisions that are perceived as unfair can ignite a social identity conflict.

*Different values* act as a trigger when members of an organization have decidedly different beliefs. What is seen as "right" by one group is seen as "wrong" by another. People feel threatened because their fundamental ideologies are brought into question when they are asked to do something that violates beliefs of right and wrong. A common example involves the changing definition of family in the United States. In many organizations, there is a reluctance of employers to extend healthcare benefits to unmarried partners. This can activate tensions between gay and straight employees, causing each group to feel threatened by the other's interpretation of family.

*Assimilation* can be a force activating faultlines in many different types of organizations. In many parts of the world, there is an expectation by the majority group that everyone else will act just like them—speak their language, practice their religion, listen to their music, celebrate their holidays, dress like them, and eat like them. Dominant group members may become uncomfortable when members of other groups express their distinctiveness. For example, speaking Afrikaans among those who do not speak the language in South Africa can engender feelings of distrust and disrespect. In French schools there is a ban against wearing religious garb such as headscarves or religious symbols; bringing in symbols of "difference" is not tolerated. A very common issue has to do with holiday celebrations privileging one culture over another, which often creates dissension in the organization when a faultline is opened up between members of different religions.

*Insults or humiliating actions* may be the most obvious triggers. These comments and behaviors are degrading to others. Every language has words intended to denigrate or demean some people and polarize a group. The threat to identity is often blatant and can escalate quickly. Typical examples include referring to others as "You people" or "those stinking X's". The insult is tied to social identity in either the mind of the insulter or in the mind of the person insulted. For example, in 2007, Isaiah Washington, a star of TV's *Grey's Anatomy,* used an epithet to refer to his gay co-star, T.R. Knight. It put the cast and the producers in a bind, detracting from their work. Ultimately, Washington left the series. Sometimes triggers grow out of a poor attempt at humor; a friendly joke may not be perceived as friendly if it emphasizes status or power differences.

Some triggers are not as obvious as the insult. *Simple contact* can sometimes be enough to set off an event. In a situation when tensions in society at large are strong, simply bringing together people whose identity groups are involved in a highly publicized and adversarial event can result in polarization. People feel threatened simply by being in the proximity of a group perceived as hostile, even if they work in the same organization. For example, Palestinians and Israelis forced to work together in the same organization may find it very difficult to do so when violent attacks against their identity groups are going on daily. Decades of conflict makes working together extremely difficult.

## WHAT TO DO

Although the activation of faultlines may result in many outcomes, social identity conflicts are very likely to follow if the faultlines are strong. So what can either an individual or an organization do to ameliorate or prevent faultline activation in an organization? Do traditional leadership approaches apply? Who should act? The answers to these questions vary depending on the context of the situation—the local cultural norms for dealing with conflict, societal issues, and organizational policies or norms.

A general strategy for considering these questions is to try to gain a deeper understanding of social identity issues in the organization. This may allow for the recognition of potential triggers. Recognizing triggers is a step toward reducing the power of a latent faultline to create an earthquake. You can't address problems you can't see. The following are some diagnostic questions that can be asked:

1. What underlying tensions may activate faultlines?
2. How strong are the perceived faultlines in the organization—how likely is it that a triggering event will lead to intergroup conflict?
3. Have employees complained of unfair treatment or filed grievances?
4. Are there patterns to these complaints or grievances?

5. How do employees respond to conflict? Do people talk things out or do they avoid one another?

6. Do certain groups feel excluded from the power circles in the organization?

7. Do holiday celebrations make any groups uncomfortable?

8. Have there been complaints about insulting remarks?

Bear in mind that social identity conflicts are emotional—they get at the very heart of who we are and what we believe. Further, they reflect social and power alignments in society at large. Social identity events can easily escalate to become aggressive and hostile. Workers may feel psychologically threatened. Any response must address these fundamental characteristics of the situation.

A basic dilemma of our times is that succeeding in today's organizational environment depends on the ability to lead across differences, yet most people don't know how to do this. Understanding and identifying triggers is a foundational skill needed to lead across differences. Although faultlines are always present, they remain invisible until primed by a trigger. Triggers act as a sign that conflict may bubble to the surface. Sometimes faultlines may erupt, and other times they may remain dormant. Recognizing the potential of triggers gives both the organization and the individual the power to address issues before a full-blown earthquake erupts.

# Organizational Faultlines

*Astrid C. Homan*
*Karen A. Jehn*

---

**Keywords:** faultlines, in-groups, out-groups, social identity, self-categorization, task conflict, relationship conflict, transformational leadership, transactional leadership

**Key Points**

- Faultlines are hypothetical lines dividing a team or an organization based on one or more attributes.

- Faultline diversity occurs when different diversity dimensions converge and group categories are created so that the members of one group trust less and are less motivated to cooperate with members of the other group.

- A team or an organization may have wide-ranging potential faultlines.

- Faultlines can increase in strength as a large number of attributes are aligned, which diminishes the number of subdivisions and increases the consensus within each subdivision.

- In contrast, the strength of faultlines decreases when attributes are not correlated and multiple subdivisions exist.

- Leadership strategies, as discussed in the Leadership Practices chapter, can be employed to deal with faultlines that cause conflict in teams.

- This chapter also shows how transformational and transactional leadership deal with relationship and task conflict in teams divided by faultlines.

**Related Exercises**

- Exercise 3: Identifying Faultlines

**Related Cases**

- Case 1: Race and Respect
- Case 2: Water Crises
- Case 3: Floating Holidays
- Case 4: Not My Weekend
- Case 5: It's Their Fault
- Case 6: The Scent of Difference
- Case 7: Not Catching On
- Case 8: Glass Ceiling at Big Boy Toys
- Case 9: Super Drugs
- Case 10: The Right to Be Pregnant
- Case 11: Local Bombing
- Case 12: Benefits Battle
- Case 13: Francois' Dilemma

---

Organizations are increasingly comprised of individuals from different social identity groups. This diversity can have detrimental and beneficial effects on the performance of work groups (van Knippenberg, De Dreu, & Homan, 2004; Williams & O'Reilly, 1998). Inevitably, work group members differ on a variety of dimensions, such as gender, age, race, nationality, educational background, religion, and organizational tenure. In this chapter, we describe how constellations of social identity differences within teams can create greater opportunity for triggers of intra-team conflicts (see the chapter "Triggers of Social Identity Conflict" to learn about the events that trigger conflicts).

A recent development in workforce diversity pertains to viewing a team or an organization as divided by faultlines. The concept of faultlines was introduced in a seminal article by Lau and Murnighan (1998). They define a faultline as a division of "group's members on the basis of one or more attributes that divides a work group into two or more smaller subgroups" (p. 325). For example, a marketing group of ten individuals may be divided into two subgroups by age, with five individuals under twenty-five years old and five individuals over fifty years old. Faultlines are stronger when there is more than one difference dividing the group (Lau & Murnighan, 1998, 2005; Thatcher, Jehn, & Zanutto, 2003). For example, in the same marketing group mentioned above, assume all the younger group members were female and all the older members were male. This team would then be characterized by two subgroups that differ from each other on age and gender; thus the faultline dividing the group would be stronger.

How faultlines effect team performance is described in research about social identity and self-categorization (Tajfel & Turner, 1986; Turner, Hogg, Oakes, Reicher, & Wetherell, 1987). Research has shown that people use information about social categories to classify others and themselves into distinct categories (Tajfel & Turner, 1986; see the chapter on "Social Identity" in this book for more information). For instance, people can use their gender to classify themselves and their co-workers into male and female subgroups. Because people prefer to interact with people who are similar rather than dissimilar to them, these categorizations or subgroup formations can lead people to make "us-them" distinctions (Byrne, 1971). Going back to our example, this could mean that the younger females evaluate their own subgroup as better and more positive than the older and male subgroup (Hewstone, Rubin, & Willis, 2002; Turner, Hogg, Oakes, Reicher, & Wetherell, 1987). These "us-them" distinctions are likely to result in reduced levels of trust between groups, reduced motivation to cooperate with members of other identity groups, less commitment to the full group (in favor of increased commitment to one's subgroup), increased interpersonal tension and conflict, and lower frequency and quality of communication (Earley & Mosakowski, 2000; Homan, van Knippenberg, Van Kleef, & De Dreu, 2007; Lau & Murnighan, 2005; Li & Hambrick, 2005; Thatcher, Jehn, & Zanutto, 2003; for a review, see vanKnippenberg & Schippers, 2007). One of the most common problems that arise in faultline groups is that of intergroup conflict (Bezrukova, Jehn, Thatcher, & Zanutto, 2004; Thatcher, Jehn, & Zanutto, 2003). In this chapter, we focus on describing the underlying faultline dynamic that results in conflicts and how to reduce them.

## TYPES OF CONFLICT IN FAULTLINE GROUPS

The existence of strong subgroups in teams (that is, strong faultlines) can lead to tension and conflict. There are primarily two types of conflict: task conflict and relationship conflict (Jehn, 1994, 1995). Task conflicts are those that members have regarding the specific jobs they are working on. Relationship conflicts are about non-task-related things such as politics, gossip, and fashion and are often more emotional and taken personally (Jehn, 1994). Relationship conflicts have been found to harm team performance and processes within the team. Interpersonal tensions have been found to enhance negative reactions such as anxiety and fear, making team members experience a decrease in their satisfaction with the team experience. When employees dislike other team members or are disliked by others on their teams, this may lead to frustration, strain, and uneasiness (Jehn, 1995). Task conflicts can potentially benefit team performance to the degree that task conflicts result in articulating divergent viewpoints and ideas, thus expanding possible solutions and strategies. Exchanging and discussing these viewpoints, perspectives, and ideas potentially could benefit team performance. However, task conflicts do not always lead to information exchange and processing.

Members of a group created by faultlines often consider others in the group part of their "in-group," and anyone not in their group is considered part of the "out-group." This in-group versus out-group distinction can in turn instigate intergroup bias, which manifests in low trust and dislike between the subgroups (that is, relationship conflicts). Intergroup bias will inhibit the potentially constructive information exchange and also increase negative attitudes and emotions. If members from subgroups distrust and dislike each other, it will be less likely that they listen to viewpoints and information provided by members from the other subgroups. In-group members will value their own information and perspectives as better than information and perspectives provided by out-group members and thus will not pay attention to or use information provided by out-group members (van Knippenberg, De Dreu, & Homan, 2004).

## LEADERSHIP THROUGH DIFFERENT TYPES OF CONFLICT

Fortunately, all is not necessarily lost when teams experience faultline tensions and conflict. A team or an organization may have wide-ranging potential faultlines. Faultlines can be triggered through structural and procedural changes in a team; for instance, implementing pay based on tenure may trigger age divisions, while women occupying positions with lower wages provokes a divide based on gender. Faultline conflict can occur when there is distrust and low motivation to cooperate with other members of the group due to the convergence of group categories in teams. Team leaders can be very effective in managing the task and relationship conflicts in a context of faultlines.

Faultlines can also differ in strength. This depends on the alignment of attributes and spillover of societal faultlines. For example, when there are religious tensions in the community in which an organization is based, religious tensions between employees are also likely to be present in the organization. Faultlines can increase in strength as a large number of attributes are aligned. For example, if members of the same faith also have nationality and race in common, but these attributes are different from those of the other faith, tensions may be even higher because there are more differences present between the two subgroups. In contrast, the strength of faultlines decreases when attributes are not correlated and multiple subdivisions do not exist.

The faultline perspective of diversity provides managers with an insight regarding the conditions under which the strength of the faultline is low so that a team or an organization can be thus composed for their maximal effectiveness (Lau & Murnighan, 1998). Leadership strategies in dealing with team conflict can be to create new faultlines, different from the ones that create conflict, or just simply to break down high-conflict potential faultlines, such as race and gender in groups.

The more leaders are capable of managing interpersonal processes and are tuned into social identity dynamics, the less likely it is that groups will experience relationship conflicts. Before conflicts get out of hand and groups experience negative interpersonal processes, leaders should take action to make sure conflicts do not escalate and result in irreparable damage within the team. The "Leadership Practices" chapter describes a variety of leadership strategies that can be employed. Groups characterized by a faultline are also likely to experience more task conflicts. While task conflicts can benefit group performance, they could also decrease performance when they are highly correlated with relationship conflicts (DeDreu & Weingart, 2003). A conflict could start out on the task level, such as discussing different viewpoints regarding how to promote a new product. If the conflict becomes heated, for instance, because neither subgroup is willing to give in, personal frictions could be instigated. Subgroup members could experience or perceive the differences of opinion as personal rather than task-related. Leaders should therefore also make sure that task conflicts are indeed focused on the task and do not spread to more personal frictions.

Burns' (1978) notion of transformational and transactional leadership can be used to illustrate how leaders can reduce the prevalence of and address task and relationship conflicts. The thinking here is that transformational leaders will be more equipped to deal with relationship conflict and transactional leaders will handle task conflict better; however, when there is high conflict in groups due to faultlines, a combination of transactional and transformational leadership is needed.

*Transformational* leaders influence followers to go beyond personal interests and aim for collective achievement (to focus on a common goal), whereas *transactional* leaders influence followers by using mutually beneficial transactions (that is, gaining rewards and avoiding punishments). It has been proposed that transformational leadership also includes behaviors that empower followers such as the delegation of responsibilities to followers, enhancing followers' capacity to think on their own, and encouraging them to come up with new and creative ideas (Dvir, Eden, Avolio, & Shamir, 2002). Focusing on the team as a whole or the "collective" might be especially relevant for a team with strong subgroups due to a faultline. The experience of subgroups might then be replaced by a "one team" "us" representation of the group, to try and draw the group closer together. Transformational leaders have the ability to intellectually stimulate their subordinates and to inspire people to get to great heights. When the transformational leader gets a collective, desirable goal across, chances are high that task conflicts will indeed stay limited to the task and not result in personal frictions. That leader is using the leadership practice called recategorization or boundary reframing, which is described in the Leadership Practices chapter.

Transactional leaders influence followers through task-focused behaviors; they clarify expectancies, rules, and procedures, emphasizing a fair deal with subordinates (Bass, 1985; Burns, 1978; House, 1996). Faultline teams that experience task-related conflicts might benefit greatly from a leader providing structure and rules regarding the task, shaping conditions that aid the exchange, and elaborating on task-relevant information. Goal-setting focused on specific task outcomes, specifically breaking down faultlines through changes in group composition, and paying for team rather than individual performance are strategies that can be used here.

The role of transactional leadership is to make sure task-related processes go smoothly (Keller, 2006), while transformational leadership behaviors have more to do with smoothing relationship-related processes and can therefore play a crucial role in improving negative group processes in teams characterized by a faultline. In the marketing group example shared previously, this team consists of strong subgroups that might experience task and/or relationship conflicts. The older and male subgroup might have a different focus on how to sell a certain product than the younger and female subgroup. When the team as a whole successfully discusses these foci, these differences of insights could potentially lead to an optimal integration of ideas. However, the older and male subgroup might experience interpersonal frictions with the younger female subgroups when working together, because the younger women feel threatened and not taken seriously. This can obstruct effective coordination and teamwork and will probably result in suboptimal performance and decision making. This means that especially the relational conflicts between the team members need to be managed, because these conflicts can be very harmful for the functioning of the team. Kearney and Gebert (2009) found positive effects of transformational leadership on the functioning of teams diverse in terms of age, nationality, and education. Transformational leadership had this positive effect because information exchange and processing were increased as well as the degree to which team members identified with their teams.

## SUMMARY

What we recommend that organizations, leaders, and group members do is to first identify whether there is a demographic faultline within the group, that is, do subgroups exist within the group. One way to assess this is to look at the extent of diversity within the group. Groups with diverse elements spread throughout the group tend to have fewer faultlines. That is, a team that consists of people of many different ages is less likely to split into subgroups than the marketing team that was used as an example throughout this chapter. People often think that the highly visible diversity characteristics are the most likely candidates for subgroup formation, but this is not necessarily the case (Harrison, Price, & Bell, 1998). Value and personality differences have also been found to exert major influence on team processes and performance, especially over time (Harrison, Price, & Bell, 1998). Thus, leaders should be aware of the diversity composition of their teams and should look for alignment of certain diversity characteristics (for example, all females are young and all males are old). Leaders could also easily ask team members what their *perceptions* are of subgroups (Homan, Greer, Jehn, & Konig, in press) to assess whether detrimental faultlines exist.

A second point to consider is whether there is conflict arising from this faultline and whether it is constructive conflict or negative conflict (which can be the case for task- or relationship-oriented conflicts). Detrimental constructs are characterized by interpersonal frictions and tension within the group. If members of subgroups tend to work in separate rooms, do not integrate ideas, shout to other subgroup members, interrupt the members of other subgroups, are not listening when the other subgroup is talking, and show signs of distrust, leaders should be aware that relationship conflicts are probably occurring (Jehn, 1995). On the other hand, if all subgroups are discussing the task at hand and this discussion stays focused on the task despite faultlines, it is more likely that you are observing task conflicts. If a leader (or group member) identifies negative relationship conflict in the group, that person should focus on showing transformational leadership behavior (that is, manage interpersonal processes). However, faultlines are not necessarily detrimental. For instance, if the faultline instigates task-focused, constructive conflicts, that may benefit task progress, or if the group is better off working in subgroups due to task requirements, faultlines might even benefit team performance. These are critical concepts to identify in faultline groups in order to promote effective functioning.

# Leadership Practices Across Social Identity Groups

*Marian N. Ruderman*
*Sarah Glover*
*Donna Chrobot-Mason*
*Chris Ernst*

**Keywords:** social identity leadership practices, decategorization, boundary suspending, recategorization, boundary reframing, sub-categorization, boundary nesting, cross-cutting, boundary weaving

## Key Points

- Identity-based conflicts arise when individuals attribute the cause of intergroup tension to social identity.

- It is practically a universal assumption that employees expect someone in a leadership role to act in the face of social identity conflicts.

- "Leadership practices" are actions addressing (or intended to prevent) social identity conflicts in organizations. Leadership practices can be taken by an individual, group, or organization. They can be taken by any person in the organization regardless of formal authority, though they are likely to use different strategies.

- The Leadership Response Cycle is a six-step process for addressing social identity conflict in organizations, with previous steps informing the next step.

- There are three distinctly different, underlying beliefs about the organization's role in managing cross-group relationships: (1) that the organization should have no role at all in such relationships (Hands Off); (2) that it is the responsibility of the organization to direct and control such relationships (Direct and Control); and (3) that the organization's role is to create the right conditions for relationships to develop in a healthy manner (Cultivate and Encourage).
- There are four types of practices that fall under the Cultivate and Encourage approach: decategorization; recategorization; subcategorization; and cross-cutting.

### Related Exercises

- Exercise 5: Approaches to Difference
- Exercise 7: Your Leadership Practices
- Exercise 8: Examining Your Leadership Networks
- Exercise 9: Taking a New Perspective

### Related Cases

- Case 1: Race and Respect
- Case 2: Water Crises
- Case 3: Floating Holidays
- Case 4: Not My Weekend
- Case 5: It's Their Fault
- Case 6: The Scent of Difference
- Case 7: Not Catching On
- Case 8: Glass Ceiling at Big Boy Toys
- Case 9: Super Drugs
- Case 10: The Right to Be Pregnant
- Case 11: Local Bombing
- Case 12: Benefits Battle
- Case 13: Francois' Dilemma

Each of the cases in this casebook describes a situation in which conflict stems from issues of social identity. Identity-based conflicts arise when individuals attribute the cause of intergroup tension to social identity. Because social identity is an important part of one's self-esteem and self-concept, we naturally feel threatened or frustrated when our social identity is challenged, and this often results in persistent conflict with another social identity group (Chrobot-Mason,

Ruderman, Weber, Ohlott, & Dalton, 2007). In some cases, conflict adds fuel to existing tense relationships. In others, the conflict escalates to a full-blown dispute involving many people and severely limiting the productivity of the organization. Leadership, or the lack thereof, is a repeating theme in these cases. Because these conflicts happened in workplaces, there was an expectation that someone from the organization would address the hostility. It is practically a universal assumption that employees expect someone in a leadership role to act in the face of social identity conflicts (Gentry, Hannum, Munusamy, & Weber, 2007). To "do nothing," say many employees in our research, is the least effective strategy a leader can take.

This chapter looks at leadership practices when social identity dynamics create problems or threaten to create problems between groups. It is based on the same data set that yielded the cases, as well as other research. "Leadership practices" are actions addressing (or intended to prevent) social identity conflicts in organizations. Leadership practices can be taken by an individual, group, or organization. They can be taken by any person in the organization, regardless of formal authority, although they are likely to use different strategies.

Because social identity clashes are inherently complex, involving feelings, status, and resources, they are very difficult to resolve. These struggles get into the question of the value of a group an individual identifies with and consequently the individual's own value (Rothman, 1997). There is no map or formula that can be mechanistically followed that will lead to a positive outcome in every situation.

Social identity conflicts are an example of what Heifetz (1998) calls an adaptive challenge, a problem for which there is no technical remedy and which calls into question closely held beliefs. Social identity conflicts truly call for "creative leadership," the ability to think beyond current boundaries, to learn new skills and behaviors, and to act both strategically and flexibly. In this chapter, we outline a Leadership Response cycle containing six broad steps leaders can follow to determine the best course of action.

## THE LEADERSHIP RESPONSE CYCLE

The six steps shown in Figure 4.1 create a cycle; learning from previous steps informs the next step. If appropriate action is taken, an organization or an individual should be able to apply learning from one social identity conflict toward prevention of similar conflicts in the future, although it is important to remember that every situation is different. Because of the subjectivity inherent in social identity conflicts, it is essential that you be aware of your part in each step in the cycle. That is because you are an important part of the picture; you also bring your social identity to the conflict. When tensions escalate, people tend to take sides and make assumptions based on the identity groups they belong to. For each step you will see a subsection titled "Your Part" with questions to help you become more aware of the important role you play in each step.

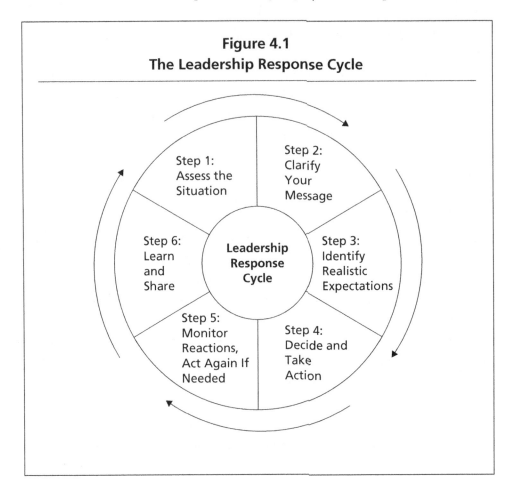

**Figure 4.1**
**The Leadership Response Cycle**

### Step One: Assess the Situation

The first step is a crucial one: to see the whole picture. This requires understanding the many factors that influence collisions between social identity groups in organizations. Given that social identity conflicts are ambiguous and characterized by mistrusting and contentious relationships, it is critical to see how the pieces fit together before attempting a solution. Figure 4.2 contains a schematic showing the range of factors that influence social identity conflicts—both their emergence and resolution. It was developed based on interview data collected as part of the Leadership Across Differences research project and depicts a series of rings showing the embedded nature of these factors. The factors shown in the outer rings are further away from the organization (more distal), and those shown in the inner rings are closer to the immediate conflict (more proximal) and may therefore have more direct influence on the situation. Keep in mind that reality is "messier" than this figure depicts. Each of the rings interacts with the others. In reality, a variety of factors influence social identity clashes, some which are right in front of us and others which are more embedded in the context and more difficult to see and recognize.

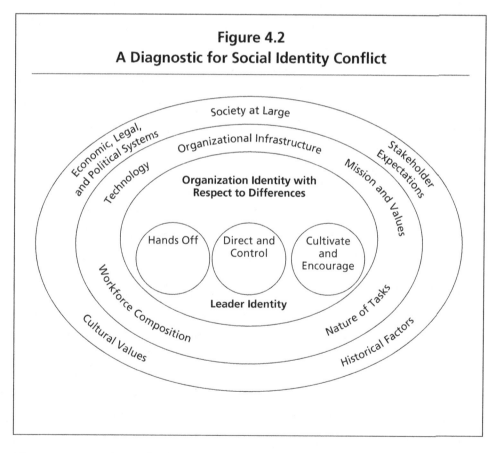

**Figure 4.2**
**A Diagnostic for Social Identity Conflict**

The outermost ring refers to society. Analysis of the cases suggests that societal influences, including the history of the conflict; the legal, economic, and political systems; pressures from external stakeholders; and the prevailing cultural values, influence the course of social identity relationships in organizations. Members of non-dominant groups use laws, media, and other external parties to hold the organization accountable for fair behavior (however that may be defined). Society influences the nature and duration of the conflict by creating the legal, economic, and political backdrop that helps to resolve and/or fan the flames of a conflict event. Additionally, the culture in which an organization resides often influences perceptions of fairness, appropriate behavior, and effective leadership (see the Social Justice and Dignity chapter for more information). These factors interact to influence how we interpret the behavior of other group members. Simon and Klandermans (2001) suggest that political or ideological events and issues may politicize a collective identity group such that its members consciously engage in a power struggle on behalf of their group. Shared identity group membership heightens awareness of shared grievances, and shared grievances serve to reinforce collective group identity.

The next ring deals with the infrastructure of the organization. It includes the technology, workforce demographics, mission, and the interdependence of work tasks. These variables influence the number and magnitude of identity conflicts. An obvious example is the composition of the workforce—does the workforce contain groups that are at odds with one another? A less obvious example has to do with task interdependence—do people need to work as a group or team in the organization or are tasks independent of one another? Interdependence creates greater contact, creating the opportunity for both positive and negative intergroup relationships, as compared to task independence, which separates individuals. In our data, we found that the organizational mission was important in the sense that organizations with clear overarching goals seem to have fewer conflicts than other organizations. As discussed later, a strong mission or goal can serve as a powerful force to bind groups together.

The third embedded ring addresses the intangibles of the organization, representing the internal context or organizational culture. It includes the identity of the organization with regard to differences; its views on professionalism; its values around discourse, justice, and respect; and how relationship-oriented the organization is. Organizational norms or standards of behavior play an important role in the dynamics of identity-based conflict. Constructive interaction is supported when social norms and organizational expectations predispose individuals toward trusting members of the other group. Organizations that have norms for holding difficult conversations are better positioned for dealing with social iden-tity conflicts when they arise. Further, conflict between groups may be reduced when both groups perceive justice and a climate of respect. Fair treatment fosters feelings of being valued. Our data suggests that, when one group perceives that they have been treated unfairly in comparison to another group, they will likely feel devalued in the organization. A climate unsupportive of respect allows social identity issues to fester (Hannum & Glover, in press).

Another intangible included in this ring is the identity of the leader or person in formal authority, either in general (for example, the CEO) or relative to the conflict in question. Social identity theories of leadership predict that the identity of a leader matters. Employees are more likely to respond favorably to someone who is a "prototypical" leader, or someone whose social identity is typical of the group (Haslam, 2001). People in formal leadership roles are expected to model appropriate behaviors around inclusion, set norms around respect, and make sure that employees feel psychologically safe. In our research, we saw quite a few examples of leaders who were seen as positive role models for resolving conflicts and improving cross-group relationships.

Finally, in the heart of the ring, there are three circles representing general beliefs about the role of the organization in addressing relationships across groups. They are pictured in the innermost part of the drawing because they are embedded in and influenced by all the other factors. We will discuss these factors in more detail later.

In addition to understanding the many causes and moderators of social identity tension or conflict in organizations, it is important to realize that different players in the situation see the conflict differently. Factors that influence conflict are subjective and are seen through different lenses (for example, power or powerlessness). The most important point is that people in different identity groups have different stakes in the situation and as such can see the same event in contradictory ways. One constant across many situations is that members of the dominant group in an organization or society are likely to see the situation differently than do members of the non-dominant group. Typically, the non-dominant group is more likely to see some type of injustice, such as those mentioned in the chapter on triggers. Based on their own experiences, the non-dominant group may be more likely to recognize triggers. The dominant group is less impacted by these triggers so they are far less likely to see the issue. Sometimes dominant groups are very eager to maintain the status quo, keeping themselves in a dominant position. Other times the "blindness" exhibited by dominant group members is simply due to lack of awareness. Different groups have different sets of information available about the relevant social history. We saw in our study that individuals did not necessarily know the history or values of another group and overlooked something disrespectful or offensive because they literally did not know about the historical underpinnings and hidden meaning of a joke or action. In trying to address these situations, it is critical to consider both the different lenses through which people see events and the different resources that they have for interpreting them.

**Your Part** If you are faced with a social identity conflict, one of the key issues to consider is "Where am I in the picture?" It is important to understand what your role in the conflict may be and the lenses through which you view the situation. Your own vantage point affects the information and resources you have for acting, and your perceived identity affects how people will interpret your actions.

You may be one of the players in the conflict yourself, an observer, or someone with perceived responsibility for resolving it. If you are in a position of authority, you should realize that there is always pressure on a formal leader to do something, at a minimum to acknowledge what is happening. If you are in a formal role and don't take action, employees will likely assume that you condone the situation or see it as unimportant. In this way, doing nothing is, in fact, seen as an action rather than "nothing." No matter what you do, your behavior as the leader will be scrutinized. It is a difficult spot to be in, because taking action can upset the status quo and not taking action can destroy morale. Either way, productivity is likely to be affected.

If you are in a human resource role, it is possible to take action by developing or executing human resource management policies in a way that improves the situation. Human resource professionals can also act as intermediaries between the groups, coach the individuals involved, or influence others by serving as role models for demonstrating respect.

If you are not in a formal leadership or human resource role, it is still possible to take powerful actions. Leading when you don't have authority is different from leading from a position of authority. Yet, a review of the cases both in this book and the larger data set show that one person can make a difference in addressing these situations and mobilizing a community to act. These actions can be taken by an observer of the conflict or someone embroiled in it, from any point in the organizational chart, or even by someone in the broader community. Such actions take courage, but they can be the seed for positive transformation.

In addition to considering your role, it is important to consider how emotionally close you are to the conflict. What are the stakes for you? What is your social identity relative to the dispute? How have various political, legal, or economic factors shaped the way you look at the conflict? What influence do cultural values and past historical events have on your perspectives? Do you identify with one of the groups involved? Do others associate you with one of the groups? If you do belong to one of the groups involved, is it the dominant group with power in the organization or a less dominant group? Before acting, it is necessary to be acutely aware of your role and social identity relative to the conflict because these characteristics affect how other employees or stakeholders will view your actions.

## Step Two: Clarify Your Message

Once you have figured out your part in the picture, it is important to consider what message you want to send. The goal of this step is to ensure your actions are aligned with your values (see the "Cultural Values" chapter for more information). Because a leader's behavior will be scrutinized, and because emotions are probably high, you can reduce the chance of misunderstanding by carefully thinking through what you want to convey to employees and colleagues. Some of this thinking and communicating can be done even before a conflict arises. For example, it is important to ask yourself: What values or beliefs do I want to reinforce? In our data, we found a variety of messages sent through leadership practices such as the following: "We will not tolerate disrespect toward anyone, no matter what"; "We trust you to solve your own conflicts"; "Every voice should be heard"; and "We respect authority and will not allow authority to be overlooked." These messages are normally a combination of personal, organizational, and cultural values, which people tend to hold deeply. People will read something into a leader's actions (or non-actions) and fill in the blanks for themselves. Messages can always be misconstrued, but it is less likely to happen if the message is carefully considered and aligned with values at its origin.

**Your Part**   Responding to a social identity conflict requires clarifying the organization's values as well as your own and figuring out how to connect them to the situation at hand. What are your core values related to the conflict? What are the organization's core values? What are the overlaps and the potential gaps? Hopefully, your personal values align well with your organization's values, especially if you represent the organization in the conflict situation. If not, you may feel the need to explain how these values differ when you respond.

Even when your values align and you are very clear what message you want to convey, it is important to remember (as discussed in Step One) that your identity affects how people react to you. Is it possible that your role and/or social identity will filter your desired message somehow? If so, it is important to obtain feedback from a variety of constituencies to determine whether your desired message was indeed received.

## Step Three: Identify Realistic Options

Once the message is determined, it is important to apply a reality filter. Of all the things you could do that convey the right message, what is actually practical to do? The goal of this step is to identify realistic options. Often there are ideal actions that you may consider, but they are not practical. For example, an intervention that involves getting a team of people from different locations together in the same room may not be possible for budgetary reasons. Or an initiative that takes lots of planning may not be reasonable when action is needed quickly. Some interventions are unrealistic just because the person doesn't have the appropriate sphere of influence. For example, it can be hard for one person to change organizational policy in a short time frame. Further, it can be hard for someone without formal authority to act in a directive or controlling manner.

The readiness and the cultural intelligence of the different groups matters as well (see the Cultural Intelligence chapter for more information). Where are the group members in terms of intergroup awareness and cultural sensitivity? How much contact do the groups have with one another? Someone might want to do a trust-building intervention, for example, but might feel that the group is not ready for it.

The point is to pick a course of action that is realistic given the resources available. The good news here is that many possible actions literally do not cost a thing. Apologies or conversation can happen for free.

**Your Part**  In applying your reality filter, you should consider your own skills, resources, and relationships. If you do not have the communication skills, time, or access that would be ideal for the leadership practice that seems warranted, is there someone else who could do it? Do you have a good relationship with someone in one of the identity groups involved, someone who could be a sounding board for you and provide you with feedback?

## Step Four: Decide and Take Action

Having clarified your message and identified practical constraints, it is time to evaluate specific actions you can take. In our research, we have observed many ways in which leaders have acted to address conflict between groups. Table 4.1 lists a variety of actions from the cases presented in this book as well as other cases drawn from our research. Unfortunately, we do not have data on the relative effectiveness of these practices. Future research is necessary in order to determine when and where these practices are most effective.

In Table 4.1, leadership practices are organized into columns representing three distinctly different, underlying beliefs about the organization's role in managing cross-group relationships: (1) that the organization should have no role at all in such relationships (Hands Off); (2) that it is the responsibility of the organization to direct and control such relationships (Direct and Control); and (3) that the organization's role is to create the right conditions for relationships to develop in a healthy manner (Cultivate and Encourage). Although organizational actions may be influenced by all three beliefs, our data suggest that many organizations adopt one predominant belief that guides the prevention of and initial response to social identity conflicts.

### The "Hands-Off" Approach

The first approach involves a passive or "hands-off" approach to cross-group relationships. The belief behind this approach is that the workplace is not the appropriate venue to deal with societal issues or that the organization should not be responsible for intervening in cross-group relationships. There are very different ways this belief played out in the organizations we studied.

In a few of the organizations, cultural and organizational values suggest that tension between religious or ethnic groups should be kept separate from the work of the organization. The organization prefers a non-disruptive view of events. The assumption is that, if social identity differences are not recognized, then the stability of the organization can be maintained.

In different cases, "doing nothing" was a common leadership practice. This occurs when the person with formal authority does nothing to intervene and

## Table 4.1
### Leadership Practices for Cross-Group Relationships

| Approach | Direct and Control | Hands-Off | Cultivate and Encourage |
|---|---|---|---|
| Basic Principle | Uses authority of the organization to manage relationships | The workplace should not deal with societal issues. The organization does not deal with identity-based conflict | Encouraging cross-group relationships will enhance the viability of the organization |
| Examples | • Policies punishing discrimination and harassment;<br>• Performance management systems emphasizing feedback, rewards, and punishment;<br>• Formalized conflict-management procedures providing a structure for complaints;<br>• Staffing policies emphasizing mission and protecting organization boundaries;<br>• Published code of conduct;<br>• Organize work so groups are separated;<br>• Intranet decision-making system to allow for input throughout the system | • Doing nothing; letting the situation resolve on its own;<br>• Denial of a problem;<br>• Blame the victim;<br>• Venting of emotion without taking action;<br>• Emphasize only professional identities; do not recognize or encourage other identities | • Diversity/Sensitivity/Cultural training and education to increase awareness of value of diversity;<br>• Encouraging contact across groups/ decategorization;<br>• Creating a shared identity/recategorization;<br>• Creating affinity groups/subcategorization;<br>• Cross-cutting groups; creating diverse work teams;<br>• Whole-system interventions;<br>• Creating boundary-crossing or bridging roles;<br>• Climate of respect;<br>• Apology and acceptance of apology;<br>• Encouragement of individual initiative to resolve problems and conflicts;<br>• Mentoring to facilitate integration of non-dominant groups;<br>• Creation of a "safe" format for discussing conflict that promotes questioning, challenging debate, and open discussion |

neither does anyone else in the system. It may be difficult to understand why a leader would choose to do nothing. Our cases tell the story only from one vantage point, making it difficult to determine reasons for the absence of an intervention. However, our interviewees attributed doing nothing to several different mindsets, which we describe below.

One mindset is denial of the problem: "If I don't see the problem, there is no problem." A leader may apply his or her own definitions and perspectives to the situation and make little or no attempt to understand the issue from the point of view of other group members. Another mindset, often appearing to onlookers as denial, is fear. Social identity conflicts are characterized by heightened anxiety. Some people are simply afraid to get involved, and others are paralyzed by fear of doing the wrong thing. Our data demonstrate that leadership actions can, on occasion, accidentally fuel an escalation. Indeed, this is understandably frightening, as a well-intentioned leader doesn't want to make a painful situation worse.

A third mindset is that no action is necessary because the conflict will resolve on its own. This is the idea, perhaps, that "time heals all wounds." This indeed seemed to happen in some organizations, yet in others a grievance was probably intensified because the lack of response signaled to the parties that no one cared.

Still another mindset is that the very act of naming a problem will draw too much attention to it, only encouraging more complaints. This may be described as "blaming the victim"—punishing the person who identifies a potential trigger of a social identity conflict.

One final example of this approach was to allow different groups to vent about one another with the expectation that no actions would be taken in response to the venting. Employees were given space to air their feelings and let out steam, but the underlying issues were ignored. One of the Spanish organizations in our dataset relied on this approach when tensions got high.

*Note:* As social scientists trained in the United States, those of us authoring this chapter find the "hands-off" approach difficult to accept because the underlying problems remain intact. As outsiders to these situations, we saw the hands-off attitude as a cover to prevent the inevitable discomfort that comes from change. However, the reality is that we are not in these situations and that the actors in these situations saw this separation of the organization from social identity issues as a preferred strategy in many cases. It is a very normal human response to stay away from the types of threats social identity conflicts pose. Further, we don't know how these situations might have unfolded if there was action. The groups might not have been sufficiently skilled to have dealt with the conflicts in a healthy way and the situations might have deteriorated even further.

**Direct and Control**   Organizations with a direct-and-control approach use the authority of the organization to manage relationships. The fundamental belief underlying these kinds of leadership practices is to protect the organization, and its employees, so that work tasks and outcomes can be accomplished. The overriding goal is to reduce the impact of xenophobia, the dislike or fear of people who are different from oneself, on behavior in organizations.

Formal and informal rewards and punishments are used to influence behavior, holding employees accountable for acting in a certain way. Punishments were often found in our study. For example, we observed many organizations that had policies stating that certain forms of harassment or discrimination would not be tolerated and describing various levels of penalties associated with such behavior (verbal warning, written warning, firing). In the United States and South Africa, we found this was a common approach. Policies were often written in employee handbooks, posted on company intranets, and included in new employee orientation. Employees were penalized for acting in a way that demonstrated prejudice.

Sometimes a directive approach is used to reward appropriate behavior, although we did not see many specific examples of rewards. One example of rewards is a situation in which an organization has a competency model that emphasizes respect for all and employees are rewarded in their performance appraisal for behaving in a respectful way. In the United States, bonuses are sometimes tied to meeting staffing goals with regard to inclusion.

A conflict-management process is another manifestation of a direct-and-control philosophy. In this leadership practice, information about the conflict is typically gathered and processes are followed for taking complaints up the chain of command. Employees can find the formal steps involved in the organizational policies. These processes allow for review of the issue at multiple levels, providing an opportunity for resolution at each one. They are intended to control the conflict by reaching an organizationally acceptable agreement between groups.

Another way to direct and control relationships across groups is to try to prevent them. The mindset behind this strategy is that the risk of conflict is too high and too disruptive to the work. One of the organizations that we studied in Jordan used the practice of segregating different ethnic groups so that interaction between groups was minimal. This was done in one of the organizations studied in Spain as well. The expectation of negative interactions is so high that the organization prevents it by structuring itself in a way that keeps groups apart. Boundaries are put in place to keep the organization stable and to maintain order.

Related to the above is a tactic we observed whereby employees were expected to keep social identity out of the workplace. Organizations may ask workers, either explicitly or implicitly, to avoid displaying aspects of their personal identity. For example, in one organization, members of a non-dominant religion were told to keep their observance in private. The underlying philosophy is that professional competency is what matters, not group differences. A common expression consistent with this philosophy is that "We are all professionals here." The organizations from France in our study exemplified this approach.

Direct-and-control practices are intended to be preventative in hopes of extinguishing behaviors that create conflict; however, they are sometimes first initiated in response to an actual conflict. Direct and control is essentially a behavioral approach to relationship management. It is common in countries that rely on laws and regulations to address differences. Direct and control approaches are used to protect the organization from serious social identity conflicts and to maintain equilibrium in the organization.

**Cultivate and Encourage**   The third approach to cross-group relationships is to cultivate and encourage them. The belief behind this approach is that the organization should create the right conditions for positive contact among different groups and reinforce informal norms of valuing differences. Pittinsky (2005) refers to the promotion of positive attitudes between groups as *allophilia*. Leaders employing these practices believe that they will naturally lead to healthier relationships and improve attitudes about other groups, allowing the organization to better respond to changes by being more inclusive. These strategies are often loosely based on the early work of Allport (1954) and more recently Pittinsky (in press) and propose methods for positive interactions between groups in order to improve cross-group relationships. The cultivate-and-encourage approach was found in each country we studied. There were many different practices that could be considered part of this approach, both preventative and reactive.

One of the most basic examples of cultivate and encourage from our study is diversity or cultural sensitivity training. We saw this offered both routinely and in special cases after conflict situations occurred. The rationale is that both dominant and non-dominant employees can learn to better get along with one another by being aware of, appreciating, and valuing differences. The hope is that employees will act more responsibly if they are sensitized to differences.

An extremely low-cost strategy is to foster cross-group friendships so that members of different groups see one another as individuals rather than in terms of identity groups. We found many examples of this practice. The psychological process of removing stereotypical categories is called *decategorization* (Brewer & Miller, 1984). Organizations create situations such as parties, community projects, or luncheons during which people from different groups can get to know each other as friends. Ernst and Yip (2009) call the practice of getting individuals to decategorize *boundary suspending*. The field of social psychology has demonstrated that contact between members of social identity groups is a very powerful tool for prejudice reduction. Organizations don't necessarily need to take the initiative here; individuals can do this on their own from any position in the hierarchy.

A similar practice endorsed in our research, especially as a prevention strategy, is to encourage a shared identity to bind people from different social identity groups together. This psychological process is known as *recategorization*, in that groups are recategorized to encourage all groups to pursue a shared overarching goal (Dovidio, Gaertner, & Bachman, 2001). When an organization tries to create this, it is called *boundary reframing* (Ernst & Yip, 2009). Goals and the mission of the organization are constructed so they bind people from different identity groups together by emphasizing a common destiny or identity. For example, several of the organizations in our study emphasized a common professional identity (for example, lawyers, social workers) to help employees feel part of the same group and resolve differences respectfully. Nonprofit organizations may find that a mission of helping others or promoting justice compels people to put aside differences. Profit is also a very powerful mission and encourages people to work together. Boundary reframing practices can be done formally by an organization or more informally by individuals.

*Subcategorization* is another approach to prejudice reduction. This has to do with recognizing subgroup membership in the context of a larger organization (Hewstone & Brown, 1986). Many organizations have affinity groups; for example, women or employees of various racial groups may form a professional network group that provides information and support to its members as a unique subgroup within the larger organization. When an organization intentionally employs this strategy, it is called *boundary nesting* (Ernst & Yip, 2009) in that the affinity groups are nested within the larger organization. These affinity groups can be either formally arranged by the organization or informally sponsored. They allow for identity groups to be recognized and supported within the context of the larger organization.

Another psychologically based approach is that of establishing *cross-cutting* groups (Brewer, 1995). This is a way of structuring groups so that faultlines are less prominent (see the Organizational Faultlines chapter in this casebook). Work teams may be composed in such a way that weaker rather than stronger faultlines are created. For example, instead of having a team on which all the engineers are Japanese and all the sales people are American, the team is more mixed, including engineers and sales people from both countries. The intentional use of this strategy in the composition of teams is called *boundary weaving* (Ernst & Yip, 2009). There is often a greater possibility to do this with virtual teams than with co-located teams.

Cross-group relationships can also be fostered directly by creating some type of organization-wide intervention for dialogue and discussion. Several of the organizations in our study had a process or structure for facilitating conversations between groups. Some organizations had committees or meetings wherein conflict could be aired in a constructive manner. When there is instability, these systems allow the tension to be constructively addressed. These were difficult conversations and allowed groups with competing views of the world to acknowledge their differences and the impact they had on the organization.

In yet a different practice, some organizations in our study encouraged inter-group relationships by placing someone in a linking or boundary spanning role with responsibility for building connections between groups. Boundary spanners act so as to blur the boundaries between groups so that ideas, information, and resources can mix. In terms of behaviors, leaders playing this role can actively build positive relationships between groups; they can represent the interests and needs of divergent groups to one another; they can scan and amplify information across groups; and, when necessary, they can attempt to reconcile or transform situations of potential conflict. We found boundary spanning individuals at all levels in the organization, ranging from the shop floor to the CEO.

In our research, we also saw actions taken by individuals purely on their own in the spirit of cultivating and encouraging cross-group relationships. People who were naturally skilled at cross-group interactions were willing to act as coaches to others and as role models. Finally, one behavior frequently mentioned in our interviews that most anyone in an organization can do proved to be helpful almost every time—apologizing. Across countries and identity groups, a heartfelt "I'm sorry" made a significant difference to the situation (Miller, 2001). An apology is a direct way of reducing fear and normalizing relationships. It is best if it takes the form of a genuine apology from the person(s) involved, yet organizations also have a role to play: leaders can choose to mandate an apology to show *they* take the conflict seriously (even if it comes across as insincere from the individual), or they may suggest an apology for groups and individuals to consider.

Finally, it is important to realize that single isolated practices may not be enough. In fact, we found that the organizations we considered most skilled at dealing with social identity conflicts employ multiple practices and have redundant systems. They encourage and cultivate cross-group relationships and also have policies that show they really value and measure good relationships. They expect changes in attitudes *and* behaviors. They know when "hands off" is the right thing to do and not an avoidance tactic. They use multiple strategies under the assumption that a single strategy will not be enough to adequately deal with the situation. Redundancy may be one of the most important principles in dealing with social identity conflicts.

**Your Part**   It is important for you to determine which approach you want to take and why. Which of the three approaches seems to be preferred by your organization? Are you comfortable with it? If you must represent your organization's preference versus your own, how can you adapt your response to make yourself more comfortable and authentic as you take action? Thinking through the consequences of your actions (or inaction) is important when considering which approach to adopt.

### Step Five: Monitor Reactions, Act Again If Needed

After taking initial action, it is important to monitor the situation and to see how well the first response worked. The goal of this step is to ensure that actions improve rather than aggravate the conflict. Don't expect an initial response to completely calm the situation. In our study we saw that some leadership responses (or lack thereof) can actually make the situation worse. Monitoring the situation requires asking the various actors how things are going. There is risk in assuming that things are going well without checking to ensure that it really is the case. Try to keep an eye on the big picture and understand what different people can and cannot do. All the actions described above take time to put into place.

Monitoring reactions is a particularly difficult step. It can be hard to tell whether initial leadership practices are simply not working or whether others are just strongly resistant to doing things differently. According to Heifetz (1998), people often resist painful learning situations. When responding to social identity conflicts, it is important to check in with others as to what is going on and to determine the impact of intentional (or unintentional) actions. It is also important to check in with yourself. Attempting to intervene in an intergroup conflict can be stressful and exhausting. It is important to manage your energy and well-being, given it may take several actions or a period of time for a situation to improve.

**Your Part**   Are you in a close enough position to monitor the situation yourself, or will you need to rely on others for information? What indicators will tell you that the situation is improving? How/when will you know when further action is necessary? Who else can serve as an additional set of "eyes and ears" for you?

You should pay attention not only to the impact of a leadership practice on others, but also on yourself. If you initiated or implemented a practice, what are your associated thoughts and feelings? Have your own perceptions or ways at looking things changed? How might you want to do things differently for additional actions? Addressing these types of questions will help guide your thinking for any further actions you will need to take.

## Step Six: Learn and Share

The previous step involves monitoring the response to your actions. It takes place "in the heat of the moment" during a conflict situation. In this final step, Learn and Share, you have the opportunity to reflect back on the event after its resolution. It is critically important that you capture the learning from conflict events, so you can apply what you've learned to future situations. Learning from the event and sharing this knowledge with others is the goal of Step Six and, ultimately, the Leadership Response Cycle.

Dealing with social identity conflicts is inherently risky. According to Linsky and Heifetz, "To lead is to live dangerously because when leadership counts, when you lead people through difficult change, you challenge what people hold dear—their daily habits, tools, loyalties, and ways of thinking, with nothing more to offer perhaps than a possibility" (2002, p. 2). The cases in this volume represent highly challenging situations. A key point is that these can be learning situations. Actions that fail and those that succeed can be powerful teachers. Learning is the best path to success in the future because without it people cannot make changes necessary to thrive in organizations with multiple ethnicities, races, and religions. Individuals, groups, and organizations can all learn from social identity conflicts and use this knowledge to better address social identity conflicts in the future. Developmental outcomes are important. Learning can influence future cycles of conflict and improve the organization's skills in dealing with them. Lessons learned that can be applied to prevent or ameliorate the harmful effects of conflict are particularly valuable.

**Your Part** What have *you* learned from each experience? Has the conflict changed you? What new goals might you set for yourself? What else do you want to learn about the broader societal factors described in Step One? Have any of your core values been influenced or changed as described in Step Two? Have your opinions of other social identity groups changed? Have your opinions of other individuals changed? What have you learned about how you are perceived in the organization? What have you learned about how you perceive yourself?

## CONCLUSION

Organizations play a vital role in society. Leadership practices to address social identity clashes influence not just the organization but also society at large. Early organizational theorists such as Max Weber (1968) thought that organizations could function independent of larger society. The modern reality is, however, quite different. The schematic in Figure 4.2 shows how embedded work relationships are in society; organizations are built from society and contain underlying societal fractures. As such, cross-group relationships in organizations cannot be seen as independent of society. The hope for change lies in the fact that society not only influences organizations, but organizations also influence society. In the context of social identity conflicts, organizations have the opportunity to be role models for the larger community. They have the chance to show how to creatively respond to divides created by social identity disputes and to demonstrate that people of different histories and backgrounds can work together to achieve a common destiny.

# Cultural Values

*Shalom Schwartz*

---

**Keywords:** cultural values, autonomy, embeddedness, egalitarianism, hierarchy, harmony, mastery

## Key Points

- One of the most useful ways to think about cultural differences is to identify the key value emphases that prevail in a society.
- Cultural values shape the common beliefs, practices, symbols, social norms, and personal values in a society and provide a degree of coherence.
- The approach that scholars find most convincing is to seek dimensions of values that identify differences in preferred ways of pursuing key societal goals.
- Various sources point to three societal problems as most critical: (1) defining the boundaries between the person and the group and the optimal relations between them; (2) ensuring coordination among people to produce goods and services in ways that preserve the social fabric; and (3) regulating how human and natural resources are utilized. Cultural value emphases reflect and justify preferred societal responses to these problems.
- There are three bipolar, conceptual dimensions of culture that represent alternative resolutions to each of three problems that confront all societies: autonomy versus embeddedness, egalitarianism versus hierarchy, and harmony versus mastery.

- Leaders who recognize and take account of the cultural value orientations that influence their own beliefs and actions and those of the people with whom they work are more likely to successfully lead in contexts of difference.

## Related Exercises

- Exercise 1: Mapping Your Social Identities
- Exercise 2: Your Experience with Triggers
- Exercise 3: Identifying Faultlines
- Exercise 4: Cultural Values
- Exercise 5: Approaches to Difference
- Exercise 6: Cultural Intelligence
- Exercise 7: Your Leadership Practices
- Exercise 8: Examining Your Leadership Networks
- Exercise 9: Taking a New Perspective

## Related Cases

- Case 1: Race and Respect
- Case 2: Water Crises
- Case 3: Floating Holidays
- Case 4: Not My Weekend
- Case 5: It's Their Fault
- Case 6: The Scent of Difference
- Case 7: Not Catching On
- Case 8: Glass Ceiling at Big Boy Toys
- Case 9: Super Drugs
- Case 10: The Right to Be Pregnant
- Case 11: Local Bombing
- Case 12: Benefits Battle
- Case 13: Francois' Dilemma

Understanding the cultural differences between the participants in the cases in this book can go a long way toward explaining their expectations, feelings, and behavior, as well as conflict across differences. One of the most useful ways to think about cultural differences is to identify the key value emphases that prevail in a society. These prevailing value emphases may be the most central feature of a culture, distinguishing it from other cultures. Values are beliefs about what is good and desirable and what is bad and undesirable. These serve as guides for how people should behave and how organizations should function. Cultural values find expression in the various beliefs, practices, symbols, specific norms, and personal values that are common in a society. These cultural values differ between cultures, and manifest in different forms of behavioral expression and practices. For example, in a society whose culture strongly emphasizes hierarchy values, it is likely that most people will believe that teachers always know more than their students (beliefs), will impose strict discipline in families (practices), will treat their national flag as sacred (symbols), will criticize workers who question their boss (specific norms), and will attribute importance to being obeyed by subordinates and to obeying superiors (personal values). In this chapter I provide a model for thinking about and understanding cultural values based on my research as well as research by others (Sagiv & Schwartz, 2000, 2007; Schwartz, 1999, 2004, 2007).

Prevailing beliefs, practices, symbols, specific norms, and personal values are the ways that the underlying culture manifests itself. Cultural values also influence organizational and leadership practices. Cross-cultural leadership studies clearly indicate that cultural differences influence individual expectations and assumptions about management and that management philosophies typically evolve in harmony with the cultures within which they function (Dorfman, 1996; Hofstede, 1980,1991,1994; House, Hanges, Javidan, Dorfman & Gupta, 2004).

People may not be able to tell us very much about their culture because they take so much of it for granted. For example, a manager may come from a society in which most people take for granted that it is important to avoid openly arguing or defying the expectations of one's boss. Another manager may come from a society in which people take for granted that you should express your ideas freely and give your boss as much information as possible for making a good decision. Each set of behaviors is appropriate with members of one society but will not work well in the other. Understanding the prevailing cultural values can help managers to behave appropriately, or at least to know when they are behaving in an unexpected way (see, for instance, the difference in values between the Malaysian and Singapore employees in the water crises as described in Case 2).

Cultural values help to shape the common beliefs, practices, symbols, social norms, and personal values in a society and to give them a degree of coherence. Thus, culture is the context in which people live and are socialized. By virtue of living in a particular society, we experience the normative value emphases of our society's culture as a set of pressures of which we are only vaguely aware. Few of us realize, for example, that whether we were given our own bedrooms as young children or not influenced our thinking about whether it is more important for people to have privacy and independence or to have close, interdependent relationships. What I call the press of culture influences our attitudes, beliefs, feelings, ways of thinking, and behavior (Schwartz, 2009). In order for us to lead effectively across difference, we must not only know and understand the presses of our own cultures, but also the presses of those cultures that we work in or work with. Chapter 7 on cultural intelligence sheds more light on these aspects.

## THE PRESS OF CULTURE

The press of culture takes many forms. First, it refers to the events and experiences that we encounter more or less frequently in our daily life. Do our daily experiences draw attention more to the individual or the group? For example, does our income depend on our individual productivity or on what our work team produces? Do events to which we are exposed direct attention more to preserving the environment or making money? For example, does the daily news celebrate the glories of nature or the life styles of millionaires? The cultural press may even be built into the language we speak. Some languages always use pronouns to make clear who is speaking and being spoken too (for example, "I," "you"). Others drop the pronouns and rely on people's ability to figure this out from the context. The first type of language unconsciously focuses people on individuals and their characteristics; the second focuses people on the context in which people act and its influence on them.

The cultural press also takes the form of the opportunities for action that are available in a society. In societies whose culture emphasizes autonomy (or independency), people have many opportunities to do things on their own, for example, to demonstrate their special talents and pursue their favorite interests. In societies whose culture emphasizes relatedness (interdependency), in contrast, people have more opportunities to work as a team and to offer sympathy and support to others. Finally, this cultural press takes the form of the expectations and constraints that we encounter as we go about enacting our roles in societal institutions. For example, are students in educational institutions encouraged to ask questions and raise doubts or constrained to accept passively what is taught? Is it culturally legitimate for parents to put their own interests ahead of their children's in using the family's resources or are they constrained to put their children's interests first? And what of the children of elderly parents—whose interests should they put first? Answers to these questions vary across societies and express the underlying normative value emphases that are the heart of the culture of the society.

Not only the expectations and constraints built into the social institutions of a society express the underlying cultural value emphases. The very ways that the institutions are organized or led also express the prevailing culture. For example, the economic system in the United States is highly competitive, the legal system in which prosecution and defense lawyers seek to defeat one another is confrontational, and the family systems emphasize achievement-oriented childrearing. All of these institutional arrangements express a cultural value emphasis on success, ambition, and self-assertion. The parallel institutions in the socialist, Scandinavian countries are much less competitive and confrontational. They express stronger cultural value emphases on cooperation, concern for others' welfare, and equality.

Most individuals develop, adopt, and/or internalize modes of thinking, behaviors, attitudes, and personal value priorities that enable them to function effectively and feel comfortable in the societal contexts to which they are exposed. In these ways, they absorb the impact of culture. Strong cultural value emphases on preserving hierarchical relations and traditional in-group solidarity in Thailand and in many sub-Saharan African countries, for example, induce widespread conformity and self-effacing behavior in their populations, attitudes of humility, and personal values that give high priority to fulfilling the expectations of the kin group.

## DESCRIBING CULTURAL DIFFERENCES

Thus far, we have seen what cultural value emphases are and how they are expressed in and influence both the functioning of institutions and the attitudes, behavior, and values of individuals. But how can we describe cultural differences systematically? When we travel from one society to another or meet people from other countries, we notice many differences. With cultures differing in so many ways, we need a manageable set of constructs on which to compare them. These constructs should be fundamental: they should identify the most important, underlying value emphases and reflect the basic nature of societies or other large groups (for example, ethnic groups).

The approach that scholars find most convincing is to seek dimensions of values that identify differences in preferred ways of pursuing *key societal goals*. Early sociological theorists identified these goals as maintaining social order, containing social conflict, encouraging productivity and innovation, and regulating social change. These are basic requirements for the successful functioning of societies.

In pursuing these goals, all societies confront and must cope with basic problems in regulating human activity if they are to survive. Various sources point to three societal problems as most critical: (1) defining the boundaries between the person and the group and the optimal relations between them; (2) ensuring coordination among people to produce goods and services in ways that preserve the social fabric; and (3) regulating how human and natural resources are utilized. Cultural value emphases reflect and justify preferred societal responses to these problems. We can derive a set of bipolar dimensions for comparing cultures by considering societal values that might underlie alternative ways of handling these problems.

These preferred cultural value orientations prescribe how institutions should function and how people should behave in order best to deal with the key problems societies face. Each pair of value orientations, described below, forms a cultural dimension with opposing preferences for dealing with one key problem. One orientation may be more effective than its opposite in some contexts, but neither is better in all contexts. No society's culture is at the extreme on any cultural dimension. Rather, societal cultures are located along the dimensions nearer to one pole and farther from the other. In describing the cultural value orientations, as identified by Schwartz (1999, 2004, 2007), their implications for the way organizations are likely to function are also pointed out.

## Autonomy vs. Embeddedness

The problem of defining the optimal relations and boundaries between the person and the group translates into the question: To what extent should people be treated as autonomous versus as embedded in their groups? *Embeddedness* cultures treat people as entities embedded in the collective. Meaning in life is expected to come largely through in-group social relationships, through identifying with the group, participating in its shared way of life, and striving toward its shared goals. Embedded cultures emphasize maintaining the status quo and restraining actions that might disrupt in-group solidarity or the traditional order. Such values as social order, respect for tradition, security, and wisdom are especially important in embedded cultures. The cultures of African and Muslim countries are especially high in embeddedness.

*Autonomy* cultures treat people as autonomous, bounded entities. They encourage people to cultivate and express their own preferences, feelings, ideas, and abilities and to find meaning in their own uniqueness. There are two types of autonomy: Intellectual autonomy encourages individuals to pursue their own ideas and intellectual directions independently (important values: curiosity, broadmindedness, creativity). Affective autonomy encourages individuals to pursue affectively positive personal experiences (important values: pleasure, exciting life, varied life). The cultures of such West European countries as Germany, France, Sweden, Denmark, and Sweden are especially high in intellectual autonomy; those of Anglo countries (United States, New Zealand, Great Britain, Ireland) are especially high in affective autonomy.

Organizations located in societies high on embeddedness are more likely to function as extended families, taking responsibility for their members in all domains of life and, in return, expecting members to identify with and work dutifully toward shared goals. Organizations located in high autonomy societies, in contrast, are more likely to treat their members as independent actors with their own interests, preferences, abilities, and allegiances. They tend to grant members more autonomy, encouraging them to generate and act upon their own ideas.

## Egalitarianism vs. Hierarchy

The problem of ensuring coordination among people to produce goods and services in ways that preserve the social fabric translates into the question: How can the unavoidable interdependence among people be managed in a way that elicits coordinated, productive activity rather than disruptive behavior or withholding of effort? *Hierarchy* cultures rely on hierarchical systems of ascribed roles to ensure responsible, productive behavior. They define the unequal distribution of power, roles, and resources as legitimate and even desirable. They socialize people to take a hierarchical distribution of roles for granted and to comply with the obligations and rules attached to their roles (important values: social power, authority, humility, wealth). Confucian influenced cultures are especially high in hierarchy.

*Egalitarian* cultures urge people to recognize one another as moral equals who share basic interests as human beings. They socialize people to internalize a commitment to cooperate, to feel concern for the welfare of all, and to act voluntarily to benefit others (important values: equality, social justice, responsibility, honesty). The cultures of West European countries other than Portugal and Greece are especially high in egalitarianism.

In hierarchical cultures, organizations are more likely to construct a chain of authority in which all are assigned well-defined roles. Members are expected to comply with role obligations and to put the interests of the organization before their own. Egalitarian organizations, in contrast, are built on cooperative negotiation among employees and management. Leaders more often use shared goal setting and appeal to the joint welfare of all to motivate members. Members are expected to enact their roles more flexibly and to influence organizational goals.

## Harmony vs. Mastery

The problem of regulating how human and natural resources are utilized translates into the question: To what extent should individuals and groups control and change their social and natural environment versus leaving it undisturbed and unchanged? *Mastery* cultures encourage active self-assertion by individuals or groups in order to master, direct, and change the natural and social environment and thereby to attain group or personal goals. They emphasize the desirability of active, pragmatic problem solving that can produce "progress" (important values: ambition, success, daring, competence). The cultures of the United States, Israel, and China are especially high in mastery.

*Harmony* cultures emphasize fitting into the social and natural world, accepting, preserving, and appreciating the way things are rather than to change, direct, or exploit. Harmony cultures discourage efforts to bring about change and encourage maintaining smooth relations and avoiding conflict (important values: accepting one's position in life, world at peace, unity with nature). The cultures of Germany, Italy, Mexico, and Ethiopia are especially high in harmony.

Organizations that emphasize mastery are likely to be dynamic, competitive, and oriented to achievement and success. They often develop and use technology to manipulate and change the environment to attain organizational goals. Where harmony is important, in contrast, organizations are expected to fit into the surrounding social and natural world. Leaders try to understand the social and environmental implications of organizational actions and to seek non-exploitative ways to work toward their goals. They may question the legitimacy of technological manipulation of the environment.

## CONCLUSION

In sum, the theory specifies three bipolar, conceptual dimensions of culture that represent alternative resolutions to each of three problems that confront all societies: *autonomy* versus *embeddedness, egalitarianism* versus *hierarchy*, and *harmony* versus *mastery*. A societal emphasis on the cultural orientation at one pole of a dimension typically accompanies a de-emphasis on the polar type with which it tends to conflict. Leaders who recognize and take account of the cultural value orientations that influence their own beliefs and actions and those of the people with whom they work are more likely to successfully lead in contexts of difference. The Leading Through Paradox chapter in this book offers a perspective on how leaders can lead in these situations.

# Approaches to Difference: Allophilia and Xenophobia

*Todd L. Pittinsky*

---

**Keywords:** allophilia, xenophobia, recategorization, decategorization, simultaneous identities

**Key Points**

- Xenophobia is the general fear or hatred of those who are considered to be in a different group than one's own. It is not necessarily based on direct experience with any particular group. Allophilia, in contrast, is a positive feeling toward the members of a particular group that is considered to be different from one's own.

- Studies on the relations between groups typically assume that, in order to have more positive feelings toward members of another group, we need to (1) see their group and our own group as part of a single larger group (this is called recategorization); (2) see individual members of the other group strictly as individuals and not as members of the other group (this is called decategorization); or (3) see ourselves and others has having dual identities—they are part of their group, we are part of our group, and we are all part of a larger group.

- The allophilia model is different because it proposes that one can have positive feelings about members of another group without seeing oneself and others as part of the same group. Put another way, one can have positive feelings about "the other" in all his or her "otherness."

- Allophilia been found to have five forms: affection (having positive feelings toward members of the other group); engagement (seeking interactions with members of the other group); kinship (believing there is a close connection with members of the other group); comfort (feeling comfortable and at ease with members of the other group); and enthusiasm (feeling impressed or inspired by members of the other group).

- Xenophobia and allophilia are not opposites in the sense that reducing one will not have the same effects as increasing the other. The reduction of xenophobia is a good predictor that there will be fewer hate crimes. The promotion of allophilia is a strong predictor of such deliberately helpful behaviors as giving money to a charity that serves the other group, supporting public policies that will benefit the other group, standing up to someone about to commit an act of hate toward the other group, and going out of one's way to become acquainted with or become friends with members of the other group. Reducing xenophobia will not, in itself, bring the benefits of increasing allophilia.

### Related Exercises

- Exercise 1: Mapping Your Social Identities
- Exercise 2: Your Experience with Triggers
- Exercise 3: Identifying Faultlines
- Exercise 4: Cultural Values
- Exercise 5: Approaches to Difference
- Exercise 6: Cultural Intelligence
- Exercise 7: Your Leadership Practices
- Exercise 8: Examining Your Leadership Networks
- Exercise 9: Taking a New Perspective

### Related Cases

- Case 3: Floating Holidays
- Case 5: It's Their Fault
- Case 6: The Scent of Difference
- Case 9: Super Drugs
- Case 11: Local Bombing
- Case 12: Benefits Battle
- Case 13: Francois' Dilemma

When we encounter those who are different from us—be it religious, ethnic, professional, national, or any other form of difference—we bring to the encounter feelings and thoughts about the groups to which they belong and dispositions to behave toward those groups in certain ways. One common way to categorize such orientations toward those who are different is to consider the degree to which the orientation is negative or positive. Xenophobia is the general fear or hatred of those who are different, not necessarily grounded in direct experience with any particular group. Allophilia, in contrast, is a positive orientation toward the members of a particular group seen as different or "other." In this chapter I describe xenophobia and allophilia and show how they help to describe a fuller range of possible relations among individuals from different social identity groups.

## XENOPHOBIA

The first use of the term *xenophobia* was by Sumner (1906). Today, xenophobia is typically used to refer to fear of what is foreign or strange. One of the earliest studied concepts of attitude toward "the other," xenophobia is frequently discussed in the context of ethnocentrism—the tendency to believe in the superiority of one's own ethnic group. Xenophobia is frequently considered the "evil twin" of ethnocentrism. Xenophobia (and, for that matter, ethnocentrism) are often cast as extensions of an evolutionarily hard-wired preference for those who are most nearly related to us and whose survival, therefore, most nearly approximates the survival of our own genes (Hamilton, 1963; Rushton, 1999; van den Berghe, 1999; van der Dennen, 1987). These negative attitudes toward others are sometimes viewed as a way of creating or strengthening one's own sense of group identity (Sherif, 1967; Tajfel & Turner, 1986). Many argue that xenophobia is an innate universal human trait that assumes different forms depending on context. When xenophobia is prevalent and powerful, it can be a strong precursor of *acts* of hatred, such as genocide or other forms of violence and oppression (Shaw & Wong, 1989; van der Dennen, 2004).

Xenophobia is widespread within and across cultures and over time. For example, multiethnic societies, including those with significant immigrant populations, are often home to xenophobic attitudes fueling social movements. Xenophobic responses can be fueled by elements of fear for the in-group's economic or cultural well-being (or perhaps its economic or cultural dominance) but also by irrational and fantastic prejudices against the out-group (Karakatsanis & Swarts, 2007; Soldatova, 2007).

## ALLOPHILIA

Orientations toward others are typically studied, discussed, and addressed in terms of negative attitudes such as xenophobia, ethnocentrism, and prejudice (Pittinsky, 2008; Pittinsky & Maruskin, 2008). But the presence or absence of negative attitudes toward the other is not the whole story; people also have positive feelings about others. For example, there are Jewish citizens of Israel who feel genuine kinship with Arab citizens and Arab citizens who feel genuine kinship with Jewish citizens (Pittinsky, Ratcliff, & Maruskin, 2008). Research on positive attitudes toward those who are seen as different counters the preponderance of attention toward negative attitudes and their reduction. The term for such positive attitudes, *allophilia,* is derived from the ancient Greek words for "liking or love of the other."

Research suggests that we will feel more positive toward the members of another group when we can (1) recategorize the other (see them as us) through a superordinate identity or goal that binds us to them; (2) decategorize the other (see the other as an individual rather than as a member of a group); or (3) emphasize dual identities (simultaneously emphasize the senses of them, us, and an overarching we). (For a review, see Pittinsky & Simon, 2007.) These processes all seek to reduce the emphasis on the *other* social identity group to which the other belongs, an emphasis that is typically presumed to provoke negative responses. The allophilia model is different because it assumes the default approach to different social-identity groups often is, and increasingly can be, positive rather than negative. It focuses on them as *them* and on the conditions under which we feel positive toward them. In short, the allophilia model argues that it is possible to have positive feelings about "the others" in all their "otherness." This perspective is important because evidence from cognitive science increasingly supports the view that people are predisposed to think categorically—to classify the world into "us" and "them." Allophilia focuses researchers and practitioners on consideration (and promotion) of cases of us liking them more, not hating them less.

Though allophilia research is an emerging field, it has yielded important findings. Allophilia for the members of another group has been found to have five forms: affection (having positive feelings toward members of the other group); engagement (seeking interactions with members of the other group); kinship (believing there is a close connection with members of the other group); comfort (feeling comfortable and at ease with members of the other group); and enthusiasm (feeling impressed or inspired by members of the other group) (Pittinsky, Rosenthal, & Montoya, forthcoming).

Research also indicates that the outcomes of promoting allophilia are different from the outcomes of reducing xenophobia. The reduction of xenophobia is a good predictor that there will be fewer hate crimes. The promotion of allophilia is a strong predictor of such positive, proactive behaviors as providing resources to another group (in the form of monetary donations to a charity), supporting institutionalized policies to benefit another group, standing up to an aggressor before an act of hate, and going out of one's way to form attachments with members of a different group (Pittinsky, Rosenthal, & Montoya, 2007; Ratcliff & Pittinsky, 2008). In other words, positive relations between groups are predicted better by how much the members of one group like members of the other group (allophilia) than by how little they dislike members of the other group (prejudice). It has also been found that a combination of positive intergroup attitudes and a more general sense of equity will motivate greater support for programs and policies to assist an out-group than either factor will motivate alone (Pittinsky & Montoya, 2009).

It is important to understand that reducing xenophobia (fear of the other) will not necessarily increase allophilia (affection for the other). Think of debt and income. They can go up and down independently. Getting a raise doesn't automatically lower your debt. If you are a spendthrift, your income and your debt can both go up at the same time. To improve your financial state, you may need to increase your income and reduce your debt—two very different tasks. In much the same way, to bring about positive relations between different groups, prejudice must be reduced and allophilia must be increased.

## XENOPHOBIA, ALLOPHILIA, AND LEADING ACROSS DIFFERENCE

Leaders are likely to find themselves leading groups made up of subgroups whose members see one other as different. What is a leader to do? While leaders understand the need to create positive relations among their subgroups, what they typically set about to do is reduce negative relations—eliminating conflict, countering prejudice, and so on (Pittinsky, 2009). But the concept of allophilia suggests that leaders can do better than that. Trying to create a cohesive group of followers out of subgroups who have negative attitudes about one another requires two independent (although related) efforts: reducing the negative intergroup attitudes so as to minimize the associated negative behaviors *and* promoting positive intergroup attitudes so as to increase the associated positive behaviors (Pittinsky, 2009).

Research is examining the antecedents of allophilia, that is, the pathways leaders can follow to increase it. For example, recent findings suggest that, while evoking sympathy (empathic sorrow) for another group does reduce prejudice, evoking symhedonia (empathic joy) for another group is a stronger predictor of creating allophilia for that group (Pittinsky & Montoya, in press). Other work looks at how groups display their pride and how other groups respond to those displays. When we believe an out-group to be hubristically proud, we actually dislike them more, but when we perceive an out-group as feeling justifiably proud, our allophilia for them actually increases (Ratcliff & Pittinsky, 2008).

Both leaders and the diverse collectives or communities they lead have to work hard if they want to reduce negative intergroup relations while increasing positive intergroup relations. But the payoff can be great: communities, organizations, and nations whose proudly distinct subgroups live and work enthusiastically with each other.

# Cultural Intelligence: A Pathway for Leading in a Rapidly Globalizing World

*Linn Van Dyne*
*Soon Ang*
*David Livermore*

**Keywords**: cultural intelligence (CQ), motivational cultural intelligence, cognitive cultural intelligence, metacognitive cultural intelligence, behavioral cultural intelligence

**Key Points**

- Cultural intelligence (CQ) builds upon and extends emotional intelligence.

- CQ focuses specifically on one's capability to effectively understand and adapt to a myriad of cultural contexts as an essential skill set needed to lead effectively across cultures. CQ is in essence the ability to function effectively in a diverse context where assumptions, values, and traditions of one's upbringing are not uniformly shared with those with whom one needs to act. Or, to put it differently, CQ is the capability of leaving behind those intelligent behaviors learned in one cultural context when what is intelligent in another cultural context differs.

- CQ is rooted in four different, yet interrelated sets of capabilities: motivational CQ (showing interest, confidence, and drive to adapt cross-culturally), cognitive CQ (understanding cross-cultural issues and differences), metacognitive CQ (strategizing and making sense of culturally diverse experiences), and behavioral CQ (changing verbal and nonverbal actions appropriately when interacting cross-culturally).

- CQ can be developed and offers us a set of steps and capabilities that allows us to show respect and dignity for others while enhancing our own effectiveness and competitive edge in multicultural and global contexts.

## Related Exercises

- Exercise 6: Cultural Intelligence (CQ)

## Related Cases

- Case 1: Race and Respect
- Case 2: Water Crises
- Case 3: Floating Holidays
- Case 4: Not My Weekend
- Case 5: It's Their Fault
- Case 6: The Scent of Difference
- Case 12: Benefits Battle

---

Cultural intelligence refers to *an individual's capability to function effectively across cultures*—this can include national, ethnic, and organizational as well as other types of culture (Ang & Van Dyne, 2008; Earley & Ang, 2003). Rather than expecting individuals to master all the norms, values, and practices of the various cultures encountered, cultural intelligence helps leaders develop an overall perspective and repertoire that results in more effective leadership. The driving question behind the idea of cultural intelligence (or CQ) is this: *Why do some leaders easily and effectively adapt their views and behaviors cross-culturally and others don't?* Your honest engagement with that question can determine whether or not you lead successfully in our rapidly globalizing world. In this chapter, we provide an overview of cultural intelligence and describe the Four-Factor Model of Cultural Intelligence (motivational CQ, cognitive CQ, metacognitive CQ, and behavioral CQ) with the aim of helping you to think more deeply about your own cultural intelligence capabilities as well as helping you to apply these ideas and the CQ framework to the cases in this book.

## WHAT IS CULTURAL INTELLIGENCE (CQ)?

Most of us know that IQ or intelligence quotient is a measurement of one's intellectual capabilities. In recent years, we've also seen the significance of EQ or emotional intelligence—one's ability to lead and interact with effective emotional sensibilities. Cultural intelligence builds upon some of these same ideas, but instead focuses specifically on one's capability to effectively understand and adapt to a myriad of cultural contexts as an additional and essential skill set needed by contemporary leaders (Ng, Van Dyne, & Ang, 2009a, 2009b).

Theories and books about cross-cultural interaction abound (Hofstede & Hofstede, 2004; House, Hanges, Javidan, Dorfman, & Gupta, 2004). A great deal of that material focuses on cultural knowledge—knowing how cultures differ in work norms, habits, and behaviors. The cultural intelligence approach goes beyond this emphasis on knowledge because it also emphasizes the importance of developing an overall repertoire of understanding, motivation, and skills that enables one to move in and out of lots of different cultural contexts (Ang & Van Dyne, 2008). Cultural intelligence considers cultural, sociological, and individual dynamics that occur for each of us in cross-cultural settings.

Research demonstrates that effective cross-cultural leadership isn't just a matter of emotional intelligence and common sense (Ang, Van Dyne, Koh, Ng, Templer, Tay, & Chandrasekar, 2007). Just as emotional intelligence focuses on a leader's ability to work effectively with people by paying attention to the emotions of self and others, cultural intelligence focuses on a leader's ability to function effectively with people and in situations involving different cultural backgrounds. When we interact with people from our own culture, we intuitively use a set of social cues to engage effectively. We have a wealth of information, most of which is subconscious, that helps us know how to relate and lead.

In contrast, when we experience a new culture, cues and information that have worked in the past are largely absent or misleading. For example, in culturally unfamiliar situations, it sometimes seems that other people's behavior and perspectives are somewhat bizarre and random. Those with high CQ have the ability to encounter these types of confusing situations, think deeply about what is happening (or not happening), and make appropriate adjustments to how they understand, relate, and lead in the context of this different culture.

Making these kinds of adjustments involves a complex set of capabilities and processes that comes from intentional effort on the part of the leader, all of which contribute to the leader's CQ. Cultural intelligence is a set of capabilities and skills that enables leaders from outside a culture to interpret unfamiliar behaviors and situations as though they were insiders to that culture. One of the most important things to assess when looking for culturally intelligent leaders is to see whether the person can identify behaviors that are universal to all humanity, behaviors that are cultural, and behaviors that are idiosyncratically personal to a particular individual in a specific situation.

## THE FOUR-FACTOR MODEL OF CULTURAL INTELLIGENCE

The cultural intelligence model is rooted in a four-factor framework that synthesizes the volumes of material and perspectives on intelligence and cross-cultural leadership. CQ is composed of four qualitatively different capabilities, and yet, each of the four factors is interrelated. For real effectiveness, leaders need all four CQ capabilities, because focusing only on one factor of CQ may actually result in increased cultural ignorance rather than enhanced cultural intelligence. This is because CQ requires an overall repertoire of adaptive capabilities. The four factors of CQ are motivational CQ, cognitive CQ, metacognitive CQ, and behavioral CQ (see Figure 7.1). Each is described below.

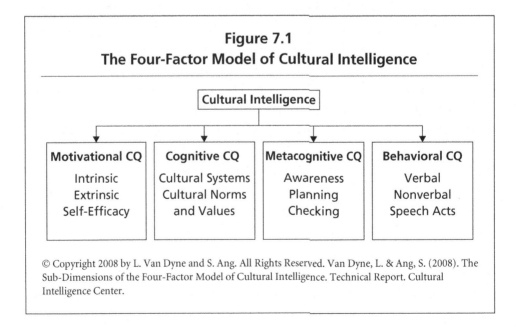

**Figure 7.1**
**The Four-Factor Model of Cultural Intelligence**

| **Cultural Intelligence** | | | |
| --- | --- | --- | --- |
| **Motivational CQ** | **Cognitive CQ** | **Metacognitive CQ** | **Behavioral CQ** |
| Intrinsic | Cultural Systems | Awareness | Verbal |
| Extrinsic | Cultural Norms | Planning | Nonverbal |
| Self-Efficacy | and Values | Checking | Speech Acts |

© Copyright 2008 by L. Van Dyne and S. Ang. All Rights Reserved. Van Dyne, L. & Ang, S. (2008). The Sub-Dimensions of the Four-Factor Model of Cultural Intelligence. Technical Report. Cultural Intelligence Center.

## Motivational CQ: Showing Interest, Confidence, and Drive to Adapt Cross-Culturally

The motivational factor of CQ refers to the leader's level of interest, *drive*, and energy to adapt cross-culturally. This refers to whether or not you have the confidence and drive to work through the challenges and conflict that often accompany cross-cultural work. The ability to be personally engaged and to persevere through cross-cultural challenges is one of the novel and most important aspects of the cultural intelligence framework. Many of the other approaches to thinking about cross-cultural competencies simply *assume* that people are motivated to gain cross-cultural capabilities. Yet employees often approach diversity training apathetically, and employees headed out on international assignments are often more concerned about moving their families overseas and getting settled than they are about developing cultural understanding. Without ample motivation, there's little point in spending time and money on training.

Motivational cultural intelligence includes intrinsic motivation—the degree to which you derive enjoyment from culturally diverse situations; extrinsic motivation—the more tangible benefits you gain from culturally diverse experiences; and self-efficacy—your confidence that you will be effective in a cross-cultural encounter. All three of these motivational dynamics play a role in how leaders approach cross-cultural situations. Stop and examine your level of drive for doing cross-cultural work. Your motivational CQ is strongly related to your level of effectiveness in new cultural contexts.

## Cognitive CQ: Understanding Cross-Cultural Issues and Differences

Cognitive CQ is the *knowledge* dimension of cultural intelligence. It refers to the leader's level of understanding about culture and culture's role in shaping the way to do business and interact with others across cultural contexts. Your cognitive CQ or knowledge is based on the degree to which you understand the idea of culture and how it shapes the way you think and behave. It also includes your overall understanding of the ways that cultures vary from one context to the next.

One of the most important parts of cognitive CQ is an understanding of cultural systems and the set of cultural norms and values associated with different societies. Cultural systems are the ways societies organize themselves to meet the basic needs of humanity. For example, every nation has cultural systems for (1) economic approaches for producing vital commodities and distributing products and services; (2) ways of codifying mating and child-rearing practices that create marriage, family, and other social structures; (3) educational practices that enable learning and cultural transmission; (4) political, legal, and social controls that reduce anarchy and destruction (obedience to social norms); (5) language conventions that facilitate interaction; and (6) religious beliefs that explain inexplicable phenomena.

Cultural norms and values are the varying ways cultures approach things like time, authority, and relationships (see the Cultural Values chapter in this book for more information). Although an understanding of how a family system works might seem somewhat theoretical, it becomes critically relevant when you're trying to develop human resource policies for employees coming from a place where the cultural norms dictate that employees will care for senior members of their extended families. Likewise, the value a culture places on time and relationships becomes highly germane when an American is trying to get a signed contract from a potential affiliate in China or Brazil or Saudi Arabia or Spain, where cultural values provide different norms for what is considered appropriate in this type of situation.

Cognitive CQ is the factor that is most often emphasized in typical approaches to intercultural competency. For example, a large and growing training and consulting industry focuses on teaching leaders this kind of cultural knowledge. While valuable, however, the knowledge that comes from cognitive CQ has to be combined with the other three factors of CQ or its relevance to the real demands of leadership is questionable and potentially detrimental.

## Metacognitive CQ: Strategizing and Making Sense of Culturally Diverse Experiences

The metacognitive factor of CQ refers to the leader's ability to strategize when crossing cultures. Metacognitive CQ, or *strategy*, involves slowing down long enough to carefully observe what's going on inside our own and other people's heads. It's the ability to think about our own thought processes and draw on our cultural knowledge to understand a different cultural context and solve problems in that situation. It includes whether we can use our cultural knowledge to plan an appropriate strategy, accurately interpret what's going on in a cross-cultural situation, and check to see whether our expectations are accurate or whether our mental model of that particular person and/or culture should be revised.

Seasoned leaders often jump into meetings with little planning. This can work well in one's home culture. By drawing on emotional intelligence and leadership experience, we can often get away with "winging it" because we know how to respond to cues and how to talk about our work. When meetings involve individuals from different cultural contexts, however, all the rules change. Relying on our ability to intuitively respond to cues in these more novel situations is dangerous. That's where this third factor of cultural intelligence, metacognitive CQ, comes in.

Metacognitive CQ includes awareness, planning, and checking. Awareness means being in tune with what's going on in one's self and others. Planning is taking the time to prepare for a cross-cultural encounter—anticipating how to approach the people, topic, and situation. Checking is the monitoring we do as we engage in interactions to see whether the plans and expectations we had were appropriate. It's comparing what we expected with our actual experience—with what happened. This factor of CQ reflects whether or not we can engage in awareness, planning, and checking in ways that result in better contemporary leadership practices. Metacognitive CQ emphasizes strategy and is the lynchpin between understanding cultural issues and actually being able to use that understanding to be more effective.

## Behavioral CQ: Changing Verbal and Nonverbal Actions Appropriately When Interacting Cross-Culturally

Behavioral CQ, the *action* dimension of CQ, refers to the leader's ability to act appropriately in a range of cross-cultural situations. It influences whether we can actually accomplish our performance goals effectively in light of different norms across cross-cultural situations. One of the most important aspects of behavioral CQ is knowing when to adapt to another culture and when *not* to do so. A person with high CQ learns which actions will and will not enhance effectiveness and acts on that understanding. Thus, behavioral CQ involves flexible actions tailored to the specific cultural context.

The behavioral factor of CQ includes the capability to be flexible in verbal and nonverbal actions. It also includes appropriate flexibility in speech acts—the exact words and phrases we use when we communicate specific types of messages. While the demands of today's intercultural settings make it impossible to master all the do's and don'ts of various cultures, there are certain behaviors that should be modified when we interact with different cultures. For example, Westerners need to learn the importance of carefully studying business cards presented by those from most Asian contexts. Also, some basic verbal and nonverbal behaviors enhance the extent to which we are seen as effective by others. As an example, the verbal tone (loud versus soft) in which words are spoken can convey different meanings across cultures. Although it is not necessary for an outsider to master the intricacies of bowing in Japan, appropriate use of touch *is* something to bear in mind. In sum, almost every approach to cross-cultural work has insisted on the importance of flexibility. With behavioral CQ, we now have a way of exploring how to enhance our flexibility.

## FOUR STEPS TOWARD ENHANCING OVERALL CQ

Although the four factors of cultural intelligence don't always develop in one particular order, Van Dyne and Ang (2008) suggest that it can be helpful to think about the four factors of CQ as four steps toward enhanced overall cultural intelligence.

- Step 1: Motivational CQ (Drive) gives us the energy and self-confidence to pursue the needed cultural understanding and planning.
- Step 2: Cognitive CQ (Knowledge) provides us with an understanding of basic cultural cues.
- Step 3: Metacognitive CQ (Strategy) allows us to draw upon our cultural understanding so we can plan and interpret what's going on in diverse contexts.
- Step 4: Behavioral CQ (Action) provides us with the ability to engage in effective flexible leadership across cultures.
- Feedback loop → Others respond to our behavior; this influences our motivational CQ; and the cycle starts over—leading to further enhancement of overall cultural intelligence.

It is an exciting time to be involved in cross-cultural leadership! Almost every day each of us has the opportunity to learn from people who are different from us—people in various walks of life who are from different cultural backgrounds. Cultural intelligence offers us a pathway—a set of steps and capabilities for this journey—that should allow us to show respect and dignity for others while enhancing our own effectiveness and competitive edge in multicultural and global contexts.

# Social Justice and Dignity

*Philomena Essed*

**Keywords:** in-group/out-group dynamic, intersectionality, cosmopolitanism, microinequities, multiple identities, simultaneous identities

**Key Points**

- The ability to acknowledge cultural experiences without stigmatizing them is at the heart of social justice and dignity.

- Social justice and dignity require, among other things, an understanding of systems of privilege and oppression, which are invariably connected to notions of power and authority in organizations.

- Recognizing an individual as only having one social identity (such as "white" or "male") undercuts the relevance and importance of other social identities and incorrectly reduces the complexity of what it means to be human. Conversely, failing to recognize a social identity important to people ignores a part of them they feel is critical to who they are.

- Intersectionality accounts for discrimination and privilege on the basis of intertwined social identities. For instance, whiteness and masculinity often converge to create privilege (often referred to as "white privilege") while blackness and femininity create a double-edged disadvantage.

- Cosmopolitanism is an all-encompassing view of the community of humankind creating the freedom for people to make choices, to liberate the self from the constraints of cultural expectations.

- Non-dominant people tend to be disproportionately asked to give up aspects of themselves in order to maintain the peace. Calls for a group to "get over it" for the sake of the organization might be met with resistance and anger when there has been a long history of a particular group having to give things up for the sake of others, when there is little evidence of the sacrifice being reciprocated.

- To create an environment of justice and dignity, leaders need to develop a clear understanding of who they are as individuals and as members (or symbols of) the various social identity groups to which they belong and to understand others in their own terms (rather than their sense of who they are or should be).

### Related Exercises

- Exercise 1: Mapping Your Social Identities
- Exercise 2: Your Experience with Triggers
- Exercise 3: Identifying Faultlines
- Exercise 4: Cultural Values
- Exercise 5: Approaches to Difference
- Exercise 9: Taking a New Perspective

### Related Cases

- Case 1: Race and Respect
- Case 2: Water Crises
- Case 3: Floating Holidays
- Case 4: Not My Weekend
- Case 5: It's Their Fault
- Case 6: The Scent of Difference
- Case 7: Not Catching On
- Case 8: Glass Ceiling at Big Boy Toys
- Case 9: Super Drugs
- Case 10: The Right to Be Pregnant
- Case 11: Local Bombing
- Case 12: Benefits Battle
- Case 13: Francois' Dilemma

---

Everybody wants to be treated fairly, but not everybody treats others fairly or sees fairness in the same way. Some cases in this book are situations in which individuals feel offended, not seen, or not acknowledged in their cultural, ethnic, racial, religious, national, or gendered social identities. Other cases illustrate that individuals feel patronized, stigmatized, or excluded because they are seen *only* or primarily in terms of their social identities. The ability to acknowledge cultural experiences without stigmatizing them is at the heart of social justice and dignity, the focus of this chapter.

Social justice and dignity require, among other things, an understanding of systems of privilege and oppression, which are invariably connected to notions of power and authority in organizations. Listening to those who feel discriminated against and hearing the message, the ability to be critiqued without immediate self-defense, the courage to take a firm stand against discrimination without demonizing anyone, and a belief in the human capacity to change are among the important tools leaders can use to create an inclusive and productive organization. However, doing so can be extremely difficult. The ability to recognize the inherent human worth of self and others without losing sight of relevant differential group experiences is what dignity is about. Leaders must balance individual and shared identities in a manner that honors themselves and those around them. In this chapter, I provide an overview of concepts and theories that can help leaders understand why it is important to acknowledge cultural experiences without stigmatizing them. I also provide some suggestions for how to begin to build the skills to do so.

## MULTIPLE IDENTITIES

While norms, values, symbols, and shared ways of life form the glue of cultural connectivity, cultures are not homogeneous. For example, there are conflicts over gender equality within cultures, political and class differences within cultures, and so on. How we relate to social worlds is fluid rather than static. To further complicate matters, individuals are members of more than one group (gender, race, class, nationality, and so on). These multiple identities are simultaneously present, but ebb and flow in their relevance and importance based on the context and situation. People cannot be reduced to only one dimension of their identity, for instance just their "race" or their "gender" (Essed, 2001). In fact, recognizing an individual as only having one social identity (such as "white" or "male") undercuts the relevance and importance of other social identities and incorrectly reduces the complexity of what it means to be human. Conversely, failing to recognize a social identity important to others ignores a part of them they feel is critical to who they are.

Another dynamic associated with multiple social identities is what Kimberlé Crenshaw (1991) calls intersectionality. Intersectionality accounts for discrimination and privilege on the basis of intertwined social identities. For instance, whiteness and masculinity often converge to create privilege (often referred to as "white privilege") while blackness and femininity create a double-edged disadvantage.

## DEFINING ONESELF

The desire to belong to a group can create a prison of cultural appropriation. This happens when other people define the behavioral conditions of group membership and pressure individuals to comply. For example, comments suggesting "If you do that, then you are not like us" can force individuals to choose between being part of the group and honoring or acknowledging another aspect of themselves. In her book, *The Space Between Us: Negotiating Gender and National Identities in Conflict*, focusing on women projects in three areas of violent conflict (Northern Ireland, Israel-Palestine, Bosnia Herzegovina), Cynthia Cockburn (1998) discusses the development of alliances between women who were members of historical enemy groups. The women came to the projects with highly politicized ethnic-national identities and political affiliations, but they created space to acknowledge these differences. There was also space to allow for closeness and shared experiences of pain and hope; they had all known violence and loss due to actions taken by the "other" group. The process of beginning to see each other as multifaceted, complex individuals involved finding their own subjectivity, where women dealt with the gap between how they felt about themselves as unique and how they thought they should feel or behave because of their ethnic, religious, gender, and political identity. The societal message suggested they should hate one another ("If you are one of us, then you have to hate them"). However, they shared critical reflections on the need to belong ("I want to be one of the group") and at the same time voiced critique of the coercion they had experienced from the dominance of ethnic and national identities ("I do not have to hate someone else to be part of that group").

An answer to deterministic racial or cultural affiliations is radical cosmopolitanism. In his book, *Becoming a Cosmopolitan*, Jason Hill (2000) defines cosmopolitanism as an all-encompassing view of the community of humankind. He calls for autonomy, the freedom to make choices, to liberate the self from the constraints of cultural expectations. Autonomy does not mean disconnection from the social or independence from relations to other human beings. Autonomy is independence of judgment—the freedom to be self-reflective, to be critical of the norms and rules one is expected to follow. Strong social identities can temper the necessary distance one needs in order to be reflective about the norms, values, and expected behavior particular social identities represent. Autonomy is the right to decide to which groups one belongs and how—not someone else defining who you are for you. It pushes against the notion that someone within a group has the "right" to define that group for others. This can be important in organizations with strong faultlines because there may be pressures (even threats) to behave a certain way or lose acknowledgement of group membership. An example of this can be leaders who are members of two social identity groups at odds with one another. The advantage the leader has is potentially being a bridge between the two groups; the disadvantage is that both groups may feel like the leader is not really "one of us" and, thus, perhaps cannot be fully trusted.

## PRINCIPLES OF JUSTICE

In the Western tradition, people often delegate some of their individual rights to a government in order to achieve political and social order. Philosophers such as Locke, Hobbes, and Rousseau hold that structured social order is necessary and is created by a legitimate governing authority sanctioned by "the people" wherein individuals choose to not do things they can and want to do in order to maintain peace and order. Classical theories of this social contract presupposed that contracting agents were male, rational, and more or less equally equipped to contribute to the economy, and thus non-dominant people were, and have been, disproportionately asked to give up aspects of themselves in order to maintain the peace. Calls for a group to "get over it" for the sake of the organization might be met with resistance and anger when there has been a long history of a particular group having to give things up for the sake of others, when there is little evidence of the sacrifice being reciprocated. It leaves a group to wonder, "Why are we always the ones asked to 'let it go'?"

In addition, sometimes inaccurate assumptions about conflicting roles have been made and held. For example, parenthood (and particularly motherhood) and professionalism are often seen as competing roles. If one wanted to be serious about being professional, than parenthood needed to be put on hold or be a more hidden aspect of oneself. However, recent research indicates that one's ability to engage oneself across all aspects of one's identity leads to more self-awareness and skill development, which increases effectiveness across categories (Graves, Ohlott, & Ruderman, 2007). Identity is not a zero-sum game. Acknowledging our multiple roles and identities may enhance rather than reduce our well-being and productivity, assuming we can see them as complementary rather than conflicting.

## DIGNITY

The protection of dignity is one of the most important challenges people face in organizations. Dignity is the ability to experience a sense of self-worth while also being principled about respecting the equal worth of other lives. Dignity is a relational concept, even when it appeals to a sense of individuality. It is easier to identify violations of dignity than to define what dignity is, in the same way that it is easier to identify illness than to define what health means. In his study, *Dignity at Work*, Randy Hodson (2001) identifies four challenges to the dignity of employees: mismanagement and abuse, overwork, limits of autonomy, and contradictions of employee involvement (harder work, more commitment without offering job security). Employees across the board are facing these challenges. But women, immigrants, ethnic minorities, people with disabilities, and other members who are not considered part of the norm (which is usually some combination of male, white, heterosexual, highly educated, able-bodied) are more vulnerable to being exposed to violations of their dignity and often experience greater negative consequences.

Microinequities in organizations and institutions are probably one of the most common forms of discrimination. These are seemingly minor events that undermine one's self-esteem and self-worth. Just as many drops of water can erode a rock, microinequities continually reinforce an in-group/out-group dynamic that threatens to erode dignity, justice, and self-worth. Statements like "It was just a joke" or "What's the big deal?" reflect a lack of understanding that a single seemingly insignificant act or statement may symbolize a much larger system of oppression or discrimination. Effective leaders understand the deeper relevance of microinequities, rather than dismissing them as isolated events.

## RESPECT

Self-respect without respect for others becomes arrogance, and respect for others without self-respect can become self-humiliation. *The balance between self-respect and respect for others is maintained through humility*, a sense of modesty about the importance of self and one's own cultural beliefs. Al Guskin (1997) calls for cultural humility, respecting the validity of other cultural beliefs, not perceiving your own culture or any other as superior, and trying to understand rather than to evaluate. Sarah Lawrence-Lightfoot (2000) wrote a well-known book about the equalizing power of respect entitled *Respect*. She studied the underlying nature of respect, its roots, its development, and its expression.

Most of the literature perceives of respect as something that emerges in situations of hierarchy. You owe people respect because of a factor deemed worthy of admiration or deference (social status, accomplishments, membership of the dominant race, gender group, and so on). Or people demand respect in order to save their honor or to avoid embarrassment. The book *Respect* offers a relational approach. Respect is not something static, not a given, but something that grows. Respectfulness means often breaking with routine and not accepting inequality. Giving respect can encourage respect in return. Respect can create symmetry, empathy, and connection in functionally unequal relations: respectfulness from employer to employees, from doctor to patient. Lawrence-Lightfoot calls attention to the careful and purposeful work involved in fostering respectful relationships.

To create an environment of justice and dignity, leaders need to develop a clear understanding of who they are as individuals and as members (or symbols of) the various social identity groups to which they belong, and to understand others in their own terms (rather than their sense of who they are or should be). A study of two service programs in England noted that respect was essentially centered on the individuals being listened to, having their experience, ideas, and views taken seriously and valued (Jones, Chant, & Ward, 2003); that is an essential skill for leaders in a context of differences.

## INTERCULTURAL DIALOGUE

In his seminal book on multiculturalism, Bhikhu Parekh (2000) provides analytical tools for intercultural dialogue. Respectful dialogue includes all parties and acknowledges the need to feel culturally embedded and to identify with particular cultures or collectivities. One can be critical of other cultures, but must also recognize that cultures deserve respect. It is relevant to separate the need to belong (a basic human need) from the contents of the culture one identifies with.

Cultures are by definition limited. No culture is completely worthless, and no culture is perfect. Elements of cultures can be compared and judged in mutually respectful dialogue in a manner that enriches and empowers rather than mystifies and oppresses. By moving beyond stereotypes about what culture "looks like" and thinking about social identity as a zero-sum game, we can develop leadership that is more inclusive and thus benefits from the advantages multiple talents and perspectives have to offer.

# Miasma: The Dynamics of Difference

*Ancella B. Livers*
*Robert F. Solomon, Jr.*

---

**Keywords:** miasma, social identity, in-group, out-group, institutional bias, microinequity

**Key Points**

- Membership in non-dominant groups often carries a concomitant reduction in the access to and privileges of power.
- Miasma is characterized by an opaque atmosphere of misperception and distortion, where social outsiders (non-dominant managers) are subjectively penalized for being different.
- Social identity, historical conditions, hegemony, and competing assumptions coalesce in the social environment to create miasma.
- As a result of this impact of miasma, the organization can suffer exponentially through the loss of employee productivity, engagement, and innovation.
- Because of their historical, group, and personal experience, non-dominant group members may have limited trust for those in the dominant group and the systems they have created. In addition, this limited trust may be significantly more fragile than those in the dominant group recognize. The same is true for issues of respect.
- Leaders must ask whether their actions are truly effective and efficient or whether they are simply habitual.

## Related Exercises

- Exercise 3: Identifying Faultlines
- Exercise 5: Approaches to Difference

- Exercise 8: Examining Your Leadership Networks
- Exercise 9: Taking a New Perspective

## Related Cases

- Case 1: Race and Respect
- Case 2: Water Crises
- Case 3: Floating Holidays
- Case 5: It's Their Fault
- Case 6: The Scent of Difference
- Case 7: Not Catching On

- Case 8: Glass Ceiling at Big Boy Toys
- Case 9: Super Drugs
- Case 10: The Right to Be Pregnant
- Case 12: Benefits Battle

---

Demographic change from relatively more homogeneous to more heterogeneous environments causes organizations and individuals to experience conflicts stemming from social identity differences (see the Triggers of Social Identity Conflict chapter for more information). As described in the Social Identity chapter, these identities are not just descriptive, but are laden with culturally construed meanings that confer on their members degrees of status and access to power and influence. Ultimately, in a society, some social identity groups are dominant and have greater access to status, power, and influence, while other groups are non-dominant or subordinate. Membership in these non-dominant groups often carries a concomitant reduction in the access to and privileges of power. The focus of this chapter is the unacknowledged and undefined space between the equitable and inequitable treatment of non-dominant groups.

As members of non-dominant groups move into organizations, many become increasingly aware that their work environments hinder their career progression. This difficult environment, called miasma, is characterized by an opaque atmosphere of misperception and distortion, where social outsiders (non-dominant managers) are subjectively penalized for being different (Livers & Caver, 2003).When miasmic conditions prevail, managers of difference perceive the social environment as tainted, which rarely allows for the managers to be at ease while working. As a result of this impact of miasma, the organization can suffer exponentially through the loss of employee productivity, engagement, and innovation.

Although miasma, by definition, is a somewhat nebulous concept, its intangible and fluid characteristics are generally visible and understood by non-dominant managers but are often invisible to those who represent the dominant power structure.

Other characteristics, however, may be visible to both non-dominant and dominant group members, but they may be perceived very differently by the groups. Two of these elements are trust and respect. Because of their historical, group, and personal experience, non-dominant group members may have limited trust for those in the dominant group and the systems they have created. In addition, this limited trust may be significantly more fragile than those in the dominant group recognize. The same is true for issues of respect. Non-dominant group members may not respect the dominant group and its iconic symbols and institutions to the degree that dominant group members do. This difference in perception and understanding can lead to significant workplace problems because, as both trust and respect, independently, decrease, miasma increases. In such circumstances, the workplace becomes more strained and difficult to navigate and the possibility increases for misunderstanding and sundering of the tenuous trust and respect that exist. The converse is also true.

Consequently, whether leaders are from dominant or non-dominant groups, they must be actively aware that widely varying levels of trust and respect can adversely affect the workplace. Further, the leaders have to be mindful of their own behaviors and assumptions as they work with their colleagues and manage their direct reports. Finally, rather than assuming that everyone feels the same levels of trust and respect, leaders need to create circumstances that build these characteristics.

The perceived experience of the nontraditional manager is tantamount to truth for that manager. For in a state of miasma, as in other social conditions, perception is reality. Nontraditional managers experience miasma in very real terms—as when it takes them longer to be promoted than it takes their dominant counterparts or when they must prove and re-prove their qualifications. However, proving miasma's existence is an exercise in providing empirical evidence for something that is not tangible. This difference in how miasma is perceived by the various groups feeds into the difficulty an organization has in understanding and managing it.

Managing miasma begins with understanding the societal conditions that produce a miasmic environment. Social identity, historical conditions, hegemony, and competing assumptions coalesce in the social environment to create miasma. These conditions combine because they support ideas of inequity between dominant and non-dominant groups. First, the creation of social identities is paramount in forming miasma. Social identities often indirectly label people as insiders and outsiders, thus establishing unnecessary tension. Second, societies do not exist in a historical vacuum; consequently, current societal attitudes evolve or emerge from their historical conditions. For instance, legacies of a caste system in India may impede the ability of lower caste members to rise in organizations. And in Northern Ireland, the religious beliefs of employees could have a negative impact on the quality of their workplace experience. Hegemony, or the social, cultural, ideological, or economic influence exerted by a dominant group, is also a precipitating factor of miasma. The existence of successful non-dominant group members may, by their very presence, threaten the hegemonic norms established by the dominant culture. In essence, dominant group members may feel their authority and status are diminished or in danger if non-dominant individuals do well. Finally, competing assumptions often exacerbate miasmic conditions. Assumptions, in general, help people to make decisions without exerting extra energy. However, incongruent assumptions that undergird peoples' interpretations of an event or behavior are fertile ground for misperceptions and distortions (Livers & Caver, 2003). For example, if co-workers are unclear about their reporting relationships, their interactions between superiors and direct reports can appear disrespectful when there may be no ill intent.

## MIASMA IN PRACTICE

Although the term miasma seeks to describe something that is an intangible phenomenon, the impact of the phenomenon can be very real on employees and organizations. This tangible effect is because miasma negatively influences perceptions and possibilities of employees and how they interact with one another.

Because of this negative influence, the perceptions people have of one another and the way they interpret each other's words and actions can cause a breakdown in trust, communication, work relationships, and performance. As one manager of difference said, "I live with this overwhelming distrust and am relatively remote with my majority colleagues." Such an undercurrent of mistrust can easily cause workplace friction that creates a reflexive loop of increasing mistrust, miscommunication, and misperceptions.

Further, when people do not have the same freedom to do their work as others, or if they must continually prove themselves, endure additional scrutiny, and/or manage through veiled suspicions or assumptions of their inferiority, their efficiency and effectiveness are impeded—as are those of the larger unit or organization. It takes time and effort to continually recheck someone's work. It takes energy and focus that could be more effectively directed to the work itself. For the out-group and in-group employees and managers, the extra energy and emotion that are inherent with creating, laboring through, and sustaining miasma reduces work capacity.

Take, for instance, a situation in which two job candidates are interviewed for a position. The respective paths of Candidates A and B are shown in Table 9.1.

## Table 9.1
## Comparison of Dominant and Non-Dominant Job Applicants

|  | Dominant/ In-Group | Non-Dominant/ Out-Group |
|---|---|---|
|  | Candidate A | Candidate B |
| Job Selection Process | One Interview | Multiple Interviews Greater examination of experience More references required |
| Impact of Job Selection Process on Candidate |  | Frustration and heightened sense of not belonging |
| Impact of Job Selection Process on Organization |  | More resources |

☐ Miasmic conditions

Candidate A is a qualified member of the in-group. Candidate B, on the other hand, is a member of the culture's out-group. While also qualified, Candidate B may have to be successful in multiple interviews to prove that she is competent and able to fit into the organizational culture. Unlike Candidate A, Candidate B is given an initial interview, but is asked more questions about her experience than is Candidate A. Candidate B is also asked to return for more interviews and asked to show more references than Candidate A is. At each juncture, Candidate B is being given more scrutiny and asked to prove herself more fully than Candidate A does. In addition, at each juncture, Candidate B has the chance of being turned away. While both candidates may eventually be offered jobs, the path Candidate B has taken is personally more grueling and potentially more confidence destroying than the path of Candidate A. The second candidate's path has also required more organizational effort and resources than that of her counterpart.

The obstacles of miasma, whether in recruitment or everyday work life, can leave an employee weary and resentful. Consequently, employees who are slogging through the morass of miasma may be more likely to leave the organization as they search for work environments that are accepting of their differences and open to the unique and often innovative viewpoints that differences may bring into organizational decision making.

## MITIGATING MIASMA

Miasma is difficult for some people to acknowledge. For many people, miasma is invisible; therefore to mitigate the negative effects of it in organizations, the invisible must be made visible. This task, however, may be more difficult than it originally seems because it relies on in-group members seeing and understanding experiences they may not have had. While a number of factors can mitigate miasma's influence, the greatest of these is leadership. Leaders who are willing to find ways to see the invisible help to set the tone around embracing difference in their organizations. This means that leaders have to be open to questioning their own actions and mindsets as well as the mindsets of the people with whom they work to see whether biases are consciously or unconsciously affecting their perceptions and decisions.

Leaders also have to judge the impact of institutional bias on the organization's employees. Institutional bias (discrimination that is embedded into the processes and systems of an institution) and microinequities (small behaviors such as gestures or tone of voice that are meant to demean non-dominant group members) make miasma more palpable and therefore problematic. Therefore, leaders need to be aware of these factors and work to reduce or moderate their impact. For instance, leaders must ask whether their actions are truly effective and efficient or whether they are simply habitual. They must also determine whether all staff members have equal opportunity to receive development, promotion, challenging assignments, visibility, profit and loss responsibilities, time with superiors, and feedback. Finally, leaders have to be open to hearing answers they do not wish to hear and to consciously change their workplace to a more inclusive one. In the current constantly changing, global environment, the need for inclusiveness has bottom-line implications that cannot easily be ignored. Consequently, embracing diversity as well as practicing inclusivity of human capital can help organizations. For example, a diverse and inclusive organization can more effectively than a less diverse one:

- Increase the productivity of its human capital
- Increase its ability to serve multiple client groups
- More effectively recruit, utilize, and retain a diverse workforce
- Access different experiences to encourage innovation

Effectively managing miasma is ultimately about developing a mindset to explore all the possibilities of human capital. To do so, leaders should:

- Establish and maintain mutual respect
- Not assume that individualized experience is everyone's experience
- Seek to understand different experiences
- Be willing to challenge assumptions—one's own and those of others
- Understand that differences and similarities among people are data points for making decisions
- Be willing to broaden their outlook
- Be consistent with the utilization of nuances and complexity for making decisions about human capital

Leaders who are serious about minimizing miasma and its impact in their organizations must be willing to look for patterns of behavior that are not readily apparent to them. Further, they have to embrace difference and recognize that to effectively manage miasma means they must engage in a continuous learning process. This constant engagement is particularly important because the social identity challenges of today may look very different from the challenges of tomorrow.

# Leading Across Cultural Groups: Implications of Self-Concept

*Dharm P.S. Bhawuk*
*Vijayan P. Munusamy*

---

**Keywords:** individualism, collectivism, idiocentrism, allocentrism, social exchange

**Key Points**

- Knowing one's self-concept can help leaders to shape intergroup dynamics while leading people from different cultures.

- Individualism and collectivism refer to self-centered and other-centered worldviews and ways of life.

- At the cultural level, the terms individualism and collectivism are used, and cultures are referred to as being either individualistic or collectivist. At the individual level, the terms idiocentrism and allocentrism are used to denote individualism and collectivism, respectively, and are thought of as personality types.

- In individualist cultures, people view themselves as having an independent concept of self, whereas in collectivist cultures people view themselves as having an interdependent concept of self.

- Self-concept leads to different expectations in social exchange. Individualists are rational in their social exchanges, whereas collectivists value relationships for their own sake and may maintain even ineffective relationships.

- Self-concept has important implications for intergroup dynamics.
- Effective leadership requires understanding such differences in motivation and adapting different approaches to motivate people from different cultural groups.

## Related Exercises

- Exercise 1: Mapping Your Social Identities
- Exercise 4: Cultural Values
- Exercise 5: Approaches to Difference
- Exercise 6: Cultural Intelligence

## Related Cases

- Case 1: Race and Respect
- Case 2: Water Crises
- Case 3: Floating Holidays
- Case 4: Not My Weekend
- Case 5: It's Their Fault
- Case 6: The Scent of Difference
- Case 7: Not Catching On
- Case 8: Glass Ceiling at Big Boy Toys
- Case 9: Super Drugs
- Case 10: The Right to Be Pregnant
- Case 11: Local Bombing
- Case 12: Benefits Battle
- Case 13: Francois' Dilemma

---

The theory of individualism and collectivism is one of the most tested theories in cross-cultural psychology and has a number of implications for leading across cultural groups. In this chapter we discuss how the self-concept (Bhawuk, 2001; Markus & Kitayama, 1991; Triandis, 1989), which is a core dimension of this theory, influences the process of leadership. We provide examples of how, when leading across cultural groups, leaders need to adjust their culturally determined rational or relational social exchanges to be effective. We also discuss and provide examples of how knowing one's self-concept can help leaders to shape intergroup dynamics while leading people from different cultures. Not understanding how self-concept impacts one's leadership roles can lead to conflicts between leaders and group members when they belong to different cultural groups. On the other hand, an appreciation of the theory of individualism and collectivism and the concept of self provides leaders a cultural lens with which to lead across diverse groups effectively.

## SELF-CONCEPT: INDEPENDENT AND INTERDEPENDENT SELF

Individualism and collectivism refer to self-centered and other-centered world-views and ways of life. When people act to maximize their personal gains, they are referred to as individualists, whereas when people behave to help their in-groups, community, or society, they are referred to as collectivists. Following the work of Geert Hofstede (1980), Harry C. Triandis and his collaborators have developed a program of research that has popularized these psychological constructs, and they can be used at the individual as well as cultural levels. At the cultural level, the terms *individualism* and *collectivism* are used, and cultures are referred to as being either individualistic or collectivist. At the individual level, the terms *idiocentrism* and *allocentrism* are used to denote individualism and collectivism, respectively, and are thought of as personality types (Triandis, Chan, Bhawuk, Iwao, & Sinha, 1995). Both idiocentric and allocentric people can be found in either culture, but more idiocentric people are likely to be found in the individualist culture; similarly, more allocentric people are likely to be found in a collectivist culture. There are clear antecedents and consequences of these constructs, and the theory of individualism and collectivism is useful in explaining and predicting many social behaviors that can help us lead people across cultural groups (Triandis, 1995b).

In individualist cultures, people view themselves as having an independent concept of self, whereas in collectivist cultures, people view themselves as having an interdependent concept of self. For example, when individualists think of themselves and others, they are clear that their self only includes themselves. "This is me, but that is not me. My mother is not a part of me. My child is not a part of me. They are separate from me." There is no overlap between their selves and others. On the other hand, when collectivists think of people in their families (parents, spouse, children, siblings, and so forth), they feel these people are a part of their selves. For example, one's thinking may proceed like this: "My father is a part of me, not completely me, but somewhat a part of me. My child is a bigger part of me compared to my father, not completely me, but, yes, a good part of me." The same feeling holds in case of other relatives, friends, and even neighbors.

Of course, the biological self is the same for individualists as well as collectivists. It is the socially constructed self that is thought of differently. And when one constructs the social self as interdependent, then even the biological body is viewed to be for the service of those others with whom the self is shared, much as it is for oneself. Hence, independent and interdependent self has clear implications for leading across cultural groups. In this chapter, we discuss three implications that are most critical in our experience observing and reflecting about leadership.

## SELF-CONCEPT AND LEADERSHIP STYLE

The link between self-concept and how people behave has been well documented (Triandis, 1990; Triandis & Bhawuk, 1997). For example, self-concept has been linked to how people communicate (Gudykunst, Matsumoto, Ting-Toomey, Nishida, Kim, & Heyman, 1996) and how they relate to each other (Endo, Heine, & Lehman, 1998). Leadership is about communication and relationship and, hence, understanding the relationship between self-concept and how we relate to and communicate with each other will shape the leadership process (Bhawuk, 1997). It is useful to note that people with an interdependent self-concept view transformational leadership as more effective than transactional leadership (MacDonald, Sulsky, & Brown, 2008). A tacit assumption of the preference for transformational leadership is that in collectivist cultures subordinates expect leaders to be nurturing before they can exact task-related outcomes of them (Sinha, 1980). This finds support in indigenous leadership research in countries like Mexico, the Philippines, and Japan, to name a few, in such constructs as *simpatia*, *pakikisama*, and *amae*.

*Simpatia* or being *simpatico* means being pleasant and interpersonally sensitive in Latin America and among Hispanics and Latinos in the United States. Similarly, in the Philippines the word *pakikisama*, which includes managerial characteristics like understanding, concern for employee welfare, kindness and helpfulness, and a pleasant and courteous disposition toward subordinates, indicates a people focus in leadership. In Japan, *amae*, which means presuming that one will be indulged by a person with whom one has an intimate relationship (Yamaguchi & Ariizumi, 2006), suggests that subordinates will expect to be supported by supervisors even if the behavior of the subordinates is not perfect. This is not the situation in individualistic cultures, where leaders are not expected to nurture the subordinates beyond maintaining a professional arms-length relationship. In fact, in individualist cultures, both superiors and subordinates tend to prefer to keep each other at arm's length. While leading people from different cultures, one has to pay attention to these cultural scripts and modify one's behavior to meet the psychological needs of the subordinates to motivate them to meet challenging work situations.

While communicating, individualists with an independent self-concept prefer to be direct and forthright, whereas collectivists with an interdependent self-concept prefer to be indirect. This creates challenges while leading in either direction, whether the leader is individualist and the subordinate collectivist, or vice versa. Individualists feel they are doing the right thing if they pointedly tell their subordinates what is working or not working and what is the responsibility of a particular subordinate. Subordinates with an interdependent self-concept, however, perceive this directness as rudeness, lack of social courtesy, or a general disregard for the well-being of the subordinate. For individualistic leaders, it becomes an impossible task to lead a subordinate through the performance appraisal process without giving direct feedback. Similarly, for a collectivist leader it is too painful to tell the individualistic subordinate everything, which from the leader's perspective, the subordinate should be able to read from the context. An appreciation of this basic difference in self-concept and its impact on how we relate to each other and communicate with each other can prepare leaders to fine-tune their style while interacting with different cultural group members.

## SELF-CONCEPT AND SOCIAL EXCHANGES

Self-concept leads to different expectations in social exchange. In individualist cultures, social exchange is based on the principle of equal exchange, and people form new relationships to meet their changing needs based on cost/benefit analysis. Thus, individualists are rational in their social exchange. But in collectivist cultures, people have an interdependent self-concept and they inherit many relationships. Therefore, people in these cultures view their relationships as long term in nature and are unlikely to break even a cost-ineffective relationship. Thus, collectivists value relationships for their own sake and nurture them with unequal social exchanges over a long period of time.

The nature of transactions that take place in relationships is different in individualist and collectivist cultures. Individualists tend to use exchange relationships, whereas collectivists tend to use communal relationships (Mills & Clark, 1982). In an exchange relationship, people give something (a gift or a service) to another person with the expectation that the other person will return a gift or service of equal value in the near future. The characteristics of this type of relationship are "equal value" and "short time frame." People keep a mental record of exchange of benefits and try to maintain a balance between what they've given and what they've received. In a communal relationship, people do not keep an account of the exchanges taking place between them; one person may give a gift of much higher value than the other person, and the two people may still maintain their relationship. In other words, it is the relationship that is valued by collectivists and not the exchanges that go on between people when they are in a communal relationship. Thus, the exchange goes on for a long time unless the series is broken by some unavoidable situation. In this type of relationship, people feel an "equality of affect" (that is, when one feels up, the other also feels up; and when one feels down, the other also feels down). In contrast, in individualist cultures, common interests bring people together to exchange goods and services, and only if the benefits justify the costs. Individualists *move on* to new relationships when a relationship does not meet their needs, but doing so for collectivists would be heart-wrenching.

For leaders leading across cultural groups, the different expectations from a relationship need to be taken into account, because displaying rational leadership in collectivist cultures may be perceived as selfish and displaying relational leadership in individualist cultures may be perceived as overstepping professional boundaries. A collectivist subordinate may bring an expensive gift for the superior to express gratitude, and the individualist superior may consider it inappropriate to accept the gift, not knowing that not accepting the gift would cost the commitment of the subordinate in the future. A collectivist leader may find it odd that a subordinate would not use his or her personal resourcefulness to help the team and may interpret the subordinate as not committed to the group. In the long run, these little behavioral misunderstandings can cause havoc in the organization due to lack of trust between the leader and the subordinate. An understanding of the dynamics of social exchange and basic differences between people of different self-concepts can better prepare a leader to create a team from subordinates from different cultural backgrounds.

## SELF-CONCEPT AND INTERGROUP DYNAMICS

Self-concept has important implications for intergroup dynamics. For example, research shows that people with an interdependent self-concept view social goals as more important than individual goals, whereas people with an independent self-concept view both goals as equally important (Van Horen, Pohlmann, Koeppen, & Hannover, 2008). Collectivism requires the subordination of individual goals to the goals of a collective, whereas individualism encourages people to pursue the goals that are dear to them and even change their in-groups to achieve those goals. The value and meaning associated with being part of a group are likely to be different for people in individualist and collectivist cultures. Individualists can more easily dissociate their identities from others, allowing them to quickly create loose relationships with different groups. Collectivists inherit more complex webs of relationships that are deeply embedded in preexisting groups.

Research also shows that, in dyadic conflicts, people with an interdependent self-concept who have more power than other parties tend to be generous in solving conflicts. However, they can be exploitative with their power in intergroup conflicts (Howard, Gardner, & Thompson, 2007). In other research, it was found that people with an independent self-concept actually displayed more pronounced in-group favoritism when their self-esteems were threatened than when this was not the case. People with an interdependent self-concept responded with less intergroup favoritism when their self-esteems were threatened than when this was not the case (Nakashima, Isobe, & Ura, 2008).

Leadership entails creating winning teams, but individualists may consider all teams as functional and short-term oriented, whereas collectivists are likely to consider team formation to be for a long time, if not a lifetime. Thus, individualist leaders may find collectivist subordinates incapable of fitting into different teams for role enlargement and career progression, and collectivist leaders may find individualist subordinates calculative and rather selfish in pushing their self goals, as opposed to sacrificing for the goal of the team. An international posting may be too far to go for a collectivist member and too much of a personal sacrifice for an individualist subordinate. Effective leadership requires understanding such differences in motivation and adapting different approaches to motivate people from different cultural groups (Bhawuk, 1997).

## SUMMARY AND CONCLUSION

Self-concept influences effective leadership. It contributes to different expectations of social exchanges and shapes intergroup dynamics. By understanding differences in self-concepts, the possibilities of leaders meeting the expectations of followers can be increased and the possibilities of leaders misattributing conflicts to other facets of culture can be reduced. Meeting the expectations of what followers perceive to be effective leadership in their cultures is important because it can help leaders set direction, align different perspectives, and gain commitment. Accurate assessment of self-concept shaped by cultures and how that can relate to leader-follower dynamic is important because misattribution can potentially lead to unwarranted conflicts. In many ways, culture is not only a shared mindset, but it also offers a toolset to bridge different mindsets. An appreciation of self-concept and how it relates to leadership styles, social exchanges, and intergroup dynamics can help leaders pick appropriate tools while interacting with subordinates from different cultural groups and avoid the one-size-fits-all approach to leading. Leading is not about developing a fixed management style like a person with a hammer who treats everything as a nail, but rather like a doctor who chooses the treatment to meet the needs of the patient. When dealing with subordinates who are from many cultural backgrounds, a clear understanding of independent and interdependent self-concept and the theory of individualism and collectivism can help leaders serve people like physicians who can read much from taking the pulse.

# Leader Values and Authenticity

*Todd J. Weber*

---

**Keywords:** authentic leadership, homogeneous groups, terminal values, instrumental values, role congruence, role incongruence, psychological capital

**Key Points**

- Values are concepts or beliefs about desirable end states or behaviors that transcend specific situations, guide selection or evaluation of behavior and events, and are ordered by relative importance. Authenticity is the unobstructed operation of one's true, or core, self in one's daily enterprise.

- A conflict that may appear to be focused on basic policies, use of resources, or interpersonal interaction may in fact be a manifestation of fundamental value conflicts or differences or role incongruence.

- Being aware of one's values does not necessarily mean that behaviors are consistent with those values. At times, people may act in ways that contradict their values or present themselves in such a way that values are misrepresented. Their espoused and enacted values are then not the same.

- The concept of authenticity refers to the consistency (or lack thereof) between who you are and how you act. While values are an important part of who you are, authenticity refers to a broader range of characteristics, attributes, and beliefs, collectively referred to as "the self."

- Individuals who are authentic can develop meaningful relationships and trust that will allow for mutual understanding and accommodation. Conversely, inauthentic behavior will lead to low-trust relationships.

## Related Exercises

- Exercise 1: Mapping Your Social Identities
- Exercise 2: Your Experience with Triggers
- Exercise 3: Identifying Faultlines
- Exercise 4: Cultural Values
- Exercise 5: Approaches to Difference
- Exercise 6: Cultural Intelligence
- Exercise 7: Your Leadership Practices
- Exercise 8: Examining Your Leadership Networks
- Exercise 9: Taking a New Perspective

## Related Cases

- Case 1: Race and Respect
- Case 2: Water Crises
- Case 3: Floating Holidays
- Case 4: Not My Weekend
- Case 5: It's Their Fault
- Case 6: The Scent of Difference
- Case 7: Not Catching On
- Case 8: Glass Ceiling at Big Boy Toys
- Case 9: Super Drugs
- Case 10: The Right to Be Pregnant
- Case 11: Local Bombing
- Case 12: Benefits Battle
- Case 13: Francois' Dilemma

Values and authenticity play an important role in an organizational context, but often go unnoticed in day-to-day life. Values are defined by Schwartz and Bilsky as "(a) concepts or beliefs, (b) about desirable end states or behaviors, (c) that transcend specific situations, (d) guide selection or evaluation of behavior and events, and (e) are ordered by relative importance" (1987, p. 878). Authenticity, on the other hand, is "the unobstructed operation of one's true, or core, self in one's daily enterprise" (Kernis, 2003, p. 13). Our values and desire to be authentic guide the way we live our lives. Situations that seem to violate our values or require us to be inauthentic can act as triggers that spark conflict among social identity groups like those reflected in the cases. It is better to understand how these concepts influence an organization than to spend time and effort recovering from the conflict that may occur when these dynamics are neglected.

## LEADER VALUES

Our values guide the way we perceive the world and shape the actions we take. More often than not, we are unaware of our values until we see or hear something that contradicts or conflicts with them, at which point they can become salient. Highly homogeneous groups share a set of values that may cause them to focus on specific topics or activities while ignoring others or to approach a task in a similar way. For example, a homogeneous product development group that does not reflect the population they hope to market to may fail to consider important aspects of the product or create a product that does not adequately or appropriately meet the needs of clients. The foundation of shared values in a homogeneous group may only be recognized when they are questioned by new team members or clients who do not share the same set of values. It is only then that the group members become aware of the assumptions being made.

Research about values initially sought to understand a broad set of values that were not tied to any particular context. Milton Rokeach (1973) developed the Rokeach Value Survey, which distinguished between instrumental and terminal values. *Terminal* values are end-state values that the individual would like (for example, inner harmony). *Instrumental* values are preferences for behaviors that are likely to facilitate reaching that end state (for example, being tolerant, cheerful, and forgiving). This work was built upon by other researchers such as Shalom Schwartz (Schwartz, 1992; Schwartz & Sagie, 2000), who studied the structure of values in a global context (see the Cultural Values chapter). As noted in the Cultural Values chapter, Schwartz's work argues that cultural values find expression in various beliefs, norms, and personal values. For example, the implicit leadership beliefs of an individual within a culture are often influenced by that culture, helping to shape which leadership practices are commonly used and develop into norms. The sixty-five-nation GLOBE study (House, Hanges, Javidan, Dorfman, & Gupta, 2004) on cross-cultural leadership also found that culture influences leaders' implicit beliefs, decisions, and practices. Recently, the values framework developed by Schwartz has been adapted to focus specifically on a work context, through the Work Values Survey developed by Dan Cable and Jeff Edwards (2004). Their research examines work-life value congruence or incongruence or the relative fit between personal values, work and role expectations, and the consequences of a good and bad fit.

Values play a key role in leading across differences. Conflicting values have led to some of the more intractable conflicts that occur in society and in organizations. When leaders face conflicts in their organizations, they should take the time to clearly identify what the underlying cause of the conflict is. A conflict that may appear to be focused on policies, the use of resources, or interpersonal interactions may be a manifestation of a fundamental value conflict. For instance, cultural values influence the perception of privilege and food preference of employees in Case 6 and lead to differential treatment between members of two cultures in Case 9. Researchers are also examining the role that the fit between the values of a leader and a follower can have on the development of a high-quality relationship (Weber & Uhl-Bien, 2009). It is conceivable that high levels of leader-follower value congruence will lead to high-quality leader-follower relationships, which will lead to higher levels of commitment, motivation, and productivity. However, in line with critical diversity theory, it is also conceivable that once understanding occurs across values (when value incongruence can be understood, and different values can be incorporated—not necessarily resolved), it will also lead to higher-quality leader-follower relations and higher productivity.

## AUTHENTICITY

Being aware of one's values does not necessarily mean that behaviors are consistent with them. The concept of authenticity refers to the consistency (or lack thereof) between what you value and how you act. For example, acting as if you advocate for a given cause or goal when you believe the opposite may result in internal tension or conflicts that are not present when your beliefs and actions are aligned. For instance, if a leader advocates for gender equality (espoused value), but only appoints men in the senior leadership positions (enacted values), then this leader appears to be inauthentic to others. If the leader is aware of the disconnect, but feels there are forces that encourage (or require) him or her to act in conflict with his or her values, then the personal consequences (such as disappointment, regret, etc.) can be great.

Michael Kernis (2003), who studied the concept of self-esteem, described optimal self-esteem in part as one's authentic self being a guide to behavioral choices. He went on to define authenticity as involving four components. The first is self-awareness, including both strengths and weaknesses. The second component is unbiased processing of self-relevant information, which means one is open to hearing both positive and negative information, rather than filtering out negative feedback or other information that may be viewed as threatening. The third component refers to whether one behaves in a way that is consistent with one's true self. The final component is relational authenticity, which involves being open and honest in one's close relationships.

Individuals who are authentic can develop meaningful relationships and trust that will allow for mutual understanding and accommodation across different values. There is a wide range of conceptual definitions of trust (see Burke, Sims, Lazzara, & Salas, 2007), but a common definition is

> "the willingness of a party to be vulnerable to the actions of another party based on the expectation that the other will perform a particular action important to the trust or, irrespective of the ability to monitor or control that other party." (Mayer, Davis, & Schoorman, 1995, p. 712)

Trust is a fundamental element of leadership and an important part of an organization's functioning properly. Trust makes it possible for people to have the interdependence needed for the complex and collective efforts required in many organizations. In contrast, a lack of authenticity may impede the development of trust (see the Social Justice and Dignity, as well as the Social Identity chapters). Role expectations and preferred mental models based on social identity groups, rather than performance, can also influence authenticity. For instance, if a workplace values a Western and male approach to leadership, it would be difficult for an African woman to be her authentic self, since it is expected of her to fit into a Western male way of leading. Conversely, it would be much easier for a white male to be his authentic self in this situation.

A lack of authenticity also means that employees may not bring their whole selves to work due to conflicting values, role incongruence, or role expectations, instead choosing to only disclose information about themselves that they feel needs to be shared. For example, lesbians or gays who choose not to disclose their sexual orientation at the workplace, due to potential conflicting values, may resent conversations in which co-workers bond socially by talking openly about their families. This limited self-disclosure goes beyond the basic distinction between work and non-work settings, with its associated range of appropriate behaviors, for instance, the expected work role behaviors, such as colleague, facilitator, and manager, versus the expected home role behaviors, like being a mother or spouse.

Instead, a lack of authenticity is a barrier to creating the meaningful work relationships that are essential to an effective organization. The lack of authenticity is a particular challenge for leaders, whose influence is often based on the relationships they develop with their followers. If a follower perceives a leader is inauthentic, the follower will be less willing to go beyond the specific requirements of his or her job, effectively reducing the leader's ability to help the group respond to opportunities or challenges.

## AUTHENTIC LEADERSHIP

Authentic leadership has been described by several researchers as a "root construct" that underlies all effective leadership theories (Avolio & Gardner, 2005). Definitions vary on this emerging construct, but often include awareness (of the context and of the self), as well as being "confident, hopeful, optimistic, resilient, and of high moral character" (Avolio, Luthans, & Walumbwa, 2004, p. 4). Most researchers on this topic have focused on authentic leadership development, which has been defined as:

> "the process that draws upon a leader's life course, psychological capital, moral perspective, and a highly developed supporting organizational climate to produce greater self-awareness and self-regulated positive behaviors, which in turn foster continuous, positive self-development resulting in veritable, sustained performance" (Avolio & Luthans, 2006, p. 2).

At the heart of this approach is the idea that people's perceptions of authenticity or the lack of authenticity can have real consequences for the effectiveness of a leader. For example, a leader who teaches that people are the most important asset of a company and then makes decisions that are inconsistent with this claim is unlikely to have credibility. Similarly, leaders who ask others to subsume their interests for the benefit of the organization will not be perceived as authentic if such leaders then allocate resources in a way that maximizes their own interests. Leaders who are authentic, however, have the potential to develop relationships and clear expectations that can help them lead effectively.

There has been a substantial amount of research on authentic leadership, including special issues of academic journals (Avolio & Gardner, 2005) and numerous books (Avolio & Luthans, 2006; Gardner, Avolio, & Walumbwa, 2005). In addition to studying authentic leadership development, several related constructs have been developed, such as psychological capital, a multi-dimensional construct that consists of efficacy, hope, optimism, and resiliency (Luthans, Youssef, & Avolio, 2007).

For a leader to successfully lead a diverse group, he or she must have relationships of trust that help to bridge the barriers formed by social identity differences. One is far more likely to trust a leader who is perceived as authentic and who allows followers to also be authentic. For example, a leader facing a conflict between two social identity groups (one of which he or she is part of) may claim to be acting impartially. The opposing group would be far more likely to trust an authentic leader than to trust one they perceive as inauthentic. The same is true for efforts by the leader to ask for self-sacrifice or extra effort in pursuit of an organizational goal. Authenticity matters, as do values, particularly for one who is in a leadership position. Leaders can help convey their authenticity through striving to be more transparent with their followers and more aware of themselves and of the context in which they work. They can also strive to create a context in which their followers are encouraged to be transparent and authentic as well. Research on authentic leadership development (Avolio & Luthans, 2006) and the related construct of psychological capital (Luthans, Youssef, & Avolio, 2007) has empirically shown that relatively simple interventions can make a big difference.

# Leading Through Paradox

*Jeffrey Yip*

---

**Keywords:** paradox, paradoxical mindset, improvisation

**Key Points**

- Paradox in an organizational context is an observation in which two contradictory elements are seen as present or operating at the same time.

- Leaders are faced with cultural paradoxes such as those between cultural forces of individualism and collectivism, achievement and ascription, long- and short-term orientation, and low- and high-power distance.

- Leaders tend to be embedded in their own perspective and treat paradoxes as cases of right and wrong. In contrast, leaders need to gain a better understanding of multiple, even contradictory, ways of leading.

- Paradoxes are important, as they force leaders to think outside the box and to rethink convenient categories and stereotypes.

- Two critical capacities are needed to lead through paradox: (1) a paradoxical mindset and (2) improvisation.

**Related Exercise**

- Exercise 9: Taking a New Perspective

## Related Cases

- Case 1: Race and Respect
- Case 2: Water Crises
- Case 3: Floating Holidays
- Case 4: Not My Weekend
- Case 5: It's Their Fault
- Case 6: The Scent of Difference
- Case 7: Not Catching On

- Case 8: Glass Ceiling at Big Boy Toys
- Case 9: Super Drugs
- Case 10: The Right to Be Pregnant
- Case 11: Local Bombing
- Case 12: Benefits Battle
- Case 13: Francois' Dilemma

---

*We do leaders a disservice then when we train them to rely too heavily—too exclusively—on management formulas and models. Leaders have no choice but to grapple with the paradoxes and complexities of human nature.*

Joan Gallos, *Learning from the Toxic Trenches* (2008)

*Our mind is capable of passing beyond the dividing line we have drawn for it. Beyond the pairs of opposites of which the world consists, other, new insights begin.*

Herman Hesse, *Stories of Five Decades* (1972)

The word paradox originates from the Greek words para (beyond) and doxa (belief). Cameron and Quinn (1988) aptly define a paradox in the organizational context as an observation in which two contradictory elements are seen as present or operating at the same time. Examples of paradoxes faced by leaders include the paradoxes between continuity and change, planning and action, and learning and performance.

In leading across differences, leaders are also faced with cultural paradoxes, such as those identified by cross-cultural researchers (Hampden-Turner & Trompenaars, 2000; Hofstede, 2001; House Hanges, Javidan, Dorfman, &

Gupta, 2004; Schwartz, 1992) between cultural forces of individualism and collectivism, achievement and ascription, long- and short-term orientation, and low- and high-power distance. Such paradoxes can be daunting for leaders who are used to unambiguous solutions and models.

The aim of this chapter is to create awareness of paradoxes faced by leaders in working across differences. In particular, I discuss how paradox presents itself across cultures and how leaders might respond. Drawing on insights from social psychology, philosophy, and the creative arts, I discuss the role of a paradoxical mindset and improvisational practice as capacities that leaders could develop in leading effectively through paradox.

## WHY PARADOX?

The ability to navigate paradoxes has been cited by organizational scholars as the mark of exemplary leadership. Mitroff described the management of paradox as "one of the most crucial of all human activities" (1995, p. 749). Pascale (1990) found that leading companies such as IBM, Honda, Ford, and General Electric orchestrate tension and harness contending opposites to stay ahead of their competition. Consider the following findings of a six-year study on leadership at Toyota:

> "Toyota deliberately fosters contradictory viewpoints within the organization and challenges employees to find solutions by transcending differences rather than resorting to compromises. This culture of tensions generates innovative ideas that Toyota implements to pull ahead of competitors, both incrementally and radically.... Toyota doesn't merely have some odd characteristics —it is steeped in contradictions and paradoxes." (Takeuchi, Osono, & Shimizu, 2008, pp. 98–99)

As described by Takeuchi, Osono, and Shimizu (2008), paradoxical forces in organizations can be a powerful, generative source for innovation. This is also true of national cultures. Consider the following example of American and Japanese managers:

> "According to Hofstede's cultural dimension of uncertainty avoidance, Americans are characterized by high tolerance for uncertainty, while Japanese have a low tolerance. Why, then, in business contracts

do Americans painstakingly spell out every possible situation, while Japanese intentionally incorporate ambiguous clauses? Also, in the United States, autocratic behavior is frequently tolerated from CEOs, even though the United States is identified as an egalitarian culture." (Fatehi, 2007, p. 138)

Cultural realities are too complex to be explained from a single viewpoint. While the cultural dimensions model by scholars such as Hofstede (2001) provide a useful language in investigating cultural differences, such dimensions should not be taken as absolutes. Instead of treating culture as static, leaders need to situate it in a larger dynamic context and to view paradox as a positive and innovative force.

## LEADING THROUGH PARADOX

Dietrich Dorner (1996), in his book *The Logic of Failure: Why Things Go Wrong and What We Can Do to Make Them Right*, observed that leaders who fail at responding to complex situations are those who rely on predictable solutions and fail to adjust their thinking and actions based on the scenarios presented to them. On the contrary, effective leaders are those who are open to opposing perspectives and are willing to revise their thinking and alter their courses.

For leaders to work effectively through paradox, they need to be able to see paradoxes from both ends and to hold them in balance. However, in most cases, leaders tend to be embedded in their own perspectives and to treat paradoxes as cases of right and wrong. In contrast, leaders need to gain a better understanding of multiple, even contradictory, ways of leading. Paradoxes are important, as they force leaders to think outside the box and to rethink convenient categories and stereotypes.

How does one lead effectively in this environment? Leaders should not only persist in uncertainty but seek it out and leverage it for organizational change and transformation. Leadership through paradox requires leaders to hold mutually divergent views among organization members from different cultures and representing diverse facets within the organization. When faced with paradoxes, leaders need to analyze situations closely and to be versatile in their response. This represents two critical capacities needed in leading through paradox: (1) a paradoxical mindset and (2) improvisation. This process is illustrated in Figure 12.1 and elaborated in the sections to follow.

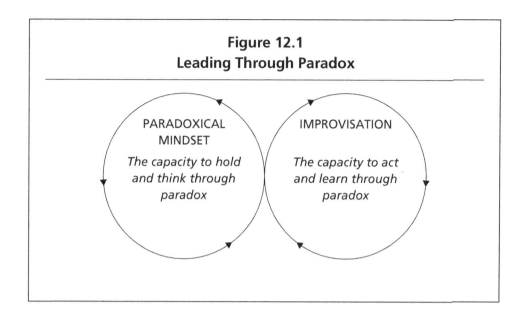

**Figure 12.1**
**Leading Through Paradox**

PARADOXICAL MINDSET

*The capacity to hold and think through paradox*

IMPROVISATION

*The capacity to act and learn through paradox*

## PARADOXICAL MINDSET

Unlike distinct and solvable problems for which an either/or decision may be chosen, paradoxical situations require leaders to see situations from multiple perspectives. A paradoxical mindset is one that accepts opposing interpretations as both plausible at the same time and does not view paradox as an uncertainty needing be removed or reduced. While a typical problem-solving mindset seeks final resolution, a paradoxical mindset views paradox as a lens for greater understanding and a catalyst for change. The difference between these two approaches is described in Table 12.1.

**Table 12.1**
**Problem Solving vs. Paradoxical Mindset**

|  | Problem-Solving Mindset | Paradoxical Mindset |
| --- | --- | --- |
| Human behavior as. . . | Predictable | Contradictory |
| Paradox as. . . | Obstacle for action | Opportunity for learning |
| Leadership as. . . | Resolute and directive | Emergent and responsive |

A paradoxical mindset is one that is able to hold and frame paradoxes in a productive manner. It can accept both ends of a paradox; even though they seem contradictory or contrasting, they are seen as meaningfully related. In complex situations such as leading across differences, black-and-white thinking can lead to problems. In contrast, a paradoxical mindset views differences as a step toward learning and can facilitate new ways of thinking about opposing and contradictory perspectives. There are two critical components to this mindset: (1) the capacity to hold paradox and (2) the capacity to think through paradox.

## The Capacity to Hold Paradox

Leaders often rush too quickly into action or, without adequate consideration, they break problems down into apparently manageable "bits" in an effort to make them seem manageable. To hold a paradox, managers must appreciate that contradictions can be productive and that they can be integrated. Fitzgerald describes this as "the ability to hold two opposed ideas in the mind at the same time, and still retain the ability to function" (1956, p. 69). Holding paradox is neither a compromise nor a split between competing tensions but is, rather, an awareness of both. This is not easy, as Palmer observed:

> "If we want to teach and learn in the power of paradox, we must reeducate our hearts. . . . [I] understand that the tension that comes when I try to hold a paradox together is not hell-bent on tearing me apart. Instead, it is a power that wants to pull my heart open to something larger than myself." (Palmer, 1998, pp. 83–84)

As Palmer describes, the act of holding paradoxes can be developmental, leading to an expanding of one's emotional capability. The concept of "negative capability" is best described in the words of the English poet, John Keats: "of being in uncertainties, mysteries, doubts, without any irritable reaching after fact and reason" (1970, p. 43). The ability to hold paradox, or negative capability, is a refusal to rush to resolution. This is often difficult for managers socialized in a problem-solving mindset that emphasizes positive capability and cognitive closure (Webster & Kruglanski, 1997), often at the expense of negative capability and the capacity to hold paradox.

## The Capacity to Think Through Paradox

To facilitate the integration of conflicting agendas and contradictory demands, Smith and Tushman suggest that managers within organizations can develop *paradoxical cognition*, which they define as "managerial frames and processes that recognize and embrace contradiction" (2005, p. 523). Paradoxical frames allow leaders to think through paradox, first by differentiating between contradicting aspects of the decision problem and then integrating them by identifying potential linkages and synergies (Smith & Tushman, 2005).

Barry Johnson (1996), in his book *Polarity Management,* suggests a practical model that leaders can use in framing paradox. As opposing ends to a paradox, Johnson describes polarities as interdependent opposites that function best when both are present to balance with each other. Due to their interdependence, neither side of a polarity can be chosen as a solution when the other side is ignored. Drawing on Johnson's approach, the following are some questions that can be used when confronted with paradox:

1. What are the opposing polarities that seem to be in conflict with each other?
2. What are the upsides to each of the poles?
3. What are the downsides to each of the poles?
4. What can be done to build on the upsides and prevent the downsides?

Polarity mapping is one example of a process in thinking through paradoxical situations. It incorporates elements of systems thinking—a dynamic process of seeing how parts are interrelated within a larger whole. Further resources on this method are included in the Resources list at the end of this casebook. The important thought processes are exploring the multifaceted sides of a paradox and a willingness to think with both poles. It requires the ability to see differences and similarities at the same time.

## IMPROVISATION

Improvisation is a unique practice that derives its energy in working through uncertain situations. While improvisation has typically been associated with jazz music and theater, it is a creative practice that builds and thrives on paradox. As Cunha, Kamoche, and Cunha describe, improvisation in leadership is the "dynamic syntheses of apparently contradictory behaviors in the process of leading a group" (2003, p. 51). It is the capacity to act and learn through paradox.

The opposite of improvisation is the use of habitual or defensive routines to guide behavior. A habitual routine exists when a person repeatedly exhibits a similar pattern of behavior in a given situation without considering alternative ways of behaving (Gersick & Hackman, 1990). In scenarios in which paradox is perceived as threatening, managers can also resort to defensive routines such as the following:

1. Rationalization: Explaining away the paradox
2. Regression: Resorting to actions that provide security
3. Denial: Refusing to accept the paradox

It is important for leaders to be aware of and recognize such defensive routines within themselves and in their organizations in order to work through paradox. Improvising through paradox requires one to step outside habitual and defensive patterns and experiment with new behaviors. To counter defensive routines, I propose three improvisational routines that leaders can consider when confronted with paradox:

1. *Anticipation:* In leadership, as in artistry, it is important for the leader to anticipate how different audiences might act or respond to their actions. To anticipate is to expect a range of plausible possibilities. The act of anticipation is an act of learning, where a leader becomes more responsive to the external environment and adapts his or her actions to that environment.

2. *Harmonization:* To harmonize is to blend apparent contradictions—a bridge between seemingly discordant parts. To use a music metaphor, harmonization involves the fusing of dominant and non-dominant tones to create a new sound. For leaders, this would involve orchestrating between seemingly contrary belief systems or ways of acting. For example, in India, Sinha (1984) found that exemplary managers harmonized a task-oriented approach with a nurturing style of management—not necessarily viewing one as opposite to the other.

3. *Experimentation:* Improvisation involves taking a risk, especially when working across contradictory belief systems. As Weick describes, improvisation involves "bringing to the surface, testing, and restructuring one's intuitive understanding of phenomena on the spot" (1995, p. 5). The experimental nature of improvisation is about challenging conventional routines, taking risks, and learning from the process. At times, the experiment may even involve silence or non-action. Experimenting with non-action can be paradoxically effective, particularly in action-oriented cultures.

The good news is that improvisation is a developable skill. In jazz music, for example, improvisation capacity is developed through preparation and experience. Similarly, many organizations have found that improvisational training through theater and music has transferable returns for leadership in the workplace. Through engaging in improvisational practice, leaders can unlearn habitual and defensive routines and begin to be more versatile and responsive to paradox, with routines such as anticipation, harmonization, and experimentation.

## CONCLUSION

Leading through paradox is not easy. One can almost feel crushed by the weight of paradox and the anxiety it creates. However, the process of leading through paradox can be developmental both for the leader and the organization, with its generative force for change. When leaders grapple with opposing insights, they are pressed to embrace complexity and contradiction. By embracing paradoxical thinking and improvisation, leaders can develop the relevant capacities for leadership in a globally diverse world.

# Exercises

The following exercises are designed to help you apply the knowledge in the preceding chapters to the situations in the cases and, more importantly, to your situation. All of these exercises are intended to be used by one person. There are group debriefing ideas and group exercises in the Facilitator's Guide.

Part 4 contains the following exercises:

- Exercise 1: Mapping Your Social Identities
- Exercise 2: Your Experience with Triggers
- Exercise 3: Identifying Faultlines
- Exercise 4: Cultural Values
- Exercise 5: Approaches to Difference
- Exercise 6: Cultural Intelligence (CQ)
- Exercise 7: Your Leadership Practices
- Exercise 8: Examining Your Leadership Networks
- Exercise 9: Taking a New Perspective

# Mapping Your Social Identities

**O**bjective: This exercise gives you an opportunity to explore your social identity by creating a social identity map and reflecting on it. You will also explore how your social identity might influence your ability to lead effectively in organizations.

**Key concepts:** social identity, given identity, chosen identity, core identity, leadership, multiple identities, simultaneity of identities, identity mapping, life roles

**Relevant cases:** All cases

### Relevant Chapters
- Chapter 1: Social Identity: Understanding the In-Group/Out-Group Phenomenon
- Chapter 4: Leadership Practices Across Social Identity Groups

**Time required:** Approximately 60 minutes

### Learning Outcomes

1. Articulate one's given identity, chosen identity, and core identity.
2. Identify the influence social identity has on others and the leadership implications.

**Materials**

- Blank Identity Map
- Pen/pencil

## EXPLANATION OF TERMINOLOGY: COMPONENTS OF IDENTITY

Your identity is a combination of three broad components: given identity, chosen identity, and core identity. Each of these components is described below.

### Given Identity

The attributes or conditions that you have no choice about are your given identity. They may be characteristics you were born with, or they may have been given to you in childhood or later in life. Elements of your given identity include birthplace, age, gender, birth order, physical characteristics, certain family roles, and possibly religion.

### Chosen Identity

These are the characteristics that you choose. They may describe your status as well as attributes and skills. Your occupation, hobbies, political affiliation, place of residence, family roles, and religion may all be chosen.

### Core Identity

These are the attributes that you think make you unique as an individual. Some will change over the course of your lifetime; others may remain constant. Elements of your core identity may include traits, behaviors, beliefs, values, and skills.

Some attributes may overlap or appear in two categories. Different people could put the same aspect of their identity in different categories depending on how much of a choice it felt like to them. For instance, your religious affiliation could be seen as either a given or a chosen aspect of your identity.

Many attributes are also subjective. One person's interpretation of "educated" may not match another's definition. Others may assume that you have chosen certain characteristics when, from your vantage point, you had little or no choice. Perhaps you were expected to go into the family business and never really made a choice about your profession.

Finally, context matters. Parts of your identity that matter to you may not matter to others, or may matter only in certain situations. Aspects of your identity that seem insignificant to you could become huge benefits or obstacles when you are working in certain situations or with particular groups. In your own country, you may leverage local culture to build rapport with others, but when traveling to other countries, you may downplay your culture and leverage your education and career credentials.

## INSTRUCTIONS

Creating a map of your identity is a way to capture and articulate how you see yourself. You can begin with surface-level begin withi dentities and then dig deeper. This can be useful in exploring how others may perceive you as a leader—who will feel more comfortable with you, who will give your words more weight, and so on. Your identity map should include the three components discussed in the previous section: given identity, chosen identity, and core identity.

Look at the sample map on the next page.

Using the blank map provided later in this exercise, follow these instructions to map your own identity.

1. In the outer ring, write words that describe your *given identity*: the attributes or conditions that you had no choice about from birth or later. You may want to include your nationality, age, gender, physical characteristics, certain family roles, possibly religion. Examples include female, only child, forty-eight, tall, blind, African-American, cancer patient, widow.

2. In the next ring, list aspects of your *chosen identity*. Consider including your occupation, hobbies, political affiliation, where you live, certain family roles, possibly religion. Examples are cyclist, mother, engineer, expatriate, college graduate, wife, leader, New Yorker, Buddhist.

3. In the center, write your *core attributes*—traits, behaviors, beliefs, values, and skills that you think make you unique as an individual. Select things that are relatively enduring about you or that are key to who you are today. For example, you may see yourself as funny, artistic, kind, conservative, attentive, creative, impatient, musical, family focused, or assertive.

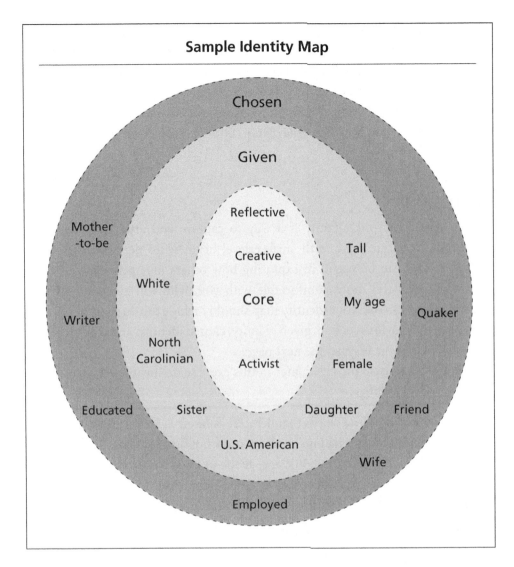

**Sample Identity Map**

Chosen

Given

Reflective

Creative

Core

Activist

Mother -to-be

Tall

White

My age

Quaker

Writer

North Carolinian

Female

Educated

Sister

Daughter

Friend

U.S. American

Wife

Employed

4. After you complete your map:

- Underline the items that are important to you personally. These are likely to be the terms you would use to describe yourself.
- Put a plus sign (+) beside the items that you believe contribute to your ability to lead effectively in your organization.
- Put a minus sign (−) beside the items that you believe detract from your ability to lead effectively in your organization.
- Put a question mark (?) beside the items that may vary in how they affect your leadership ability, depending on context.

# Blank Identity Map

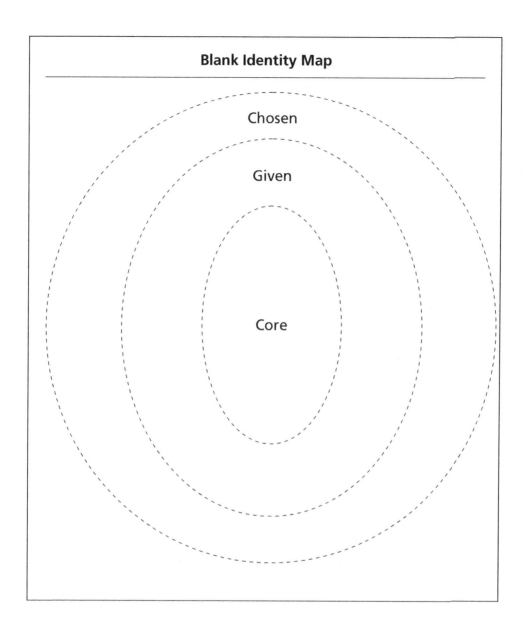

Chosen

Given

Core

## INTERPRETING YOUR MAP

Refer to your map while answering the following questions. They will help you examine your social identity in more depth.

1. When you look at the underlined items on your map, what trends do you see? Are they mainly part of your given, chosen, or core identity?

   _____

   _____

   _____

   _____

2. When you look at the items with pluses, minuses, and question marks, what trends do you see? Are they mainly part of your given, chosen, or core identity?

   _____

   _____

   _____

   _____

3. Of the aspects with pluses, minuses, and question marks, which are things you have in common with other people in the organization? Which are things that only you or a very small number of people possess? What are the leadership implications?

   _____

   _____

   _____

   _____

4. What aspects of your identity help you make connections with people at work? What aspects of your identity get in the way of making connections with people at work? What gives you the impression that this is the case?

_____

_____

_____

_____

5. Are there aspects of your identity that you keep hidden at work? What impact might that have on you and those around you?

_____

_____

_____

_____

6. How might you reveal or emphasize particular elements of your identity at work in order to build or improve relationships?

_____

_____

_____

_____

**7.** How might you hide or deemphasize particular elements of your identity at work in order to build or improve relationships?

_____

_____

_____

_____

## UNDERSTANDING OTHER PERSPECTIVES

People make assumptions about their social identities and those of others. When it comes to working with others, assumptions are often treated as reality. Assumptions can influence a person's beliefs about other people's thoughts and their motives for behaving the way they do.

Use the following questions to think through some of these assumptions. It may help to keep a particular person in mind when answering the questions (someone you've just met, someone you have problems with, etc.).

- When you are building a relationship at work, what do you want to know about another person? What do you notice first? Are you attracted to certain characteristics in others?

_____

_____

_____

_____

- What assumptions do you make about other people based on their social identities?

_____

_____

_____

_____

- If someone else were mapping your identity, what do you think he or she would notice first? What would be most relevant to the other person? Why?

_____

_____

_____

_____

- What assumptions do you think other people make about you based on your social identity?

_____

_____

_____

_____

- If you were to see the identity maps of other people with whom you work, how much do you think you would have in common with them?

_____

_____

_____

_____

- What are the areas that would probably be different?

_____

_____

_____

_____

# Your Experience with Triggers

**O**bjective: This exercise prompts you to reflect on situations that may have triggered social identity conflicts and think about how these events align with social and power conflicts in general. This exercise encourages you to examine the role your values may have played in your experience with conflict, potentially revealing your "hot buttons" when it comes to triggers.

**Key concepts:** social identity and power conflict, triggers/trigger events, differential treatment, assimilation, insults/humiliating acts, different values, simple contact

**Relevant cases:** All cases

**Relevant Chapters**
- Chapter 2: Triggers of Social Identity Conflict
- Chapter 3: Organizational Faultlines

**Time required:** Approximately 20 minutes

**Learning Outcomes**

1. Identify and understand how one's experiences with triggering events align with social and power conflicts in society at large.

2. List solutions that an individual or an organization can implement to prevent faultline activation and conflict in the future.

**Materials**

• Pen/pencil

## INSTRUCTIONS

Understanding and identifying triggers is a foundational skill needed to lead across differences. Because social identity conflicts are generally emotional in nature and often reflect social and power relationship in society at large, the ability to recognize triggering events and their connections with societal issues is key.

### Step 1: Identifying Triggers

Review the trigger description in the table below and think about situations in which you have experienced events that may have triggered social identity conflicts. Choose one or more of the triggers that you have the most experience with and jot down a few notes about each experience as it pertains to the triggers listed below. In this step, focus on describing the situation: Who was involved? What happened? Where did the situation occur? (You'll complete the Social/Power Issues column in Step 2.)

| Trigger | Description | Your Experience | Social/Power Issues |
|---|---|---|---|
| *Differential Treatment* | Occurs when one group perceives that another group has an advantage when it comes to the allocation of resources, rewards, opportunities, or punishments | | |

| | | | |
|---|---|---|---|
| *Assimilation* | Occurs when the majority group expects that others will act just like them; there is an expectation that non-dominant groups will blend into the dominant culture | | |
| *Insults or Humiliating Acts* | Occurs when a comment or behavior devalues or offends one group relative to another | | |
| *Different Values* | Occurs when groups have decidedly different values; a clash of fundamental beliefs regarding what is wrong and what is right | | |
| *Simple Contact* | Occurs when anxiety and tension between groups is high in the broader society; simple contact between these groups triggers a faultline | | |

## Step 2: Interpreting Triggers

Interpret how these triggering events are connected with social and power conflicts in society at large and how you interpret the situation. Complete the Social/Power Issues column in the previous table. See an example for the Differential Treatment trigger below.

| Trigger | Trigger Description | Your Experience | Social/Power Issues |
|---|---|---|---|
| **Example (this example is based on Case 3)** *Differential Treatment* | Occurs when one group perceives that another group has an advantage when it comes to the allocation of resources, rewards, opportunities, or punishments | I wanted to be able to take a paid holiday on a day important in my religion rather than have a paid holiday associated with another religion. | The idea that the "majority rules" can reinforce policies and norms that further marginalize groups not in the majority. I feel that those in the majority don't realize or appreciate the advantage of having rules and policies that favor them. I don't understand why it has to be such a struggle for me to get what others take for granted. |

## Step 3: Reflection: Identifying Patterns, Gathering Perspectives and Developing Ideas for Action

Being sensitive to triggers enables individuals and organizations to address issues, ideally preventing issues from deepening the divide between groups.

To assess your organization's propensity to effectively respond to triggering events, as well as your own, answer the questions on the next page:

1. Are there certain triggers with which you have numerous or particularly painful experiences? If so, what impact might that have on your ability to see other perspectives regarding similar situations?

_____

_____

_____

_____

2. How do you to express your perspective with someone very different from you without trying to convince the person that your way is the "right" way?

_____

_____

_____

_____

3. How comfortable are you listening to a perspective that is very different from your own? How do you tend to react when you feel your values are challenged or threatened?

_____

_____

_____

_____

4. What actions have you or your organization taken to gain a deeper understanding of the different perspectives related to social identity issues within the organization?

_____

_____

_____

_____

5. Do certain kinds of triggers seem to happen more often within the organization? If so, what contributes to their occurrence?

_____

_____

_____

_____

6. What are some of the things you or your organization can do to gain a deeper understanding of the potential triggers within the organization?

_____

_____

_____

_____

## IDEA FOR FURTHER EXPLORATION

Ask someone about his or her experiences with triggers and how he or she felt as a result. Listen without judging or questioning the person's perspective—just listen to the story and thank the person for sharing it.

# Identifying Faultlines

**O**bjective: This exercise is designed to help you identify potential faultlines in your work groups or other teams.

**Key concepts:** faultlines
**Relevant cases:** 5, 6, 8, 9, 10, 11, 12, 13

### Relevant Chapters

- Chapter 3: Organizational Faultlines
- Chapter 4: Leadership Practices Across Social Identity Groups

**Time required:** Approximately 30 minutes

### Learning Outcome

**1.** Identify potential faultlines in groups or teams.

### Materials

- Pen/pencil

## INSTRUCTIONS

**Step 1:** Think about a team or a group to which you currently belong or you belonged to in the past. Ideally, the team or group is work-related, but if needed you can think of a group or team from another aspect of your life. Recall the members of the team and the nature of the work you were doing together.

**Step 2:** Using the rating scale on the next page, rate the extent to which the team or group was different along the listed dimensions. There are several blank lines on which you can insert additional dimensions if appropriate.

| To what extent is the team or group similar in terms of . . . | Very Little Difference | ←——————→ | A Lot of Difference |
|---|---|---|---|
| Race | | | |
| Gender | | | |
| Religion | | | |
| Nationality | | | |
| Language spoken | | | |
| Educational level | | | |
| Age | | | |
| Functional background | | | |
| | | | |
| | | | |
| | | | |

Of the differences in the team/group you put in the chart, did (or do) any of the differences co-occur, such that members are different in terms of more than one characteristic and subgroups are similar in terms of more than one characteristic? If so, which characteristics co-occur?

_____

_____

_____

_____

Research suggests that groups that are very similar and groups that contain a lot of differences are less likely to experience faultlines, because similar groups do not have many differences and groups with a great many difference have so many differences that subgroups tend not to form. However, it is also important to note that the salience and prominence of the differences influences the degree to which faultlines may be experienced.

**Step 3:** Next, think about the context in which the group or team was (or is working).

1. How clear was the task on which the team was working?

_____

_____

2. How clear were the roles of various group or team members?

_____

_____

3. What leadership practices (see the Leadership Practices Across Social Identity Groups chapter) were used in the team and how effective were they?

_____

_____

_____

_____

4. Can you think of ways to improve your diverse interactions with work team or group members in the future? What about your work groups and teams as a whole?

_____

_____

_____

_____

# Cultural Values

**O**bjective: This exercise is designed to help you think about decisions or choices you've made that may have had an effect on a colleague, group, or organization. You are encouraged to reflect on your preferred cultural values and the roles those values typically play in your own decision making and in that of others.

**Key concepts:** cultural values, decision making, autonomy versus embeddedness, egalitarianism versus hierarchy, harmony versus mastery
**Relevant cases:** 2 through 13

**Relevant Chapters**

- Chapter 5: Cultural Values
- Chapter 10: Leader Values and Authenticity

**Time required:** Approximately 20 to 30 minutes

**Learning Outcomes**

1. Articulate the role one's preferred cultural values play in decision making and how values impact others.
2. Recognize how cultural value orientations impact decision making.

**Materials**

- Pen/pencil

## INSTRUCTIONS

First, review the Cultural Values chapter with the descriptions of the different value orientations. Think about decisions or choices you've made that may have had an effect on a colleague, group, or organization. List those decisions/choices in the first column below. Next, list your cultural value(s)—practices, symbols, specific norms, personal values—that influenced the decision or choice you made. Third, describe how your decision affected your colleagues, group, or organization. How did others react to your decision? Last, determine which value orientation is most closely related to the decision you made based on your cultural values, and circle the end of the orientation you prefer in the last column.

### Cultural Values Assessment

| Decision or choice I've made that may have had an effect (positive or negative) on a colleague or organization | Cultural values that influenced my decision and how (personal values, norms, beliefs, symbols, practices) | How my decision affected my colleague, group, or organization | Value orientation used (circle the end of the value orientation you prefer). |
| --- | --- | --- | --- |
| Decision 1 | | | Autonomy vs. Embeddedness |
| | | | Egalitarianism vs. Hierarchy |
| | | | Harmony vs. Mastery |

| | | | |
|---|---|---|---|
| **Decision 2** | | | Autonomy vs. Embeddedness |
| | | | Egalitarianism vs. Hierarchy |
| | | | Harmony vs. Mastery |
| **Decision 3** | | | Autonomy vs. Embeddedness |
| | | | Egalitarianism vs. Hierarchy |
| | | | Harmony vs. Mastery |
| **Decision 4** | | | Autonomy vs. Embeddedness |
| | | | Egalitarianism vs. Hierarchy |
| | | | Harmony vs. Mastery |

## SELF-EXAMINATION AND REFLECTION

1. "Leaders who recognize and take account of the cultural value orientations that influence their beliefs and actions and those of the people with whom they work are more likely to successfully lead in contexts of difference." Which are your preferred cultural values and what role do those values typically play in your own decision making?

_____

_____

_____

_____

2. How does understanding the role your cultural values play in your decision making affect your leadership style?

_____

_____

_____

_____

3. How did learning about the cultural value orientations impact your thinking about diverse perspectives and different ways of leading?

_____

_____

_____

_____

# Approaches to Difference

**O**bjective: The purpose of this exercise is to introduce two new orientations/perspectives that will help you understand your orientation to difference and describe working relationships with others outside of your social identity groups.

**Key concepts:** xenophobia, allophilia, social identity, in-group and out-group behavior, recategorizing, decategorizing

**Relevant cases:** 6, 9, 11, 13

## Relevant Chapter

• Chapter 6: Approaches to Difference: Allophilia and Xenophobia

**Time required:** Approximately 30 minutes

## Learning Outcomes

1. Define xenophobia and allophilia.

2. Identify one's orientation to social identity differences.

3. Develop ways to improve future encounters with individuals from different social identity groups.

## Materials

• Magazines or Internet access, from which an image can be selected

• Pen/pencil

## INSTRUCTIONS

### Step 1: Identifying an Image

Read the Approaches to Difference chapter. Then leaf through images (in magazines or online) and identify a picture that represents how you feel when you encounter someone very different from you, in general.

For example, take a look at the figure of puzzle pieces below. This image could represent an individual's sense that by encountering others those people have more perspectives to consider (and thus more puzzle pieces) and enable the individual to see a bigger picture, which creates feelings of excitement and fulfillment. However, the same image could represent an individual's sense that things are coming apart or are more divided—making it difficult to know what fits together and creating feelings of anxiety and perhaps resentment.

### Picture of Puzzle Pieces

## Step 2: Interpreting the Image

Looking at the image you selected and thinking about what it represents in terms of how you approach differences, answer the following questions:

1. What expectations do you have about the encounter?

_____

_____

_____

_____

2. What feelings tend to surface for you about the situation? Is it something positive? Uncomfortable, but necessary? Or something you'd rather avoid if possible?

_____

_____

_____

_____

3. In general, are you someone who actively seeks out those different from yourself or someone who would rather stick to his or her own kind?

_____

_____

_____

_____

**4.** What do you see as the advantages and disadvantages of each approach?

_____

_____

_____

_____

### Step 3: Applying It to Work

**1.** Think about a time when you had to work with someone or a group of people outside one of your social identity groups. Describe the situation and reflect on what worked well and what did not.

_____

_____

_____

_____

It is common for leaders to lead groups made up of subgroups whose members see each other as different. Creating a cohesive group when subgroups have negative attitudes about each other requires reducing the negative intergroup attitudes *and* promoting positive intergroup attitudes (Pittinsky, 2009).

To examine your skill level in creating cohesive groups of followers out of subgroups who have negative attitudes about each other, answer the questions below as they pertain to your past experiences with social identity conflict:

1. When leading diverse groups with negative attitudes about one another, or in-group members working with out-group members, what percent of the time do you encourage them to do the following?

   _____ Recategorize the other (see them as us) through a superordinate identity or goal that binds us to them.

   _____ Decategorize the other (see the other as an individual rather than as a member of a group).

   _____ Emphasize dual identities (simultaneously emphasize the senses of them, us, and an overarching we).

2. What approach do you tend to use and why?

   _____

   _____

   _____

   _____

3. What other tactics could you use?

   _____

   _____

   _____

   _____

# Cultural Intelligence (CQ)

**O**bjective: This exercise is designed for you to examine each factor of your cultural intelligence (CQ) for leadership effectiveness: motivational CQ, cognitive CQ, metacognitive CQ, and behavioral CQ.

**Key concepts:** cultural intelligence (CQ), motivational CQ, cognitive CQ, metacognitive CQ, behavioral CQ

**Relevant cases:** 1, 2, 3, 4, 5, 12

### Relevant Chapter

• Chapter 7: Cultural Intelligence: A Pathway for Leading in a Rapidly Globalizing World

**Time required:** Approximately 30 minutes

### Learning Outcomes

1. Define cultural intelligence and the following factors: motivational CQ, cognitive CQ, metacognitive CQ, and behavioral CQ.

2. Describe how cultural intelligence factors impact leadership effectiveness in different settings.

### Materials

• Pen/pencil

## INSTRUCTIONS

Leaders need all four CQ capabilities to be effective; thus this exercise gives you an opportunity to examine each factor of your cultural intelligence.

### Motivational CQ

How motivated are you to interact with diverse others despite challenges or conflict that may occur? How much enjoyment do you get out of working with others from different cultures? What are the barriers, if any, that prohibit you from readily interacting with diverse others? Answer these questions and jot down a few ways in which you might improve and eliminate any barriers.

_____

_____

_____

_____

### Cognitive CQ

How much do you know about other cultures? List as many common business and social practices as you are aware of for the following cultures (if there are other cultures with which you work, you may want to include them in the list):

South Africa_____

_____

Japan_____

_____

China_____

_____

Brazil_____

_____

Saudi Arabia_____

_____

Spain_____

_____

United States_____

_____

## Metacognitive CQ

If you are presented with a challenge of either garnering support from your diverse colleagues who are from very different contexts from your own or risking failure to meet a major goal, what *must* you do within your presentation to your colleagues to elicit their support? What strategies must you use to ensure success? How will you evaluate your progress?

_____

_____

_____

## Behavioral CQ

Assess your verbal and nonverbal actions by revisiting the cultures from the *Cognitive CQ* section. List verbal and nonverbal behaviors that would be appropriate/inappropriate in each of the above cultures. Think about your ability to modify these actions when necessary. Which practices are well developed? Which skills need to be enhanced?

_____

_____

_____

_____

### Self-Examination and Reflection

1. Based on what you now know about your cultural intelligence, how can you use each of the four factors of CQ to be more effective in cross-cultural and multicultural situations?

_____

_____

_____

_____

2. List four specific things you can do to enhance your leadership capabilities in this rapidly globalizing world. What has worked in the past and what must you do differently?

_____

_____

_____

3. Why is cultural intelligence a necessary ability for leading effectively in a diverse working environment? Please explain.

_____

_____

_____

For more information on CQ, how to assess CQ, and how to enhance CQ, go to http://culturalq.com.

# Your Leadership Practices

**O**bjective: The goal of this exercise is for you to explore your own responses to social identity conflict and to identify the leadership practices you typically prefer or expect an organization to use when managing social identity conflict.

**Key concepts:** leadership practices, social identity conflict, cross-group relationships, preferred social identity, conflict-management behavior
**Relevant cases:** 1, 3, 4, 5, 6, 9, 10, 11, 12, 13

**Relevant Chapter**

- Chapter 4: Leadership Practices Across Social Identity Groups

**Time required:** Approximately 15 to 20 minutes

**Learning Outcomes**

1. Identify leadership practice preferences for managing social identity conflict.

2. Articulate and aply the steps in the Leadership Response Cycle.

**Materials**

- Pen/pencil
- Calculator

## INSTRUCTIONS

How do you typically respond to cross-group relationships and conflict at work? Complete the assessment below to identify your preferences for managing social identity conflict.

Review each of the items listed below. For those items that best describe your underlying beliefs about what the organization's role in managing cross-group relationships should be, score them with a **3**. For those items that somewhat describe your beliefs, score them with a **2**. For those items that do not describe your beliefs at all, score them with a **1**. After you have scored each item, total the scores under each approach and divide by the number of items. The approach that has the largest score is typically the one you prefer and is how you believe organizations should manage cross-group relationship conflict.

    **3 = I usually prefer this approach**

    **2 = I sometimes prefer this approach**

    **1 = I rarely, if ever, prefer this approach**

### *Direct and Control* Organization Characteristics

- ☐ Policies punishing discrimination and harassment
- ☐ Performance management systems that emphasize feedback, rewards, and punishment
- ☐ Formalized conflict-management procedures providing a structure for complaints
- ☐ Staffing policies emphasizing mission and protecting organization boundaries
- ☐ Published code of conduct
- ☐ Organize work so groups are separated
- ☐ Intranet decision-making system to allow for input throughout the system

    Total/7 items = _____

## *Hands-Off* Organization Characteristics

- ☐ Doing nothing; letting the situation resolve on its own
- ☐ Denial of a problem
- ☐ Blame the victim
- ☐ Venting of emotion without taking action
- ☐ Emphasize only professional identities; do not recognize or encourage other identities

    Total/5 items = _____

## *Cultivate and Encourage* Organization Characteristics

- ☐ Diversity/sensitivity/cultural training and education to increase awareness of value of diversity
- ☐ Encouraging contact across groups/decategorization
- ☐ Creating a shared identity/recategorization
- ☐ Creating affinity groups/subcategorization
- ☐ Cross-cutting groups; creating diverse work teams
- ☐ Whole system interventions
- ☐ Creating boundary-crossing or bridging roles
- ☐ Climate of respect
- ☐ Apology and acceptance of apology
- ☐ Encouragement of individual initiative to resolve problems and conflicts
- ☐ Mentoring to facilitate integration of non-dominant groups
- ☐ Creation of a "safe" format for discussing conflict that promotes questioning, challenging debate, and open discussion

    Total/12 items = _____

## SELF-EXAMINATION AND REFLECTION

**1.** Do you prefer the *Direct and Control, Hands-Off,* or *Cultivate and Encourage* approach?

_____

**2.** Have you used any of the three approaches in your leadership practices? Which ones, and what was the outcome?

_____

_____

_____

_____

**3.** What actions/examples, if any, are missing from each group of characteristics?

_____

_____

_____

_____

**4.** If general steps are followed, an organization or individual can typically work toward preventing similar conflicts. In your past experience, have you or your organization followed the steps in the Leadership Response Cycle below before responding to a conflict?

a. Assess the situation

b. Clarify your message

c. Identify realistic expectations

5. Can you think about ways to improve your response by using the steps in the Leadership Response Cycle? The full cycle includes six steps: (1) Assess the Situation; (2) Clarify Your Message; (3) Identify Realistic Expectations; (4) Decide and Take Action; (5) Monitor Reactions, Act Again if Needed; and (6) Learn and Share.

_____

_____

_____

_____

_____

_____

_____

# Examining Your Leadership Networks

**O**bjective: In this exercise, you'll reflect on your own leadership network and the benefits of networking with individuals from different social identity groups. Having a strong and diverse network exposes you to different perspectives and provides you with access to information from different sources.

**Key concepts:** leadership network, social identity groups
**Relevant cases:** 2, 5, 6, 7, 11, 13

### Relevant Chapters

- Chapter 4: Leadership Practices Across Social Identity Groups
- Chapter 9: Miasma: The Dynamics of Difference

**Time required:** Approximately 1 hour

### Learning Outcomes

1. Describe the benefits of networking with others from different social identity groups.

2. Identify strategies to enhance one's networks and become more effective at leadership networking.

### Materials

- Flip-chart paper or notepaper
- Pen/pencil

## INSTRUCTIONS

### Step 1: Mapping Your Leadership Network

On a blank piece of flip-chart paper (or notepaper), draw large circles representing groups or individuals with whom you regularly interact or depend on to "get things done" at work. These can be people within or external to the organization. Likely categories of people to include are superiors, peers, direct reports, mentors, advisors, etc. You may also want to include the connections between the different individuals and groups with solid or dotted lines.

### Step 2: Examining Your Network

Examine your network and note the following:

1. Where do you go to get information?

   _____

2. Where do you go to get advice?

   _____

3. Where do you go to get support?

   _____

4. Whom do you trust?

   _____

5. Who do you think trusts you?

   _____

6. Are there certain types of people with whom you have a strong connection?

   _____

7. Are there certain types of people not represented or with whom you have a weak connection?

   _____

## Step 3: Applying a Social Identity Lens to Your Network

1. To what extent does the composition of your network "look like" your organization in terms of the different social identity groups?

   _____

2. To what extent does the composition of your network "look like" your customer or client base in terms of the different social identity groups?

   _____

3. To what extent does the composition of your network "look like" your community in terms of the different social identity groups?

   _____

4. Are members of different social identity groups underrepresented or not represented at all? If yes, which groups are they and what are the potential consequences of not being connected?

   _____

   _____

   _____

   _____


## Step 4: Leveraging Your Leadership Network

Having connections to different social identity groups provides important insights into differences as well as lessons about building relationships and making alliances. Networking is essential to effective leadership. Leaders who are skilled networkers have access to people, information, and resources to help solve problems and create opportunities. Leaders who neglect their networks are missing out on a critical component of their roles as leaders. While having a diverse network may sound like something that is good to do, if you do not take the time to really think about the benefits of having a strong/diverse network or the consequences of not having a strong/diverse network, you probably will not be motivated to do much about it. So take a few moments to consider your experiences with your network, describe the value to you of networking, and identify ways to expand your network.

1. How has networking with different identity groups helped or hurt you professionally?

_____

_____

_____

_____

2. Describe situations in which networking with different identity groups helped you accomplish your work or got in the way of doing work.

_____

_____

_____

_____

3. What opportunities have you potentially missed by not networking with different identity groups?

_____

_____

_____

_____

4. What work-related goals or expectations are connected with a need to network with different identity groups?

_____

_____

_____

_____

5. How would you benefit by networking with different identity groups?

_____

_____

_____

6. What steps can you take to build a more diverse network?

_____

_____

_____

_____

**Tips for Building a Diverse Network**

- Join professional organizations and seek out interest groups that will connect you with diverse perspectives.
- Ask questions about other people's experiences and listen (without judgment).
- Attend business events and community functions that will connect you with diverse perspectives.
- Become a member of an advisory board or volunteer with organizations that will increase your exposure to different perspectives.
- Invest yourself in the relationship: Try to give more than you receive.

# Taking a New Perspective

**O**bjective: The purpose of this exercise is to guide you through a "fieldwork" exercise, in an attempt to develop a deeper understanding of and empathy for a social identity group to which you do not belong.

>
> **Key concepts:** social identity
> **Relevant cases:** 1 through 13

**Relevant Chapters**

- Chapter 1: Social Identity: Understanding the In-Group/Out-Group Group Phenomenon
- Chapter 2: Triggers of Social Identity Conflict
- Chapter 6: Approaches to Difference: Allophilia and Xenophobia
- Chapter 8: Social Justice and Dignity
- Chapter 9: Miasma: The Dynamics of Difference

**Time required:** At least 1 hour prior to activity and 1 hour post-activity; length of chosen activity will vary

**Learning Outcome**

**1.** Appreciate another social identity group's perspectives and experiences.

**Materials**

- Notepaper or a journal
- Pen/pencil

## INSTRUCTIONS
### Step 1: Identifying a Group

Identify a social identity group to which you do *not* belong. You may want to choose a group you know very little about and/or a group that you anticipate working closely with in the future (or perhaps are already working with). For example, if you often work with people from another country, but do not know much about the customs or history of that country, you may want to choose that national group. To the extent possible, think about why you want to know more about that group and what specifically it would be helpful to know.

### Step 2: Identifying an Experience

Next, determine what kind of fieldwork would expose and/or immerse you in the traditions and norms of the group you selected. An extreme example could be traveling to a foreign country. However, it is probably more practical (and feasible) to think of something closer to home such as attending the services of a different religious group, visiting a low-income area within your community, or attending a celebratory or ceremonial event from another group. There are two extremes of conducting fieldwork. On one side you immerse yourself in the situation, fully participating in activities to the maximum extent possible. On the other hand, you may be more comfortable acting as an observer or witness, especially if your participation would be offensive to others and/or against your value system.

Below are some guidelines to apply when selecting your fieldwork:

- Select a situation or event that you are genuinely interested in learning about.
- If you tend to be associated with majority or dominant groups, you might want to put yourself in a situation in which you are the minority or non-dominant group.

- Make sure it is feasible for you to participate in or witness the situation.

- Gain permission, an invitation, or at a minimum be sure you won't be seen as an intruder. For instance, don't assume you can just "drop in" on a religious ceremony.

- Consider your safety. Do not take unnecessary risks! While hanging out in a crime-ridden area alone after dark may open you to a new perspective, it also puts you in harm's way.

## Step 3: Documenting the Experience

First, take some time to jot notes about what you expect to see or experience prior to beginning your fieldwork. This will allow you to more fully reflect on your experience. Next, you will need to document your fieldwork in order to make sense of it later. You can either do this in the moment (for example, by recording it or taking notes—if it is legal and acceptable) or after the fact (for example, by journaling about it). If you decide to document after the fact, do so as quickly as possible after the experience while details and emotions are still fresh. Below are some tips about the kind of things to document:

- Describe the situation.

- What is/was your reaction to the situation?

- How did others respond to you?

- What surprised you about your reaction or the reaction of others to you?

- What did you notice about leadership and power dynamics?

- How did you feel about the experience?

## Step 4: Making Sense of It All

A very rich experience will still not make you an expert in any social identity group; recognize your experience for what it is—a very small taste of something different. For example, spending a night or two in a cardboard box or living for a dollar a day in a city may illuminate challenges and perspectives associated with homelessness and poverty, but do not qualify as having the full experience of being homeless or poor. However, chances are you know more than you did before the experience. Respond to the questions below to prompt deeper learning:

1. How do your thoughts prior to taking part in the field experience compare to the actual experience? Were you accurate? Were there any surprises? What did you learn that was new?

_____

_____

_____

_____

_____

_____

2. Do you feel differently about the social identity group now than you did before? How valuable was this experience for you and what goals can you set for yourself to make any necessary changes in you and your ability to develop empathy for social identity groups outside of your own?

_____

_____

_____

_____

_____

_____

**3.** If someone were to do fieldwork based on one of *your* identities, what do you think he or she would discover? What situations or events do you think reveal the most about you?

_____

_____

_____

_____

_____

_____

# GLOSSARY

**Allocentrism** is being more concerned with the interests of others than with one's own interests.

**Allophilia** is a positive orientation toward members of a particular group seen as different or "other."

**Assimilation** is a trigger in which there is an expectation that non-dominant groups will blend into the dominant culture.

**Authentic leadership** includes the unobstructed operation of one's true self in one's day-to-day behavior. Authentic behavior promotes the development of meaningful relationships and trust.

**Autonomous cultures** treat people as independent, bounded entities. They encourage people to cultivate and express their own preferences, feelings, ideas, and abilities and to find meaning in their own uniqueness. There are two types of autonomy: Intellectual autonomy encourages individuals to pursue their own ideas and intellectual directions independently (important values: curiosity, broadmindedness, creativity). Affective autonomy encourages individuals to pursue affectively positive personal experiences (values: pleasure, exciting life, varied life).

**Behavioral cultural intelligence** is the ability to act appropriately in a range of cross-cultural situations. One of the most important aspects of behavioral CQ is knowing when to adapt to another culture and when *not* to do so. A person with high CQ learns which actions will and will not enhance effectiveness and shows flexibility in verbal and nonverbal actions.

**Chosen identity** includes the personal characteristics that you have chosen. They may describe your status as well as attributes and skills. Your occupation, hobbies, political affiliation, place of residence, family roles, and religion may all be chosen.

**Cognitive cultural intelligence** is the *knowledge* dimension of cultural intelligence. It refers to the level of understanding about culture and culture's role in shaping the way to do business and interact with others across different cultural contexts.

**Collectivism** stresses interdependence between people, rather than the importance of separate individuals.

**Communal relationships** are those in which people do not keep an account of the exchanges taking place between them; one person may give a gift of much higher value than the other person gives, and the two people may still maintain their relationship. In other words, it is the relationship that is valued and not the exchanges that go on between people.

**Core identity** includes the attributes that you think make you unique as an individual. Some will change over the course of your lifetime; others may remain constant. Elements of your core identity may include traits, behaviors, beliefs, values, and skills.

**Cosmopolitanism** is an all-encompassing view of the community of humankind, creating the freedom for people to make choices, to liberate the self from the constraints of cultural expectations.

**Cross-cutting** or **boundary weaving** is a way of structuring groups so that faultlines are less prominent.

**Cultural intelligence** (CQ) is an individual's capability to function effectively across cultures. This can include national, ethnic, and organizational as well as other types of culture.

**Cultural values** are the common beliefs, practices, symbols, social norms, and personal values in a society that give the society a degree of coherence.

**Decategorization** or **boundary suspending** is learning to see another as an individual rather than as a member of a group. It is the psychological process of removing stereotypical categories.

**Different values** are triggers represented by a clash of fundamental beliefs regarding what is wrong and what is right.

**Differential treatment** is a trigger in which one group perceives that another group has an advantage when it comes to the allocation of resources, rewards, opportunities, or punishments.

**Egalitarian cultures** urge people to recognize one another as moral equals who share basic interests as human beings. They socialize people to internalize a commitment to cooperate, to feel concern for the welfare of all, and to act voluntarily to benefit others. Values such as equality, social justice, responsibility, and honesty are important in egalitarian cultures.

**Embeddedness cultures** treat people as entities embedded in the collectivity. Meaning in life is expected to come largely through in-group social relationships, through identifying with the group, participating in its shared way of life, and striving toward its shared goals. Embedded cultures emphasize maintaining the status quo and restraining actions that might disrupt in-group solidarity or the traditional order. Such values as social order, respect for tradition, security, and wisdom are especially important in embedded cultures.

**Ethnocentricism** is the tendency to perceive things from the perspective of one's own culture and to believe that one's own cultural group is the most important and that some or all aspects of the culture are superior to those of other groups.

**Exchange relationships** are those in which people give something (a gift or a service) to another person with the expectation that the other person will return a gift or service of equal value in the near future. The characteristics of this type of relationship are "equal value" and "short time frame." People keep a mental record of exchange of benefits and try to maintain a balance between what they've given and what they've received.

**Faultlines** are the compositional dynamics of the multiple demographic attributes that can potentially subdivide a group. Faultlines may or may not be active in an organization, but they are always present. Faultlines may form along attributes such as gender, race, age, religion, nationality, or other demographic factors.

**Given identity** includes your personal attributes or conditions about which you have no choice. They may be characteristics you were born with, or they may have been given to you in childhood or later in life. Elements of your given identity include birthplace, age, gender, birth order, physical characteristics, certain family roles, and possibly religion.

**Harmony cultures** emphasize fitting into the social and natural world, accepting, preserving, and appreciating the way things are rather than changing, directing, or exploiting them. Harmony cultures discourage efforts to bring about change and encourage maintaining smooth relations and avoiding conflict. Important values in this type of culture include accepting one's position in life, world peace, and unity with nature.

**Hierarchy cultures** rely on hierarchical systems of ascribed roles to ensure responsible, productive behavior. They define the unequal distribution of power, roles, and resources as legitimate and even desirable. They socialize people to take a hierarchical distribution of roles for granted and to comply with the obligations and rules attached to their roles. Important values in this culture include social power, authority, humility, and wealth.

**Idiocentrism** is being centered on one's own, individual ways.

**Implicit leadership** theory indicates that leaders are more effective when they fit the leadership concepts held by followers.

**Improvisation** is a creative practice that builds and thrives on working through uncertain situations (paradox). The opposite of improvisation is the use of habitual or defensive routines to guide behavior.

**Individualism** stresses the importance of independence of individuals rather than the collective.

**In-groups** are social identity groups to which one belongs and feels loyalty, pride, and respect.

**Institutional bias** is discrimination that is embedded into the processes and systems of an institution.

**Instrumental values** are preferences for behaviors that are likely to result in a desired end state (for example, being tolerant, cheerful, and forgiving with the end goal of inner harmony).

**Insults/humiliating acts** are triggers wherein a comment or behavior devalues or offends one group relative to another.

**Intergroup anxiety** is the apprehension social identity groups feel toward one another.

**Intersectionality** is the intertwining of social identities that often forms the basis for discrimination or privilege. For instance, whiteness and masculinity often converge to create privilege (often referred to as "white privilege"), while blackness and femininity create a double disadvantage.

**Leadership network** consists of the people, information, and resources to which a leader has access. Maintaining a network takes effort, but it is essential to effective leadership.

**Leadership practices** are actions addressing (or intended to prevent) social identity conflicts in organizations. Leadership practices can be taken by an individual, group, or organization. They can be taken by any person in the organization regardless of formal authority, although different people are likely to use different strategies.

**Mastery cultures** encourage active self-assertion by individuals or groups in order to master, direct, and change the natural and social environment and thereby to attain group or personal goals. They emphasize the desirability of active, pragmatic problem solving that can produce "progress." Important values in this culture include ambition, success, daring, and competence.

**Mental models of leadership** are the ideas we carry about what effective leadership is and the characteristics of effective leaders.

**Metacognitive cultural intelligence** is *strategizing* and *making sense of* culturally diverse experiences. It includes whether we can use our cultural knowledge to plan an appropriate strategy, accurately interpret what's going on in a cross-cultural situation, and check to see whether our expectations are accurate or whether our mental model of that particular person and/or culture should be revised.

**Miasma** is an opaque atmosphere of misperception and distortion, where social outsiders are subjectively penalized for being different.

**Microinequities** are seemingly minor events that undermine one's self-esteem and self-worth. Just as many drops of water can erode a rock, microinequities continually reinforce an in-group/out-group dynamic that threatens to erode dignity, justice, and self-worth.

**Motivational cultural intelligence** is a leader's level of interest, *drive*, and energy to adapt cross-culturally. It includes *intrinsic motivation*—the degree to which you derive enjoyment from culturally diverse situations; *extrinsic motivation*—the tangible benefits you gain from culturally diverse experiences; and *self-efficacy*—your confidence that you will be effective in a cross-cultural encounter.

**Multiple identities** is the recognition that we each belong to multiple social identity groups simultaneously.

**Out-groups** are social identity groups to which one does not belong.

**Paradox** occurs when two contradictory elements are seen as present or operating at the same time.

**Paradoxical mindset** is one that accepts opposing interpretations as both plausible at the same time and does not view paradox as an uncertainty needing to be removed or reduced.

**Prototypical leader** is someone whose social identity is typical of the group he or she represents, often evoking or representing what is perceived to be the best aspects of the group.

**Recategorization** or **boundary reframing** is learning to see members of a different social identity group through a superordinate identity or goal that binds us to them. Groups are recategorized to encourage all members to pursue a shared overarching or superordinate goal.

**Relationship conflicts** are about non-task related things such as politics, gossip, and fashion and are often more emotional and taken personally.

**Self-categorization** is the process of identifying the social group(s) to which one belongs.

**Self-concept** is what one thinks about one's physical, psychological, and social attributes, including one's value or worth.

**Simple contact** is a trigger that occurs in situations in which tensions in society at large are strong and when bringing together people whose identity groups are involved in a highly publicized and adversarial event can result in polarization.

**Simultaneous identities** is the recognition that we each belong to multiple social identity groups simultaneously.

**Social exchange** is another way of referring to an interaction or relationship.

**Social identity** is the group(s) to which people belong on the basis of shared characteristics such as gender, religion, race, class, sexuality, and so forth.

**Social identity conflict** is triggered by events that activate latent tensions in society. Such tensions may result from disparities of wealth and power or a long history of intergroup conflict and distrust.

**Social identity theory (SIT)** describes how people categorize themselves as members of social groups, the emotional and behavioral effects of social group memberships on individual identity, and the intergroup dynamics resulting from social group comparisons.

**Spillover** is the process by which social identity differences in the society at large influence organizational dynamics.

**Structural racism** is intentional or unintentional systematic differential access to goods, services, and opportunities on the basis of race.

**Subcategorization** or **boundary nesting** has to do with recognizing subgroup membership in the context of a larger organization.

**Superordinate goal** is a goal shared by everyone in an organization.

**Task conflicts** are those that members have regarding the specific jobs they are working on.

**Terminal values** are end-state values that an individual would like to achieve (for example, inner harmony).

**Transactional leaders** influence followers by using mutually beneficial transactions (such as rewards and punishments).

**Transformational leaders** influence followers to go beyond personal interests and aim for collective achievement.

**Triggers/triggering events** can be an action or series of actions that make an inequity or inequality, related to social identity, noticeable. A trigger is an event that involves at least two social identity groups, men and women, for example, and that causes social identity to become activated in varying degrees. For an event to be a trigger, at least two members from the same identity group attribute the event or action to their social identity group or the social identity group of the other party.

**Xenophobia** is the general fear or hatred of those who are different, not necessarily grounded in direct experience with any particular group.

# RECOMMENDED READING/RESOURCES

## Part 1: Leading Across Differences Framework

Argyris, C. (1993). *Knowledge for action: A guide to overcoming barriers to organizational change.* San Francisco: Jossey-Bass.

Ernst, C., & Chrobot-Mason, D. (manuscript in preparation). *Boundary spanning leadership: A manager's guide to leadership across intergroup boundaries (tentative title).* New York: McGraw-Hill.

## Part 2: Cases

*Note:* The materials for the cases are organized by topic rather than specific case.

### Cultural Intelligence

Early, P.C., & Peterson, R.S. (2004). The elusive cultural chameleon: Cultural intelligence as a new approach to intercultural training for the global manager. *Academy of Management Learning and Education, 3*(1), 100–115.

### Dealing with Faultlines

Kossek, E.E., Lobel, S.A., & Brown, J. (2005). Human resource strategies to manage workforce diversity. In A. Konrad, P. Prasad, & J.K. Pringle (Eds.), *Handbook of workplace diversity* (pp. 53–74). London: Sage Publications.

### Gender at Work

Booysen, L. (1999, Winter/Spring). Male and female managers: Gender influences on South African managers in retail banking. *South African Journal of Labour Relations, 23*(2&3), 25–35.

Booysen, L., & Nkomo, S.M. (2006). Think manager—think (fe)male: A South African perspective. *The International Journal of Interdisciplinary Social Sciences, 1*(2), 23–33.

Eagly, A.H., & Carli, L.L. (2003). The female leadership advantage: An evaluation of the evidence. *The Leadership Quarterly, 14,* 807–834.

Eagly, A.H., & Carli, L.L. (2003). Finding gender advantage and disadvantage: Systematic research integration is the solution. *The Leadership Quarterly, 14,* 851–859.

Vecchio, R.P. (2002). Leadership and gender advantage. *The Leadership Quarterly, 13*(6), 643–671.

Vecchio, R.P. (2003). In search of gender advantage. *The Leadership Quarterly, 14,* 835–850.

### Same-Sex Orientation Workers

Colgan, F., Creegan, C., McKearny, A., & Wright, T. (2007). Equality and diversity policies and practices at work: Lesbian, gay and bisexual workers. *Equal Opportunities International, 26*(6), 590–609.

### Social Identities

Nkomo, S.M., & Stewart, M. (2006). Diverse identities in organizations. In S. Clegg, C. Hardy, & W. Nord (Eds.), *The Sage handbook of organizational studies* (2nd ed.). London: Sage Publications.

### Structural Discrimination

Bell, E.E., & Nkomo, S.M. (2001). Gender and cultural diversity in the workplace. In L. Diamant & J. Lee (Eds.), *The psychology of sex, gender and jobs: Issues and solutions.* Westport, CT: Praeger.

Cox, T., Jr., & Nkomo, S.M. (2001). Race and ethnicity: An update and analysis. In R.T. Golembiewski (Ed.), *Handbook of organizational behavior* (2nd ed.) (pp. 255–286). New York: Marcel Dekker.

Plummer, D.L. (2003). *Handbook of diversity management: Beyond awareness to competency based learning.* Lanham, MD: University Press of America.

### Whiteness in South Africa

Booysen, L. (2001, Summer). The duality in South African leadership: Afrocentric or Eurocentric. *South African Journal of Labour Relations, 25*(34), 36–64.

Booysen, L. (2007). Barriers to employment, equity implementation, and retention of blacks in management in South Africa. *Southern African Journal of Labour Relations, 31*(1), 47–71.

Booysen, L. (2007). Societal power shifts and changing social identities in South Africa: Workplace implications. *Southern African Journal of Economic and Management Sciences, 10*(1), 1–20.

Booysen, L., Kelly, C., Nkomo, S.M., & Steyn, M. (2007). Rethinking the diversity paradigm: South African practices. *International Journal on Diversity in Organisations, Communities & Nations, 7*(4), 1–10.

Booysen, L., & Nkomo, S.M. (2007). The tea incident: Racial division at Insurance Incorporated—A teaching case. *International Journal on Diversity in Organisations, Communities & Nations, 7*(5), 97–106.

Horwitz, F.M., Browning, V., Jain, H., & Steenkamp, A.J. (2002). Human resource practices and discrimination in South Africa: Overcoming the apartheid legacy. *International Journal of Human Resource Management*, *13*(7), 1105–1118.

Soudien, C. (1998). Equality and equity in South African education: Multiculturalism and change. In M. Cross & Z. Mkwanazi Twala (Eds.), *Unity, diversity and reconciliation: A debate on the politics of curriculum in South Africa*. Cape Town: Juta.

Steyn, M.E. (2002). "Whiteness" in the rainbow: The subjective experience of loss of privilege in the new South Africa. In C.H. Hamilton, L. Huntley, N. Alexander, A.S. Guimaraes, & W. James (Eds.), *Beyond racism: Race and inequality in Brazil, South Africa, and the United States*. Atlanta, GA: Lynne Rienner Publishers.

## Part 3: Perspectives

*Note:* The materials for the perspectives section are organized by chapter.

### Chapter 1

Cox, T., Jr., & Beale, R. (1997). *Developing competency to manage diversity*. San Francisco: Berrett-Koehler.

This book offers a set of readings, cases, and structured activities as a tool kit for practitioners. There is an excellent exercise (Identity Pie Chart) pertinent to understanding how people think about their identities as members of different social groups. I have used the exercise many times as an introduction to a discussion of the complexity of identity and its relevance to in-groups/out-groups.

Dovidio, J.G., Glick, P., & Rudman, L.A. (2005). *On the nature of prejudice: Fifty years after Allport*. Malden, MA: Blackwell.

This book provides a helpful compendium of the most current thinking about prejudice. It covers topics from in-group/out-group prejudice and stereotyping to socio-cultural factors influencing intergroup relations. The authors of these chapters are some of the top scholars in the field. There is also a chapter on religion and prejudice.

Haslam, S.A., van Knippenberg, D., Platow, M.J., & Ellemers, N. (Eds.). (2003). *Social identity at work: Developing theory for organizational practice*. Philadelphia, PA: Psychology Press.

This book of edited chapters offers a good overview of social identity theory and provides many practical insights into social identity theory in the workplace.

Plummer, D.L. (2003). Handbook of diversity management: Beyond awareness to competency-based learning. Lanham, MD: University Press of America.

The theoretical foundation section has a useful discussion on theories of difference in organizations. Section II contains several tools for developing skills in managing differences. The last section of the book includes a chapter on diversity and difference in specialized settings: nonprofit, faith-based, school organizations, community and government agencies.

*Eye of the Storm* (Jane Elliott, DVD)

This is probably one of the most powerful DVDs for demonstrating the power of in-group/out-group categorization. It captures Jane Elliott's approach to helping her third graders understand the meaning of prejudice. There are also additional versions of the experiment with adult participants. The DVD comes with a facilitator's guide.

## Chapter 2

Chrobot-Mason, D., & Ruderman, M.N. (2004). Leadership in a diverse workplace. In M.S. Stockdale & F.J. Crosby (Eds.), *The psychology and management of workplace diversity* (pp. 100–121). Malden, MA: Blackwell.

This chapter looks at the critical role that organizational leaders should play in bringing workers from diverse backgrounds together. It offers a perspective on the multicultural competencies relevant to addressing triggers of social identity conflict.

Chrobot-Mason, D., Ruderman, M.N., Weber, T.J., Ohlott, P.J., & Dalton, M.A. (2007). Illuminating a cross-cultural leadership challenge: When identity groups collide. *The International Journal of Human Resource Management, 18*(11), 2011–2036.

This article provides an academic description of social identity conflicts, explaining what causes them and connecting the idea of social identity conflicts to information about cultural values. The article provides information as to why it is important to take cultural differences into account when working with multiple social identity groups.

Ernst, C., & Yip, J. (2009). Boundary spanning leadership: Tactics to bridge social identity groups in organizations. In T.L. Pittinsky (Ed.), *Crossing the divide: Intergroup leadership in a world of difference.* Boston: Harvard Business School Press.

This chapter provides a rich view of different practices for helping people on different sides of faultlines work together effectively. It is intended for practitioners and scholars alike who want to better understand how to lead across differences. Four different leadership practices are described.

Gratton, L., Voigt, A., & Erickson, T. (2007). Bridging faultlines in diverse teams. *MIT Sloan Management Review, 48*(4), 22–29.

This article provides another view regarding recognition of the potential for divisive faultlines in organizations. The article offers a short survey for team leaders for the purposes of rating the strength of faultlines in a team.

Ruderman, M.N., & Munusamy, V. (2007). Know thyself. *Concepts & Connections, 15*(2), 1, 3–4.

Targeted toward educational leaders, this article explains how important it is to be aware of your own social identity. It explains how social identity ties can "bind and blind" and provides rich suggestions as to how to understand self in terms of social identity processes.

http://www.pbs.org/wgbh/pages/:frontline/shows/divided/

This website features a "Frontline" show about an Iowa teacher who gave her class a lesson on discrimination the day after the murder of Martin Luther King, Jr. Jane Elliot divided the class into "brown-eyed" and "blue-eyed" groups creating a faultline that influenced group behavior. Tapes, transcripts, and discussion questions are provided.

### Chapter 3

### Assessment of Leadership Style: Multi-Factor Leadership Questionnaire (MLQ)
Bass, B.M. (1998). *Transformational leadership: Industry, military, and educational impact*. Mahwah, NJ: Lawrence Erlbaum Associates.
Bass, B.M., & Avolio, B.J. (1990). *Manual for the multifactor leadership questionnaire*. Palo Alto, CA: Consulting Psychologists Press.

### Assessment of Relationship and Task Conflict
Jehn, K.A. (1995). A multimethod examination of the benefits and detriments of intragroup conflict. *Administrative Science Quarterly, 40*, 256–282.

### Diversity in Organizations
Harvey, C.P., & Allard, M.J. (Eds.). (2005). *Understanding and managing diversity: Readings, cases, and exercises* (3rd ed.). Upper Saddle River, NJ: Prentice-Hall.
Jackson, S.E., & Associates (1992). *Diversity in the workplace*. New York: Guilford Press.

### Measurement of Faultlines
Bezrukova, K., Jehn, K.A., Thatcher, S., & Zanutto, E. (in press). A field study of group faultlines, team identity, conflict, and performance in diverse groups. *Organization Science*.
Thatcher, S.M.B., Jehn, K.A., & Zanutto, E. (2003). Cracks in diversity research: The effects of diversity faultlines on conflict and performance. *Group Decision and Negotiation, 12*, 217–241.

### Chapter 4
Early, C., & Ang S. (2003). *Cultural intelligence: Individual interactions across cultures*. Palo Alto, CA: Stanford University Press.

This book explains the concept of cultural intelligence and its importance in today's multicultural world. It provides a useful way of looking at how important cultural intelligence is to understanding other people.

Hammer, M., & Bennett, M. (1998). *Manual: The intercultural development inventory (IDI)*. Portland, OR: The Intercultural Communication Institute.

This instrument is a sixty-item inventory that measures intercultural sensitivity based on the work of Milton Bennett. This instrument can be used for assessment and feedback for the purpose of helping individuals understand intercultural sensitivity.

Stone, D., Patton, S., & Heen, S. (1999). *Difficult conversations: How to discuss what matters most*. New York: The Penguin Group.

This book from the Harvard Negotiation Project provides a step-by-step approach to prepare for and to have difficult conversations. The authors say that each conversation that feels difficult and stressful is really three conversations: what happened, feelings, and identity.

## Chapter 5

Hall, E.T. (1990). *Understanding cultural differences*. Boston: Intercultural Press.

Hall provides research on universal cultural dimensions comparing different cultures.

Hofstede, G. (1980). *Culture's consequences: International differences in work related values*. Thousand Oaks, CA: Sage.

Hofstede, G. (1994). *Uncommon sense about organizations, cases, studies, and field observations*. London: Sage.

Hofstede, G., & Hofstede, G.J. (1991). *Cultures and organizations: Software of the mind*. New York: McGraw-Hill.

House, R., Hanges, P., Javidan, M., Dorfman, P., & Gupta, V. (Eds.). (2004). *Leadership, culture and organizations: The GLOBE study of 62 societies*. Thousand Oaks, CA: Sage.

Hofstede and House provide research that specifically links universal cultural dimensions with preferred leadership practices that can be valuable further reading in understanding how cultural values impact behavior. While Schwartz identifies only three dimensions (as discussed in Chapter 6), Hofstede uses five dimensions in his research, and House and colleagues use nine dimensions in their sixty-two-nation GLOBE study on cross-cultural leadership.

Triandis, H.C. (1995). Theoretical framework for the study of diversity. In M.M. Chemers, S. Oskamp, & M.A. Costanzo (Eds.), *Diversity in organizations: New perspectives for a changing workplace* (pp. 11–36). London: Sage.

Triandis provides research on universal cultural dimensions comparing different cultures.

## Chapter 6
www.allophilia.org

This website has all the latest information on allophilia research, including contact information for copies of the Allophilia Scale and an interchange on creating and nurturing allophilia in workplaces, schools, neighborhoods, nations, and the world.

www.adl.org

This website contains resources of the Anti-Defamation League (ADL), whose purpose is to oppose anti-Semitism and all forms of bigotry and to defend democratic ideals and civil rights.

www.tolerance.org

The Teaching Tolerance website is sponsored by the Southern Poverty Law Center and is dedicated to reducing prejudice, improving intergroup relations, and supporting equitable school experiences for children. Teaching Tolerance provides free educational materials, including downloadable curricula for teachers and other classroom activities.

## Chapter 7
http://www.culturalq.com

The Cultural Intelligence Center (CQC) website contains resources dedicated to improving the understanding of cultural intelligence (CQ).

## Chapter 12
Handy, C. (1994). *The age of paradox*. Cambridge, MA: Harvard Business School Press.

Charles Handy, a well-known management scholar, describes the changing dynamics of organizational life and suggests nine global paradoxes that leaders will be faced with. Handy suggests three senses (continuity, connection, direction) by which leaders can make meaning out of paradox; and through the use of curvilinear logic and sigmoid curves, Handy suggests possible pathways for leaders to work through paradox.

Johnson, B. (1996). *Polarity management*. Amherst, MA: HRD Press.

Johnson presents an excellent framework for making visible and explicit the paradoxes in organizational life. According to Johnson, the goal of managing polarities is to benefit from the tensions that exist between opposing poles and to draw out the synergy between the two pools to achieve a higher purpose. He describes the application of his framework in various contexts, with detailed case studies.

Smith, K., & Berg, D. (1987). *Paradoxes of group life*. San Francisco: Jossey-Bass.

Smith and Berg suggest that paradoxes are an inherent part of group life and must be accepted, confronted, and managed. Of particular relevance is the paradox of identity and belonging, which Smith and Berg describe as the struggle of individuals and the group to each establish a meaningful identity that is an integral part of the other. Other paradoxes identified by Smith and Berg include the paradox of engaging—around disclosure, trust, intimacy, and regression—and the paradox of speaking—around authority, dependency, creativity, and courage.

# REFERENCES

Abrams, D., & Hogg, M.A. (2004). Metatheory: Lessons from social identity research. *Personality and Social Psychology Review, 8*(2), 98–106.

Allport, G.W. (1954). *The nature of prejudice.* Reading, MA: Addison-Wesley.

Ang, S., & Inkpen, A.C. (2008). Cultural intelligence and offshore outsourcing success: A framework of firm-level intercultural capability. *Decision Sciences, 39*(3), 33–358.

Ang, S., & Van Dyne, L. (2008). *Handbook on cultural Intelligence: Theory, measurement and applications.* Armonk, NY: M.E. Sharpe.

Ang, S., Van Dyne, L., & Koh, C. (2006). Personality correlates of the four-factor model of cultural intelligence. *Group and Organization Management, 31,* 100–123.

Ang, S., Van Dyne, L., Koh, C.K.S., Ng, K.Y., Templer, K.J., Tay, C., & Chandrasekar, N.A. (2007). Cultural intelligence: Its measurement and effects on cultural judgment and decision making, cultural adaptation, and task performance. *Management and Organization Review, 3,* 335–371.

Ashforth, B.E., & Mael, F. (1989). Social identity theory and the organization. *Academy of Management Review, 14*(1), 20–39.

Avolio, B.J., & Gardner, W.L. (2005). Authentic leadership development: Getting to the root of positive forms of leadership. *Leadership Quarterly, 16,* 315.

Avolio, B.J., Gardner, W.L., Walumbwa, F.O., Luthans, F., & May, D.R. (2004). Unlocking the mask: A look at the process by which authentic leaders impact follower attitudes and behaviors. *Leadership Quarterly, 15*(6), 801–823.

Avolio, B.J., & Luthans, F. (2006). *The high impact leader: Moments matter in accelerating authentic leadership development.* New York: McGraw-Hill.

Avolio, B., Luthans, F., & Walumbwa, F.O. (2004). Authentic leadership: Theory-building for veritable sustained performance. Working paper. Gallup Leadership Institute, University of Nebraska, Lincoln.

Bass, B.M. (1985). *Leadership and performance beyond expectations.* New York: The Free Press.

Bezrukova, K., Jehn, K.A., Thatcher, S., & Zanutto, E. (2004, September). A field study of group faultlines, team identity, conflict, and performance in diverse groups. *Journal of Organizational Behavior, 25*(6), 703–729.

Bhawuk, D.P.S. (1997). Leadership through relationship management: Using the theory of individualism and collectivism. In R.W. Brislin & K. Cushner (Eds.), *Improving intercultural interactions: Modules for cross-cultural training programs, 2*. Thousand Oaks, CA: Sage.

Bhawuk, D.P.S. (2001). Evolution of culture assimilators: Toward theory-based assimilators. *International Journal of Intercultural Relations, 25*(2), 141–163.

Booysen, L. (2007). Societal power shifts and changing social identities in South Africa: Workplace implications. *Southern African Journal of Economic and Management Sciences, 10*(1), 1–20.

Brewer, M. (1995). Managing diversity: The role of social identities. In S. Jackson & M. Ruderman (Eds.), *Diversity in work teams* (pp. 47–68). Washington, DC: American Psychological Association.

Brewer, M., & Miller, N. (1984). Beyond the contact hypothesis: Theoretical perspectives on desegregation. In N. Miller & M. Brewer (Eds.), *Groups in contact: The psychology of desegregation* (pp. 49–65). New York: Academic Press.

Brickson, S. (2000). The impact of identity orientation on individual and organizational outcomes in diverse settings. *Academy of Management Review, 25*(1), 82–101.

Burke, C.S., Sims, D.E., Lazzara, E.H., & Salas, E. (2007). Trust in leadership: A multi-level review and integration. *The Leadership Quarterly, 18*(6), 606–632.

Burns, J.M. (1978). *Leadership*. New York: Harper & Row.

Byrne, D. (1971). *The attraction paradigm*. New York: Academic Press.

Cable, D.M., & Edwards, J.R. (2004). Complementary and supplementary fit: A theoretical and empirical integration. *Journal of Applied Psychology, 89*(5), 822–834.

Cameron, K.S., & Quinn, R.E. (1988). Organizational paradox and transformation. In R.E. Quinn & K.S. Cameron (Eds.), *Paradox and transformation: Toward a theory of change in organization and management* (pp. 1–18). Cambridge, MA: Ballinger.

Christian, J., Porter, L.W., & Moffitt, G. (2006). Workplace diversity and group relations: An overview. *Group Processes & Intergroup Relations, 9*(4), 459–466.

Chrobot-Mason, D., Ruderman, M.N., Weber, T.J., & Ernst, C. (2009). The challenge of leading on unstable ground: Triggers that activate social identity faultlines. *Human Relations, 62*(11), 1763–1794.

Chrobot-Mason, D., Ruderman, M.N., Weber, T.J., Ohlott, P.J., & Dalton, M.A. (2007). Illuminating a cross-cultural leadership challenge: When identity groups collide. *The International Journal of Human Resource Management, 18*(11), 2011–2036.

Cockburn, C. (1998). *The space between us: Negotiating gender and national identities in conflict*. London: Zed Books.

Cox, T., Jr. (1993). *Cultural diversity in organizations: Theory, research and practice*. San Francisco: Berrett-Koehler.

Cox, T., Jr. (2001). *Creating the multicultural organization: A strategy for capturing the power of diversity*. San Francisco: Jossey-Bass.

Crenshaw, K. (1991). Mapping the margins: Intersectionality, identity, politics, and violence against women of color. *Stanford Law Review, 43*(6).

Crenshaw, K. (2005). Mapping the margins: Intersectionality, identity, politics, and violence against women of color (1994). *Violence against women: Classic papers* (pp. 282–313). Auckland, New Zealand: Pearson Education New Zealand.

Cunha, M.P., Kamoche, K., & Cunha, R.C. (2003). Organizational improvisation and leadership: A field study in two computer-mediated settings. *International Studies of Management and Organization, 33*, 34–57.

De Dreu, C.K.W., & Weingart, L.R. (2003). Task and relationship conflict, team performance, and team member satisfaction: A meta-analysis. *Journal of Applied Psychology, 88*, 741–749.

Drath, W.H., McCauley, C., Paulus, C.J., Van Velsor, E., O'Connor, PMG., & McGuire, J.B. (2008). Direction, alignment, commitment: Toward a more integrative ontology of leadership. *Leadership Quarterly, 19*, 635–653.

Dorfman, P.W. (1996). Part II: Topical issues in international management research. In J. Punnitt & O. Shanker (Eds.), *International and cross-cultural leadership* (pp. 267–349). Cambridge, MA: Blackwell.

Dorner, D. (1996). *The logic of failure: Why things go wrong and what we can do to make them right*. New York: Holt.

Dovidio, J.F., Gaertner, S.L., & Bachman, B.A. (2001). Racial bias in organizations: The role of group processes in its causes and cures. In M.E. Turner (Ed.), *Groups at work: Theory and research* (pp. 415–444). Mahwah, NJ: Lawrence Erlbaum Associates.

Dvir, T., Eden, D., Avolio, B.J., & Shamir, B. (2002). Impact of transformational leadership on follower development and performance: A field experiment. *Academy of Management Journal, 45*, 735–744.

Earley, P.C., & Ang, S. (2003). *Cultural intelligence*. Stanford, CA: Stanford University Press.

Earley, P.C., & Mosakowski, E. (2000). Creating hybrid team cultures: An empirical test of transnational team functioning. *Academy of Management Journal, 43*, 26–49.

Ely, R.J., & Thomas, D.A. (2000). Cultural diversity at work: The effects of diversity perspectives of work group processes and outcomes. *Administrative Science Quarterly, 46*, 229–273.

Endo, Y., Heine, S.J., & Lehman, D.R. (2000). Culture and positive illusions in close relationships: How my relationships are better than yours. *Personality and Social Psychology Bulletin, 26*, 1571–1586.

Ensari, N.K., Christian, J., & Miller, N. (2006). Workplace diversity and group relations: An overview. *Group Processes & Intergroup Relations, 9*(4), 459–466.

Ernst, C., & Yip, J. (2009). Boundary spanning leadership: Tactics to bridge social identity groups in organizations. In T.L. Pittinsky (Ed.), *Crossing the divide: Intergroup leadership in a world of difference*. Boston: Harvard Business School Press.

Essed, P. (2001). Multi-identifications and transformations: Reaching beyond racial and ethnic reductionisms. *Social Identities, 7*(4), 493–509.

Fatehi, K. (2007). *Managing internationally: Succeeding in a culturally diverse world.* Thousand Oaks, CA: Sage.

Fitzgerald, F.S. (1956). *The crack-up.* New York: New Directions.

Gallos, J.V. (2008). Learning from the toxic trenches: The winding road to healthier organizations—and to healthier leaders. *Journal of Management Inquiry, 17*(4), 354–367.

Gardner, W.L., Avolio, B.J., & Walumbwa, F. (Eds.). (2005). *Authentic leadership theory and practice: Origins, effects and development.* New York: JAI, an imprint of Elsevier Science.

Gentry, W., Hannum, K., Munusamy, V., & Weber, T. J. (2007, July). Managing identity conflicts: Perspectives across organisational level and culture. Social Identity Conflicts in Organisational and Cultural Context: Triggers, Responses and Leadership Practices Symposium at the Internal Academy for Intercultural Research 2007, Groningen, Netherlands.

Gersick, C.J., & Hackman, J.R. (1990). Habitual routines in task-performing groups. *Organizational Behavior and Human Decision Processes, 47,* 65–97.

Graetner, S.L., & Dovidio, J.F. (2000). *Reducing inter-group bias: The common in-group identity model.* Philadelphia, PA: Psychology Press.

Graves, L.M., Ohlott, P.J., & Ruderman, M.N. (2007). Commitment to family roles: Effects on managers' attitudes and performance. *Journal of Applied Psychology, 9*(1), 44–56.

Gudykunst, W.B., Matsumoto, Y., Ting-Toomey, S., Nishida, T., Kim, K., & Heyman, S. (1996). The influence of cultural individualism-collectivism, self-constructuals, and individual values on communication styles across cultures. *Human Communication Research, 22*(4), 510–543.

Guskin, A. (1997). Cultural humility: A way of being in the world. In *Notes from a pragmatic idealist: Selected papers 1985–1997* (pp. 143–147). Yellow Spring, OH: Antioch University.

Hamilton, W.D. (1963). The evolution of altruistic behavior. *American Naturalist, 97,* 354–356.

Hampden-Turner, C., & Trompenaars, F. (2000). *Building cross-cultural competence: How to create wealth from conflicting values.* Hoboken, NJ: John Wiley & Sons.

Hannum, K.M., & Glover, S.L. (in press). Respect. In R.A. Couto (Ed.), *Political and civic leadership.* Thousand Oaks, CA: Sage.

Harrison, D.A., Price, K.H., & Bell, M.P. (1998). Beyond relational demography: Time and the effects of surface- and deep-level diversity on work group cohesion. *Academy of Management Journal, 41,* 96–107.

Haslam, S.A. (2001). *Psychology in organizations: The social identity approach.* London: Sage.

Heifetz, R. (1998). *Leadership without easy answers*. Boston: Harvard Business School Press.

Hesse, H. (1972). *Stories of five decades*. New York: Farrar, Straus and Giroux.

Hewstone, M., & Brown, R. (1986). Contact is not enough: An inter-group perspective on the contact hypothesis. In M. Hewstone & R. Brown (Eds.), *Contact and conflict in inter-group encounters* (pp. 1–44). Oxford: Blackwell.

Hewstone, M., Rubin, M., & Willis, H. (2002). Inter-group bias. *Annual Review of Psychology, 53,* 575–604.

Hill, J. (2000). *Becoming a cosmopolitan: What it means to be a human in the new millennium*. Lanham, MD: Rowman & Littlefield.

Hodson, R. (2001). *Dignity at work*. Cambridge, UK: Cambridge University Press.

Hofstede, G. (1980). *Culture's consequences: International differences in work-related values,* Thousand Oaks, CA: Sage.

Hofstede, G. (1994). *Uncommon sense about organizations, cases, studies, and field observations*. London: Sage.

Hofstede, G. (2001). *Culture's consequences: Comparing values, behaviors, institutions and organizations across nations*. Thousand Oaks, CA: Sage.

Hofstede, G., & Hofstede, G.-J. (2004). *Cultures and organizations: Software of the mind*. New York: McGraw-Hill.

Hogg, M.A., & Terry, D.J. (2000). Social identity and self-categorization processes in organizational contexts. *Academy of Management Review, 25*(1), 121–140.

Homan, A.C., Greer, L.L., Jehn, K.A., & Koning, L. (in press). Believing shapes seeing: The impact of diversity beliefs on the construal of group composition. *Group Processes and Intergroup Relations*.

Homan, A.C., & Jehn, K.A. (in press). How leaders can make diverse groups less difficult: The role of attitudes and perceptions of diversity. In S. Schuman (Ed.), *The handbook for working with difficult groups: How they are difficult, why they are difficult, and what you can do*. San Francisco: Jossey-Bass.

Homan, A.C., van Knippenberg, D., Van Kleef, G.A., & De Dreu, C.K.W. (2007). Bridging faultlines by valuing diversity: The effects of diversity beliefs on information elaboration and performance in diverse work groups. *Journal of Applied Psychology, 92,* 1189–1199.

Hornsey, M.J. (2008). Social identity theory and self-categorization theory: A historical overview. *Social and Personality Psychology Compass, 2*(1), 204–222.

House, R.J. (1977). A 1976 theory of charismatic leadership. In J.G. Hunt & L.L. Larson (Eds.), *Leadership: The cutting edge*. Carbondale, IL: Southern Illinois University Press.

House, R.J. (1996). Path-goal theory of leadership: Lessons, legacy and a reformulated theory. *Leadership Quarterly, 7,* 323–352.

House, R., Hanges, P., Javidan, M., Dorfman, P., & Gupta, V. (Eds.). (2004). *Leadership, culture and organizations: The GLOBE study of 62 societies*. Thousand Oaks, CA: Sage.

Howard, E.S., Gardner, W.L., & Thompson, L. (2007). The role of the self-concept and the social context in determining the behavior of power holders: Self-construal in inter-group versus dyadic dispute resolution negotiations. *Journal of Personality and Social Psychology, 93*(4), 614–631.

Jehn, K.A. (1994). Enhancing effectiveness: An investigation of advantages and disadvantages of value-based intra-group conflict. *International Journal of Conflict Management, 5,* 223–238.

Jehn, K.A. (1995). A multi-method examination of the benefits and detriments of intra-group conflict. *Administrative Science Quarterly, 40,* 256–282.

Jehn, K.A., Northcraft, G.B., & Neale, M.A. (1999). Why differences make a difference: A field study of diversity, conflict, and performance in work groups. *Administrative Science Quarterly, 44,* 741–763.

Johnson, B. (1996). *Polarity management: Identifying and managing unsolvable problems.* Amherst, MA: HRD Press.

Jones, H., Chant, E., & Ward, H. (2003). Integrating children's services: A perspective from England. In N. Trocme, D. Knoke, & C. Roy (Eds.), *Community collaboration and differential response: Canadian and international research and emerging models of practice.* Ottawa: Centre of Excellence for Child Welfare.

Karakatsanis, N.M., & Swarts, J. (2007). Attitudes toward the Xeno: Greece in comparative perspective. *Mediterranean Quarterly, 18,* 113–134.

Kearney, E., & Gebert, D. (2009). Managing diversity and enhancing team outcomes: The promise of transformational leadership. *Journal of Applied Psychology, 94*(1), 77–89.

Keats, J. (1970). *The letters of John Keats: A selection* (R. Gittings, Ed.). Oxford: Oxford University Press.

Keller, R.T. (2006). Transformational leadership, initiating structure, and substitutes for leadership: A longitudinal study of research and development project team performance. *Journal of Applied Psychology, 91,* 202–210.

Kernis, M.H. (2003). Toward a conceptualization of optimal self-esteem. *Psychological Inquiry, 14*(1), 1–26.

Lau, D.C., & Murnighan, J.K. (1998). Demographic diversity and faultlines: The compositional dynamics of organizational groups. *Academy of Management Review, 23,* 325–340.

Lau, D.C., & Murnighan. J.K. (2005). Interactions within groups and subgroups: The effects of demographic faultlines. *Academy of Management Journal, 48,* 645–659.

Lawrence-Lightfoot, S. (2000). *Respect: An exploration.* Cambridge, MA: Perseus Books.

Leung, K., & Ang, S. (2008). Culture, organizations, and institutions: An integrative review. In R.S. Bhagat & R.M. Steers (Eds.), *Cambridge handbook of culture, organizations and work* (pp. 23–45). New York: Cambridge University Press.

Li, J., & Hambrick, D.C. (2005). Factional groups: A new vintage on demographic faultlines, conflict, and disintegration in work teams. *Academy of Management Journal, 48,* 794–813.

Linsky, M., & Heifetz, R. (2002). *Leadership on the line: Staying alive through the dangers of leading*. Boston: Harvard Business School Press.

Livermore, D. (2009). *Leading with cultural intelligence: The new secret to success*. New York: AMACOM.

Livers, A.B., & Caver, K.A. (2003). *Leading in black and white: Working across the racial divide in corporate America*. San Francisco: Jossey-Bass.

Luthans, F., Youssef, C.M., & Avolio, B.J. (2007). *Psychological capital: Developing the human competitive edge*. New York: Oxford University Press.

MacDonald, H.A., Sulsky, L.M., & Brown, D.J. (2008). Leadership and perceiver cognition: Examining the role of self-identity in implicit leadership theories. *Human Performance, 21*(4), 333–353.

Markus, H.R., & Kitayama, S. (1991). Culture and the self: Implications for cognition, emotion, and motivation. *Psychological Review, 98*, 224–253.

Mayer, R.C., Davis, J.H., & Schoorman, F.D. (1995). An integrative model of organizational trust. *Academy of Management Review, 20*(3), 709–734.

Miller, D.T. (2001). Disrespect and the experience of injustice. *Annual Review of Psychology, 52*, 527–553.

Milliken, F.J., & Martins, L.L. (1996). Searching for common threads: Understanding the multiple effects of diversity in organizational groups. *Academy of Management Review, 21*, 402–433.

Mills, J., & Clark, M.S. (1982). Exchange and communal relationships. In L. Wheeler (Ed.), *Review of personality and social psychology* (Vol. 3) (pp. 121–144). Thousand Oaks, CA: Sage.

Mitroff, I, (1995). Review of *The Age of Paradox*. *Academy of Management Review, 20*, 748–750.

Nakashima, K., Isobe, C., & Ura, M. (2008). Effect of self-construal and threat to self-esteem on in-group favouritism: Moderating effect of independent/interdependent self-construal on use of in-group favouritism for maintaining and enhancing self-evaluation. *Asian Journal of Social Psychology, 11*(4), 286–292.

Ng, K.Y., Ang, S., & Van Dyne, L. (2009). Beyond international experience: The strategic role of cultural intelligence for executive selection of international human resource management. In P.R. Sparrow (Ed.), *Handbook of international human resource research: Integrating people, process, and context*. Oxford: Blackwell.

Ng, K.Y., Van Dyne, L., & Ang, S. (2009a). Developing global leaders: The role of international experience and cultural intelligence. In W.H. Mobley, Y. Wang, & M. Li (Eds.), *Advances in global leadership*. Greenwich, CT: JAI.

Ng, K.Y., Van Dyne, L., & Ang, S. (2009b). From experience to experiential learning: Cultural intelligence as a learning capability for global leader development. *Academy of Management Learning & Education, 8*(4).

Nkomo, S.M., & Stewart, M. (2006). Diverse identities in organizations. In S. Clegg, W. Nord, & C. Hardy (Eds.), *Handbook of organization studies* (2nd ed.) (pp. 520–540). London: Sage.

Palmer, P.J. (1998). *The courage to teach: Exploring the inner landscape of a teacher's life.* San Francisco: Jossey-Bass.

Parekh, B. (2000). *Rethinking multiculturalism: Cultural diversity and political theory.* London: Macmillan Press.

Pascale, R.T. (1990). *Managing on the edge: How the smartest companies use conflict to stay ahead.* New York: Simon & Schuster.

Pittinsky, T.L. (2005). Allophilia and inter-group leadership. In N.N. Huber & M. Walker (Eds.), *Building leadership bridges: Emergent models of global leadership.* College Park, MD: International Leadership Association.

Pittinsky, T.L. (2008). Prejudice. In V.N. Parrillo (Ed.), *Encyclopedia of social problems* (pp. 705–709). Thousand Oaks, CA: Sage.

Pittinsky, T.L. (Ed.). (2009). *Crossing the divide: Intergroup leadership in a world of difference.* Boston: Harvard Business School Press.

Pittinsky, T.L. (in press). A two-dimensional theory of intergroup leadership: The case of national diversity. *American Psychologist.*

Pittinsky, T.L., & Maruskin, L. (2008). Allophilia: Beyond prejudice. In S.J. Lopez (Ed.), *Positive psychology* (Vol. 2) (pp. 141–148). Westport, CT: Praeger.

Pittinsky, T.L., & Montoya, R.M. (2009). Is valuing equality enough? Equality values, allophilia, and social policy support for multiracial individuals. *Journal of Social Issues,* 65(1), 151–163.

Pittinsky, T.L., & Montoya, R.M. (in press). Symhedonia in inter-group relations: The relationship of empathic joy to prejudice and allophilia. *Psicologia Sociale.*

Pittinsky, T.L., Ratcliff, J.J., & Maruskin, L.A. (2008). *Coexistence in Israel: A national study.* Cambridge, MA: Harvard Kennedy School, Center for Public Leadership.

Pittinsky, T.L., Rosenthal, S.A., & Montoya, R.M. (2007, May). Prejudice and allophilia: A two-dimensional model of inter-group attitudes and relations. Poster session presented at the 19th annual meeting of the Association for Psychological Science, Washington, D.C.

Pittinsky, T.L., Rosenthal, S.A., & Montoya, R.M. (forthcoming). Attitudes beyond tolerance: Allophilia in intergroup relations. In L. Tropp & R. Mallett (Eds.), *Beyond prejudice reduction: Pathways to positive inter-group relations.* Washington, DC: American Psychological Association.

Pittinsky, T.L., & Simon, S. (2007). Inter-group leadership. *The Leadership Quarterly,* 18(6), 586–605.

Ratcliff, J.J., & Pittinsky, T.L. (2008, February). Baleful and beneficent behavior toward out-groups: The distinct roles of prejudice, motivation to respond without prejudice, and allophilia. Poster session presented at the Groups and Intergroup Relations pre-conference to the 9th annual meeting of the Society for Personality and Social Psychology, Albuquerque, New Mexico.

Rokeach, M. (1973). *The nature of human values.* New York: The Free Press.

Rothman, J. (1997). *Resolving identity-based conflict in nations, organizations, and communities.* San Francisco: Jossey-Bass.

Rushton, P. (1999). Genetic similarity theory and the nature of ethnocentrism. In K. Thienpont & R. Cliquet (Eds.), *In-group/out-group behaviour in modern societies: An evolutionary perspective.* Brussels, Belgium: NIDI CBGS.

Sagiv, L., & Schwartz, S.H. (2000). A new look at national cultures: Illustrative applications to role stress and managerial behavior. In N.N. Ashkanasy, C. Wilderom, & M.F. Peterson (Eds.), *The handbook of organizational culture and climate* (pp. 417–436). Thousand Oaks, CA: Sage.

Sagiv, L., & Schwartz, S.H. (2007). Cultural values in organizations: Insights for Europe. *European Journal of International Management, 1,* 176–190.

Schwartz, S.H. (1992). Universals in the content and structure of values: Theoretical advances and empirical tests in 20 countries. In M. Zanna (Ed.), *Advances in experimental social psychology* (Vol. 25) (pp. 1–65). New York: Academic Press.

Schwartz, S.H. (1999). Cultural value differences: Some implications for work. *Applied Psychology: An International Review, 48,* 23–47.

Schwartz, S.H. (2004). Mapping and interpreting cultural differences around the world. In H. Vinken, J. Soeters, & P. Ester (Eds.), *Comparing cultures, Dimensions of culture in a comparative perspective* (pp. 43–73). Leiden, The Netherlands: Brill.

Schwartz, S.H. (2006). A theory of cultural value orientations: Explication and applications. *Comparative Sociology, 5,* 137–182.

Schwartz, S.H. (2007). Cultural and individual value correlates of capitalism: A comparative analysis. *Psychological Inquiry, 18,* 52–57.

Schwartz, S.H. (2009). Causes of culture: National differences in cultural embeddedness. In A. Gari & K. Mylonas(Eds.), *Q.E.D. From Herodotus' ethnographic journeys to cross-cultural research.* Cambridge, MA: Pedia Electronic Publishing.

Schwartz, S.H., & Bilsky, W. (1987). Toward a universal psychological structure of human values. *Journal of Personality and Social Psychology, 53*(3), 550–562.

Schwartz, S.H., & Sagie, G. (2000). Value consensus and importance: A cross-national study. *Journal of Cross-Cultural Psychology, 31*(4), 465–497.

Shaw, R.P., & Wong, Y. (1989). *Genetic seeds of warfare: Evolution, nationalism, and patriotism.* Boston: Unwin Hyman.

Sherif, M. (1967). *Social interaction: Process and products.* Chicago: Aldine.

Simon, B., & Klandermans, B. (2001). Politicized collective identity: A social psychological analysis. *American Psychologist, 4,* 319–34.

Sinha, J.B.P. (1980). *The nurturant task leader.* New Delhi: Concept.

Sinha, J.B.P. (1984). A model of effective leadership styles in India. *International Studies of Management and Organization, 14*(3), 86–98.

Smith, W., & Tushman, M. (2005). Managing strategic contradictions: A top management model for managing innovation streams. *Organization Science, 16*(5), 522–536.

Soldatova, G. (2007). Psychological mechanisms of xenophobia. *Social Sciences, 38*(2), 105–121.

Stephan, W.G., & Stephan, C. (1985). Intergroup anxiety. *Journal of Social Issues. 41*, 157–176.

Stryker, S. (2007). Identity theory and personality theory: Mutual relevance. *Journal of Personality, 75*(6), 1083–1102.

Sumner, W.G. (1906). *Folkways: A study of the sociological importance of usages, manners, customs, mores, and morals*. New York: Mentor.

Tajfel, H. (1972). "Social categorization," English version of "La categorisation sociale." In S. Moscovici (Ed.), *Introduction a la psychologie sociale* (Vol. I. ). Paris: Larousse.

Tajfel, H., & Turner, J.C. (1979). An integrative theory of inter-group conflict. In W.G. Austin & S. Worchel (Eds.), *The social psychology of inter-group relations*. Monterey, CA: Brooks/Cole.

Tajfel, H., & Turner, J.C. (1986). The social identity theory of inter-group behavior. In S. Worchel & W.G. Austin (Eds.), *Psychology of inter-group relations* (2nd ed.) (pp. 7–24). Chicago: Nelson-Hall.

Tajfel, H., & Turner, J. (2001). An integrative theory of intergroup conflict. *Intergroup relations: Essential readings* (pp. 94–109). New York: Psychology Press.

Takeuchi, H., Osono, E., & Shimizu, N. (2008). *Extreme Toyota: Radical contradictions that drive success at the world's best manufacturer*. Hoboken, NJ: John Wiley & Sons.

Thatcher, S.M.B., Jehn, K.A., & Zanutto, E. (2003). Cracks in diversity research: The effects of diversity faultlines on conflict and performance. *Group Decision and Negotiation, 12*, 217–241.

Triandis, H.C. (1989). The self and social behavior in differing cultural contexts. *Psychological Review, 96*(3), 506–520.

Triandis, H.C. (1990). Cross-cultural studies of individualism and collectivism. In J. Bremen (Ed.), *Nebraska symposium on motivation* (pp. 41–133). Lincoln: University of Nebraska Press.

Triandis, H.C. (1995a). A theoretical framework for the study of diversity. In M.M. Chemers, S. Oskamp, & M.A. Costanzo (Eds.), *Diversity in organizations: New perspectives for a changing workplace* (pp. 11–36). London: Sage.

Triandis, H.C. (1995b). *Individualism and collectivism*. Boulder, CO: Westview Press.

Triandis, H.C. (2008). Cultural intelligence. In S. Ang & L. Van Dyne (Eds.), *Handbook on cultural intelligence: Theory, measurement and applications* (pp. xi–xiv). New York: M.E. Sharpe.

Triandis, H.C., & Bhawuk, D.P.S. (1997). Culture theory and the meaning of relatedness. In P.C. Earley & M. Erez (Eds.), *New perspectives on international industrial/organizational psychology* (pp. 13–52). New York: New Lexington Free Press.

Triandis, H.C., Chan, D., Bhawuk, D.P.S., Iwao, S., & Sinha, J.B.P. (1995). Multi-method probes of allocentrism and idiocentrism. *International Journal of Psychology, 30*(4), 461–468.

Tsui, A.S., Egan, T.D., & O'Reilly, C.A. (1992). Being different: Relational demography and organizational attachment. *Administrative Science Quarterly, 37*(4), 547–579.

Turner, J.C., Hogg, M.A., Oakes, P.J., Reicher, S.D., & Wetherell, M.S. (1987). *Rediscovering the social group*: *A self-categorization theory*. Oxford, UK: Blackwell.

Van den Berghe, P.L. (1999). Racism, ethnocentrism, and xenophobia: In our genes or in our memes? In K. Thienpont & R. Cliquet. (Eds.), *In-group/out-group behaviour in modern societies: An evolutionary perspective* (pp. 21–33). Brussels, Belgium: NIDI CBGS.

Van der Dennen, J.M.G. (1987). Ethnocentrism and in-group/out-group differentiation: A review of the literature. In V. Reynolds, V. Falger, & I. Vine (Eds.), *The sociobiology of ethnocentrism: Evolutionary dimensions of xenophobia, discrimination, racism, and nationalism* (pp. 1–47). Athens, GA: University of Georgia Press.

Van der Dennen, J.M.G. (2004). Self-cooperation, loyalty structures, and proto-ethnocentrism in inter-group agonistic behavior. In F. Salter (Ed.), *Welfare, ethnicity and altruism: New findings and evolutionary theory* (pp. 195–231). London: Frank Cass.

Van Dyne, L., & Ang, S. (2008). The sub-dimensions of the four factor model of cultural intelligence. Technical Report. East Lansing, MI: Cultural Intelligence Center.

Van Dyne, L., Ang, S., & Koh, C. (2009). Cultural intelligence: Measurement and scale development. In M.A. Moodian (Ed.), *Contemporary leadership and intercultural competence: Exploring the cross-cultural dynamics within organizations* (pp. 233–254). Thousand Oaks, CA: Sage.

Van Dyne, L., Ang, S., & Nielsen, T.M. (2007). Cultural intelligence. In S. Clegg & J. Bailey (Eds.), *International encyclopedia of organization studies* (pp. 345–350). Thousand Oaks, CA: Sage.

Van Horen, F., Pöhlmann, C., Koeppen, K., & Hannover, B. (2008). Importance of personal goals in people with independent versus interdependent selves. *Social Psychology*, 39(4), 213–221.

van Knippenberg, D., De Dreu, C.K.W., & Homan, A.C. (2004). Work group diversity and group performance: An integrative model and research agenda. *Journal of Applied Psychology*, 89, 1008–1022.

van Knippenberg, D., & Haslam, S. (2003). Realizing the diversity dividend: Exploring the interplay between identity, ideology and reality. In S. Haslam, D. van Knippenberg, M. Platow, & N. Ellemers (Eds.), *Social identity at work: Developing theory for organizational practice* (pp. 61–77). New York:

van Knippenberg, D., & Schippers, M.C. (2007). Work group diversity. *Annual Review of Psychology*, 58, 515–541.

Vince & Broussiere (1996)

Weber, M. (1968). *Economy and society: An outlined interpretive sociology* (R. Guenther & C. Wittich, Eds.). New York: Bedminster Press.

Weber, T. J. & Uhl-Bien, M. (2009, April). Values congruence and relationship quality. Paper presented at the Annual Society for Industrial and Organizational Psychology Conference, New Orleans.

Webster, D., & Kruglanski, A. (1997). Cognitive and social consequences of the need for cognitive closure. *European Review of Social Psychology, 18*, 133–173.

Weick, K.E. (1995). *Sensemaking in organizations.* Thousand Oaks, CA: Sage.

Williams, K.Y., & O'Reilly, C.A. (1998). Demography and diversity in organizations: A review of 40 years of research. *Research in Organizational Behavior, 20*, 77–140.

Yamaguchi, S., & Ariizumi, Y. (2006). Close interpersonal relationships among Japanese: *Amae* as distinguished from attachment and dependence. In U. Kim, K.S. Yang, & K.K. Hwang (Eds.), *Indigenous and cultural psychology: Understanding people in context* (pp. 163–174). New York: Springer.

# ABOUT THE CONTRIBUTORS

**Soon Ang** is Goh Tjoei Kok Distinguished Chair and professor in management at the Nanyang Business School, Nanyang Technological University, Singapore. She pioneered cultural intelligence (CQ) and specializes in its measurement and assessment.

**Dharm P. S. Bhawuk** is a professor of management and culture and community psychology at the University of Hawaii at Manoa. His research interests include, among others, intercultural training, sensitivity and leadership, individualism and collectivism, and indigenous psychology and management.

**Donna Chrobot-Mason** is an assistant professor at the University of Cincinnati in the Center for Organizational Leadership. She is also the graduate director for the Master's in Labor and Employment Relations Program. Dr. Chrobot-Mason received her doctorate from the University of Georgia in 1997 and has applied human resources experience with Xerox Corporation.

**Chris Ernst** is a senior enterprise associate at the Center for Creative Leadership (CCL), where he focuses on developing collaborative, intergroup leadership capabilities within and across individuals, organizations, and communities through integrating research and practice.

**P**hilomena *Essed* is professor of critical race, gender, and leadership studies at Antioch University. She received her Ph.D. in social science from the University of Amsterdam. She is an affiliated researcher at Utrecht University in The Netherlands, Graduate Gender Program, and deputy member of the national Equal Treatment Commission.

**S**arah *L. Glover* contributed to international research at the Center for Creative Leadership for over seven years. She is a writer focusing on cross-cultural and social issues, innovation, and community-building.

**A**strid *C. Homan* is an assistant professor at the work and organizational psychology department of the VU University in Amsterdam, The Netherlands. Her main research interests are work group diversity and performance, leadership, and information elaboration in organizations.

**K**aren *A. Jehn* is a professor of social and organizational psychology at Leiden University in The Netherlands. Her research focuses on intra-group conflict, group composition and performance, and lying in organizations.

**D**avid *Livermore* is the executive director of the Global Learning Center in Grand Rapids, Michigan. He is the author of three books on cultural intelligence, including his newest release, *Leading with Cultural Intelligence* (AMACOM, 2009).

**A**ncella *Livers* is the executive director for the Institute for Leadership Development & Research at the Executive Leadership Council. She is the co-author of the book, *Leading in Black and White: Working Across the Racial Divide,* and the *Harvard Business Review* article "Dear White Boss."

**V**ijayan Munusamy is a senior research associate at the Center for Creative Leadership–Asia. He received his Ph.D. in international management from The University of Hawaii. Among other recognitions, he is a recipient of *The Wall Street Journal* Student Achievement Award, Booz Allen Hamilton Outstanding Recognition Award, and East-West Center Distinguished Service Award.

**S**tella M. Nkomo teaches courses in the Department of Human Resource Management, Faculty of Economic and Management Sciences, University of Pretoria. She is a former chair of the Department of Management in the Belk College of Business Administration at the University of North Carolina, Charlotte, and on the faculty of the Graduate School of Business Leadership at the University of South Africa. Professor Nkomo is the co-author of two books, *Applications in Human Resource Management* (South-Western/Cengage Publishers) and *Our Separate Ways: Black and White Women and the Struggle for Professional Identity* (Harvard Business School Press).

**T**odd L. Pittinsky is an associate professor and research director of the Center for Public Leadership at the Harvard Kennedy School. His current research on positive intergroup relations includes the edited volume *Crossing the Divide: Intergroup Leadership in a World of Difference* (Harvard Business School Press, 2009).

**M**arian N. Ruderman is director, Americas and EMEA Research at the Center for Creative Leadership (CCL), where she conducts research on diversity, global leadership, and work/life integration.

**S**halom H. Schwartz is Emeritus Professor of Psychology at the Hebrew University of Jerusalem, Israel. His theories and measures of basic human values and of cultural value orientations guide a world-wide project that he coordinates.

**R**obert Solomon is the research manager at The Executive Leadership Council's Institute for Leadership Development & Research. His responsibilities include management and production of key developmental research initiatives and oversight of independent research projects.

**L**inn Van Dyne is a professor of management at Michigan State University, where she does research on discretionary behavior and cultural intelligence, serves on seven editorial boards, and is associate editor of *Organizational Behavior and Human Decision Processes*.

**T**odd J. Weber is a post-doctoral research associate at the University of Nebraska–Lincoln, where he studies leadership with a focus on how values influence the development of high-quality relationships among leaders and followers.

**J**effrey Yip is a research associate with the Center for Creative Leadership and a research fellow with the Learning Innovations Laboratory at Harvard University. His work is focused on the dynamics of effective leadership and learning across boundaries.

**K**<i>elly M. Hannum</i> is manager of research for the EMEA Region at the Center for Creative Leadership. She holds a Ph.D. in educational research, measurement, and evaluation from the University of North Carolina at Greensboro. In addition to her work at CCL over the last fifteen years, Kelly has conducted research and evaluation projects with organizations in a variety of sectors and countries. She is a visiting faculty member at Catholic University's IESEG School of Management in Lille, France, and teaches graduate-level courses at the University of North Carolina at Greensboro. Her work has been published and presented internationally in a variety of venues. She is the recipient of the Marcia Guttentag award from the American Evaluation Association and Young Alumni Awards from the University of North Carolina at Greensboro and Guilford College.

**B**<i>elinda B. McFeeters</i> is an independent contractor with faculty affiliations with the evaluation center at the Center for Creative Leadership, the Leadership Studies, Ph.D. Program at North Carolina A&T State University, and the Leadership Development group at the N.C. Rural Economic Development Center. She is also a freelance writer for EBSCO Publishing. Belinda earned a Ph.D. in educational leadership and policy studies from Virginia Polytechnic Institute and State University. Her primary research, evaluation, and assessment focus is on leadership development (national and global) and diversity education. Belinda has authored or co-authored several articles, book chapters, and books on higher education, multicultural education, K-12 education, cross-cultural leadership, and sociological issues.

**L**ize Booysen is a full professor of leadership and organizational behavior at Antioch University. Lize is an internationally recognized scholar in the field of diversity, race, gender, and leadership and a management consultant. She holds a doctorate in business leadership as well as master's degrees in clinical psychology, research psychology, and criminology, all with distinction. Prior to joining Antioch in 2009, Lize was full professor at the Graduate School of Business Leadership, University of South Africa, since 1992. She was also the editor of the *South African Journal of Labour Relations*. Some of Lize's many awards include the GLOBE Research Award (1997) and Best Academic Achievement, University of South Africa (2004). She is also included as one of fifty role models for South African women and as leadership expert in the book *Inspirational Women @ Work* (Lapa Publishers, 2003).

Made in the USA
Monee, IL
06 January 2023